PROMISING FUTURES

The Unexpected Rewards
of Engaged Philanthropy

MARGOT WELCH

COPYRIGHT © 2006 MARGOT WELCH

Published by
Font & Center Press, Inc.
P.O. Box 95
Weston, MA 02493
www.fontandcenter.com

Cover Photograph by Gene Ritvo © 2006

Library of Congress Cataloging-in-Publication Data

Welch, Margot.
    Promising Futures :

ISBN: 978-1-883280-18-5

*Copyright law requires that the "I Have a Dream" Foundation® be identified as
carrying a Restricted name. In the text, the acronym IHAD is used consistently
to refer to both the "I Have a Dream" Foundation® and the "I Have a Dream"
program. After the introductory pages, the Restricted ® symbol is not appended
to every full mention of the "I Have a Dream" Foundation® or the "I Have a
Dream" program.*

FIRST PRINTING 2006

Printed in the United States of America

1   2   3   4   5   6   7   8   9   10

To the people who make dreams come true:
Eugene Lang,
"I Have a Dream"® sponsors,
and my parents, Tom and Emily Adler

ACKNOWLEDGMENTS

It is almost painful not to be able to identify by name the "I Have a Dream" sponsors who made themselves available for this book. Confidentiality makes it much more likely that people are able to express and even discover themselves in interviews. Nonetheless I have a funny feeling that if I could give the real names of these sponsors, no one would doubt that such extraordinarily courageous and bountiful souls exist. But, as they know well, promises are promises. For sharing their stories and their dreams so openly with me I am forever grateful. As one said, "The great thing about I Have a Dream is that you can put your arms around it." I will always feel profoundly privileged to have had the chance to try.

    I also want to acknowledge the special help of editors and book producers, Chris Kochansky, Ilene Horowitz and Becky Allen Mixter. Financial support for the publication of the book came from the I Have a Dream Foundation. Over the years, staff from the IHAD national office—Rich Ungerer, Marina Winton, Terry Boyd, and Noelle Dong—has given me valuable help. Wonderful teachers, Catherine Osgood Foster, Sara Lawrence Lightfoot and Robert Selman showed me ways, and never doubted. I am also deeply grateful for all kinds of help from many special friends and relations—Martha Ransohoff Adler, Page Ashley, Andrew Bundy, Tiziana Casciaro, Linda and Bill Cotter, Elizabeth Ferrara, Rose Frisch, Marilyn Glater, Alicia Haller, Dorothy Miller Klubock, Ruth Leshen, Larisa Mendez-Penate, Mary Henderson Moskowitz, Ed Selig, Susan Semple, Richard Weissbourd, and my wonderful aunt, Peggy Frank Crawford.

I shall never be able to adequately thank my skilled and dearly beloved editor-partner-husband, Alan Harwood. His faith in the value of this project has never wavered, nor has my thankfulness for the good fortune of our love And there are cherished dream makers who will never know the role they played in helping me to realize this book. These include my sons, Joshua and Sam Welch, and Seth and Jessica Harwood, Zoe Adler Resnick, Will and Rachel Adler, Max Adler Resnick, and my precious grandchildren, Emilia, Nicolas and Mateo Welch. These dear souls are the future. Let us pledge to work together to make the world safer and more hopeful for everyone's grandchildren.

CONTENTS

PROLOGUE

"Think about Chantal," said the school principal.

She's fourteen, her mama has served three years for cocaine distribution and use, and she lives in the basement of a homeless shelter with other women and children. "The scary guys are all on the second, third, and fourth floors," she says, so she gets up at 4:00 in the morning to wash her uniform before anybody else is awake because of the way the guys look at her—she feels she's being undressed.

Chantal's breakfast today was canned Vienna sausages, six of them. I saved the can because I saw her coming into school this morning and I want to remember this for a talk I'm giving about our school this Saturday. The name of the talk is "Why Rich People Aren't Going to Heaven." There was just something about watching this child come out of that shelter this morning with rats running all over the place, a big old pile of books in her arms, her crummy little Vienna sausages and that blue-colored drink they sell at the corner for twenty-five cents—about knowing she got up in the dark because she didn't want to be around the guys when she washed her uniform—about knowing Mom's in there with six kids and going nowhere and Daddy's produced sixteen kids by five different women.

Chantal doesn't get the time of day from anybody at home. But at our school, she's on the honor roll. She's working hard. She's going to New York for a summer college prep program. Sometimes she comes to our house to use our computer and my wife gives her piano lessons. This is a resilient kid. But it takes my breath away: just how poor

poor is. They sell drugs around the corner from the shelter and this girl has every reason in the world to get high as a kite every day.

Why do we let kids in America go through this? Chantal had the misfortune of being born into the wrong zip code. She was in the wrong womb. But she's making it—because she's in a school community that loves her, and mostly because she wants it. There are people here who will support her every inch of the way. We will push, pull, prod, celebrate, kick her when we have to—but with Chantal, we don't have to do much kicking. She's had enough of that already. She knows what the alternative is and she doesn't want it.

This is not another book about poor children. It's not about the resilience of kids like Chantal—which is stunning—but the hearts of those who want to see her become a responsible, productive citizen of a country that all too often simply turns its back on her and many other children living in neighborhoods plagued by chaos and poverty. It's a book about people who have decided to invest money, time, and heart in the future of all our children. These people are engaged philanthropists who believe in the power of education and are able to make big promises. They will do whatever it takes to get the kids to whom they are committed on a personal level through high school. They'll stand by them for many years, and, what's more, they'll help pay their college tuitions. And what's in it for the philanthropists?

CHAPTER I

THE JAVELIN

Did you ever hear of the guy who won the coin toss in the javelin-throwing contest and elected to receive? Well, that was me.

—Eugene Lang, founder of the
"I Have a Dream"® Foundation

For the past few years, I've been living with the voices of people who, like Eugene Lang, made a big decision, sometimes without much information, and found themselves stormed by consequences they would never have imagined. I've been interviewing engaged philanthropists who have become involved with Lang's I Have a Dream program. And I've been living with their stories. If Lang felt astounded by what he was about to learn, so did others. Hal Davies, for example, said

> I've learned about a part of my life I'd never had a way to discover. But when you think about it, there are so many reasons not to do this! The issue of liability alone is enormous! And if you let these thoughts get in the way, you just stop. You tell yourself what any sane person would say: "This is going to get in the way in my life." When you start one of these projects, you have no idea what the upside is going to be. You can see the downside all right, and you know you can lose plenty. But taking it on comes from some place in each individual soul where you are able to look through all the risks and keep going ahead, without ever knowing what the upside will be. Of course the upside does come. It turns out that there was no risk!

Anybody who is serious about change, says Bill Shore, has to be serious about story-telling.[1] Because stories carry history. They can instruct, influence, and inspire. And engaged philanthropists have some powerful tales to tell. I began listening to them in 1997 when I put together a conference on "Mentoring: Relationships, Programs, Possibilities" at the Harvard Graduate School of Education.

Throughout the mid-1990s, mentoring programs had been rapidly gaining public attention. People were beginning to understand that because relationships are central to our lives, mentoring—pairing a younger person with a somewhat older one who can become guide, advisor, consistent friend—helps to nurture the achievement of many who are not being well served by more conventional kinds of education or training, including interventions or outreach programs designed for children.[2] I invited a variety of conference presenters to describe how mentoring programs were being organized and implemented in different kinds of settings: business leaders to explain how they were organizing workplaces to encourage employees to become engaged in local communities; school principals and leaders from various community agencies to share the kinds of mentoring relationships they had benefitted from personally while they were growing up. And, to kick off the day, I enlisted a well-known philanthropist, Eugene Lang, to be the keynote speaker.

In his opening address, Lang described how he had begun his own extraordinary mentoring initiative, the I Have a Dream program (IHAD). Since its inception in 1981, IHAD has engaged more than 14,000 young people in low-income communities all over the country, pairing them with sponsors, project coordinators, mentors, and tutors who accompany the students—the "dreamers"—all the way through secondary school and beyond, to help them define and reach their goals. I found Lang's account of how he started IHAD astonishing. Then in his early sixties, he had crossed a line from being a conventional philanthropist to committing himself to intimate engagement in the lives of inner-city children—for years.

Before 1981, Gene Lang had spent a great deal of his money on good causes. At the Harvard conference he spoke of himself as "a businessman who, with lots of luck, parlayed the streets of Harlem during the Great Depression into a good education and a rewarding business." Prior to 1981, his conventional investments in higher education alone had already cost him more than $75 million, because, he said,

> Like most businessmen concerned with risk-reward ratios, I originally focused on helping college students with the greatest promise. Meanwhile, millions of kids—largely minority poor—were dropping out, building an increasingly massive claim on the conscience and resources of our nation. Then, on June 25, 1981, while traveling education's privileged road to Damascus, I had a moment of epiphany. I spoke to an assembly of sixth graders graduating that day from P.S. 121 in East Harlem—the school from which I had graduated fifty-three years previously.

> Most of you have heard the story—how I got carried away by impromptu rhetoric and promised sixty-one black and Hispanic youngsters a college education. That night I woke up with a chilling thought. I hadn't done the mathematics associated with my promise. College tuition for sixty-one kids! Did you ever hear of the guy who won the coin toss in the javelin-throwing contest—and elected to receive? Well, that was me.

Explicating Lang's speech briefly now helps me recapture the astonishment I felt as he told his story. He began with a confident reference to successful business people whose accomplishments are usually achieved by putting their money where it's most likely to pay off: if you want to make a difference in the world, you invest your resources where you are most likely to get a return. Thus, if you want to give money away, higher education—which engages young people who have survived the throes of early childhood and much of adolescence—is a good bet. But Lang did not attempt to explain why, even while he was supporting those who were already likely to succeed, he had become increasingly aware of the "millions of kids" who were dropping out. Instead he told us about a very impulsive moment—one in which he was "carried away."

This was the behavior I found startling. When I thought about successful businessmen, I assumed that stringent, methodical calculations always preceded major financial commitments. But Lang was talking about a moment when he'd lost control of his reason, in a way. On the spot, impulsively, he had made an enormous promise that would cost him, in ways he could not possibly know, much more than he had anticipated. And in his speech at the Harvard conference he referred to that moment as an epiphany.

The etymology of the word 'epiphany,' from the Greek, emphasizes the phenomenon of manifestation. Its several definitions include "an intuiting grasp of reality through something (as an event) usually simple and striking," and the "sudden perception of the essential nature or meaning of something." But in ancient Greece, epiphany was also the name given to rituals of rebirth. And in some ways, when he took that leap in Harlem, Lang moved beyond his comfortable, secure identity to redefine himself. It was indeed a kind of rebirth, an entrance into a new world. And, as he now says, "If I had known what I was getting into, I wouldn't have done it. But if I hadn't done it—well, that would have been the biggest regret of my life."

Four years after the Harvard speech, in an address celebrating the twentieth anniversary of I Have a Dream, in 2001, Lang again described his seminal experience at P.S. 121.

> I slowly stumbled forward, wondering anxiously what I should say to an audience from which I felt completely disconnected. Having given and heard many commencement speeches, I expected conventional rhetoric to see me through. Too late, I realized that for the P.S. 121 audience such talk wouldn't go.
>
> At the podium, groping for a theme, a timely recollection— an incandescent recollection flashed through my mind: August 28, 1963, in front of the Lincoln Memorial, when Martin Luther King told the world, "I have a dream." That recollection triggered a stream of consciousness that culminated with my impulsive promise to the sixty-one minority pre-teeners, "When you graduate from high school, I promise each of you a scholarship so that you can go on to college." There was no suggestion of a program. I just promised scholarships.

In this version of the tale he has retold many times, Lang says he felt "disconnected" from the children and families who were sitting exactly where he had sat more than five decades earlier. He was unprepared for this experience, even momentarily disoriented by the distance between himself and his audience. But he was determined to be taken seriously. And suddenly he wanted those children to know that someone in their lives expected them to move right through middle and high school, on to college and occupational success. Without any forethought, he offered to help put sixty-one kids through college—*if* they finished high school. What, he wondered that night, would that mean?

> I consulted the school principal who told me not to worry—
> at least three quarters of these graduates would be drop-
> outs—and even with high school diplomas, few, if any,
> would qualify for college. So, my promise was reduced
> to commencement rhetoric—and the javelin hit its target.
> I resolved to make my promise a real opportunity. That
> resolve was the genesis of the I Have a Dream program—a
> program dedicated to the proposition that, as a mandate of
> democracy, every child in America has a birthright entitle-
> ment to a genuine opportunity for a quality education.

Surely the principal hadn't consciously meant to question the sincerity of his illustrious commencement speaker. But what had happened? A wealthy, accomplished businessman had made an impulsive remark and now, as he thought about its consequences, he was goaded on by an insinuation that he needn't worry about the cost of keeping his promise. Few of the kids "would qualify for college" anyway. This made Lang angry. As he thought about those children and their families, living where he himself had grown up fifty years earlier, Lang realized that they were as deserving of dreams for their futures as he himself had been long ago. He resolved that he would help them find paths to good futures—all of them. And in so doing he stepped out of the world of standard philanthropy and into the world of inner-city children and families whose lives are riddled with all kinds of startling javelins, both real and metaphorical.

Impulsive actions change lives. Lang became directly and personally involved in the establishment of his new project because from the beginning he insisted that the success of his dreamers would hinge on what he calls "the protoplasm" of the sponsor-dreamer relationships. "To each child," he said later, after the establishment of IHAD, perhaps "for the first time, IHAD provides an enduring human association that combines the attributes of affection and concern with power and resources."

To this end, Lang began to design a detailed model of outreach, one that offered extended supports and services to children. He hired a project coordinator (PC) to help him keep track of his dreamers. And after a few years, Lang discovered that unlike many of their peers, his "adopted children" were still enrolled in school. They were being promoted from one grade to the next. They were not dropping out.

Lang's initial project was to become a model of a kind of philanthropy that is quite different from other forms of largesse that he had bestowed in his generous life. Sometimes called "engaged" or "personalized" philanthropy, this practice transforms conventional ways of giving—away from what tend to be one-way benevolent behaviors and toward relational initiatives in which the donor can become as involved in the process of change as the beneficiary.

And it seems that Lang's impulsiveness—his unpremeditated decision to see how he could make a significant difference in the lives of many low-income children, rather than just a few—hit the mark for many other people too. After an article in the New York Times and a television interview on 60 Minutes, in 1986, Lang started getting calls and letters from people all over the country who wanted to do what he had done: sponsor classes of children, support them in their school years, and help them move on to higher education. Lang's charismatic account of his epiphany was rather contagious. Many people who heard him felt infected, one might say, by his vision, energy, and determination. And soon, to coordinate all the new projects that were springing up, he founded the national I Have a Dream Foundation. Since 1986, one hundred and eighty projects have been carried out in twenty-seven states and sixty-six cities. Thousands of children have participated in personalized, future-oriented initiatives designed to give them every possible educational opportunity and lead them into healthy and responsible citizenry. In 2004–2005, sixty-two active IHAD projects were engaging more than five thousand students.

WHY THIS BOOK

As I listened to his address at our 1997 conference, Lang's javelin struck me as well. I had worked for decades with and for a variety of public and private institutions dedicated to bettering the lives of children and youth. For the most part, the people my colleagues and I were trying to help were under-served kids and families with every kind of challenge—people who were all tangled up in the webs of inadequate support systems provided by courts, schools, health care systems, and community agencies. Over the years I had felt fierce affection for children—not only mine but others, not only the lucky, hopeful ones but also the victims, the runaways, the sad ones, even the troublemakers. To some extent my academic training in psychology and education had prepared me for the slings and arrows of caring for such children. I had learned to analyze, to maintain perspective. But I had never had the kind of intense, unstructured relationships with other people's children over the course of many years that Lang went on to describe. I couldn't stop wondering what it was like for him and subsequent IHAD sponsors to make such personal long-term commitments.

As Lang spoke about his personal relationships with his own first cohort of dreamers—the model for all subsequent IHAD efforts—he said his first step was to make it very clear to the children that he was not going to abandon them until they got through high school. If and when they needed him, they should call. He would be in their lives—not in a professional, bounded role but available at all times of day and night, all year long, for at least six years. I kept wondering how he and other sponsors who were accustomed to living well above the fray of poverty and danger felt when this actually began to play itself out in their comfortable lives. What was it like to be startled from sleep by a midnight phone call and hear a young voice on the other end saying he or she was in jail, on the street, hurt, frightened? "You said you'd stick with me," I imagined a kid saying. "If you meant what you said, come downtown now and help me get out of jail." Or "Find me a safe place to sleep tonight."

Several other IHAD sponsors came to our Harvard conference, and during the morning break I spoke with one, whom I'll call Ben, who was both surprised and intrigued by my interest in understanding what it was like to be a sponsor. He would love to talk with me sometime, he said, with an eagerness that reminded me of the people I'd interviewed for my doctoral research, which focused on the experience of job satisfaction and success in what I call "multi-problem" human service agencies. These are settings that many find hopeless and bleak, but I was interested in the meaning of "helping" to those who simply love this work—"thrivers," as I call them, who can't imagine doing anything else. They had been excited when I said I wanted to talk with them about their work—and Ben had the same kind of eagerness in his voice when he offered to talk with me about being an IHAD sponsor. I was still intrigued, apparently, by the phenomenon I thought of simplistically as "giving."

As I thought about it, I wondered if my curiosity was connected, somehow, to my own family experiences. I come from a family of generous hearts. My mother always devoted enormous amounts of time and energy to the community—teaching, helping to develop a multiracial settlement house, a community theater, and a creative dramatics program for children. She read to the blind, worked for the local chamber music and horticultural societies, and, like her own father and mother, she volunteered at hospitals. I don't remember that she ever told us to follow in her footsteps. But I think she assumed that everybody knew why she did these things and how fundamental it was to be unstintingly generous. My father, on the other hand, was a gifted but quiet man who spent his life working in a small, successful family manufacturing business. Although he served on the board of the local art museum for many years, he spent much of his spare time hunting with his dogs and playing jazz piano. He never talked with us about the meaning of social engagement, but he was widely respected for the integrity with which he ran the mill, and he provided for his family with a determination that has secured us during trials that he could never have foreseen.

As I listened to Lang, I found myself wondering about my father and wanting to understand more about how successful business people make philanthropic decisions. In particular, what motivated people, who were probably pretty focused and self-contained like Dad, to make what seem to have been such radical, long-term commitments to large numbers of low-income children who were struggling to make their way? I decided to find out.

Just who were these people? Were they simply philanthropists for whom IHAD was an extension of similar kinds of charitable activities? Had they rolled up their shirtsleeves to coach little league teams? Served on local boards of national charities? Run foundations? Used their own resources to build hospitals and endow cultural centers? Or were there ways that IHAD sponsorship was a new kind of philanthropic experience for them, as it had been for Lang? How does personalized or engaged philanthropy differ from more conventional giving behaviors? What is its impact on the philanthropist? What are its particular costs and benefits?

These are the questions that kept ringing in my head. And so, four years after the Harvard conference, I visited Gene Lang and told him that I was still intrigued when I thought about what IHAD sponsorship must have been like for the sponsors. He talked openly, with powerful feeling, about the experience. He described how his own personal, psychological investment and engagement had led to the most meaningful kind of receiving he had ever known. This was much more than giving dollars or sitting on a board. And I was captivated. Using the I Have a Dream program as a template for engaged philanthropy, I decided I would try to find out what kinds of people might decide to head down such a personal path toward giving—and what happened to them along the way.

With Lang's encouragement, over a period of several years I interviewed more than thirty IHAD sponsors, mostly in taped telephone conversations that lasted about an hour. Some I spoke with twice. A few I met with personally. In every case, my goal was to find out what made these people choose to become engaged philanthropists and how these decisions had affected their lives. In this book, I will let the people I talked to speak for themselves. To protect their privacy I have given all of them—except Lang himself—new names, and I have been circumspect about other details that might identify them specifically.

THE HEART FACTOR

After a few months of phone interviewing, I arranged to meet two sponsors in person when I was passing through their home town.

Right in the middle of our country, theirs is one of our largest, poorest cities. Between morning and afternoon interviews, the sponsors—Lou Irving, and Sam and Ann Hull (with two of their three daughters)—insisted on taking me out to lunch. It was the mid-day meal in the heart of the city's proud business district, and the large room was filled with the sounds of a workday crowd and the noises of waitresses shuttling glasses and crockery as quickly as possible. At some point, I had a fleeting memory of my father and my uncle, who had each, maybe once or twice and with no particular reason, asked me out to lunch, in the middle of their own workdays, in the Midwestern city where I had grown up. I felt special then, and again now—the way kids feel when grownups give them precious time. Lunchtime in a noisy downtown restaurant was perhaps not the best setting for contemplating the meaning of engaged philanthropy, but when Sam Hull began talking about how amazed he was by people's gratitude for his involvement in their lives, what he had to say was compelling.

The first story was simple: the father of one of his dreamers, Luis, was a watchmaker, and whenever Sam saw him the man said, "Anytime I can make a watch for you, will you tell me?" The second was more moving.

> [Another one of my] dreamers told me his dad wanted to see me. So there I am, having to walk up three floors in a filthy housing project and thinking to myself, "This guy is going to beat me up. He has a mentally deficient son and he's going to ask me to take care of the kid. I don't know what he's going to do to me but I am not looking forward to this." I go into the apartment—there's broken TVs all around—and I see the man, sitting there, spitting blood into a pan. He was dying. And he says to me, "I only had one request of my son. That was to let me talk to you. I just wanted to say 'thank you' for what you've done for me."
>
> You know, you go through all that worrying and then here's this man, sitting there, dying. He's living in incredible circumstances, trying to repair broken TV sets to get a few bucks, and he's sitting there saying "Thank you." And all you've done is give away things that are spending money, from my point of view. Some things break your heart.

Well, I thought, some things break your heart if you have a heart to break. After a dozen interviews, I was already sure that IHAD sponsors were people with big hearts and a tremendous love of life.

When I called the O'Donnells—Meg and Mike—for an interview, Meg insisted that I come to spend the night. There was much too much to say for us to talk on the phone, she said, and I needed to see all the pictures of the dreamers that Mike had taken over the years. After several hours of taped conversation, they too took me out for a meal, in the downtown district of a medium-sized New England city. And again, this time amidst the hubbub of cocktails and a seven o'clock dinner after a busy work day, these sponsors regaled me with stories—about their own pasts and about their dreamers who, by now, had been in their lives for more than a decade. Mike and Meg were well known in their town. During the meal, several people came over to greet them—talking about changes afoot at civic organizations, internecine law-office gossip, recent headlines in the local paper. And along with a great fish chowder came vivid stories about everything—Peace Corps experiences, art school training, political campaigns, local foundation work, what their grandparents had done during the Depression, drug busts and runaway children, and, over and over again, their sense of personal gratitude toward the kids whom they'd sponsored for so many years. And with certainty they insisted that they were absolutely sure they had gotten more out of IHAD—more from their long involvement with dreamers in their home town—than they had ever put in. Eventually they happened on the word "acceptance." For the O'Donnells, it has been being accepted in spite of all the differences—age, class, ethnicity—that has meant the most to them. Bridging gaps and belonging. Being taken into these children's hearts.

The heart factor. Whatever it meant, I'd have to be open to exploring it as I proceeded to interview and analyze. One of the strongest feelings I had about the sponsors with whom I'd spoken so far was that, like Lang, like the people who loved me when I was young, they were powerful connectors. They wanted to move beyond difference. To stay in touch as things changed. And choosing to have caring relationships with kids over time gave them a deep kind of joy within themselves. They were open to the rewards of connection. I'd had earlier, more rational hypotheses about findings that might emerge from these interviews. I'd assumed I'd find that IHAD sponsors shared certain frames of mind, histories, temperaments, and ambitions. But the heart factor was the most powerful of them all.

In fact, among IHAD sponsors I have found both striking commonalities and a great many differences. It's been a wonderful privilege to get to know a small group of people so dedicated to improving the lot of those in need. It's not so easy to stay hopeful in today's world. But to experience the vigorous connectedness of these IHAD sponsors—the way they shake your hand firmly, look deeply into your eyes, listen to everything you say, and share their own stories as generously and warmly as they have shared their resources with young people— makes you understand the power of human initiative and caring. And many of the sponsors with whom I've spoken repeat, in one way or another, what Lang himself says: they had no idea what they were getting into when they began but their lives have been irrevocably altered by their commitment and engagement. What's more, they're sure they have gotten even more from the experience than the young people they have helped. For many, this kind of giving has been transformative.

ENGAGED PHILANTHROPY

This book is not meant as a promotion of the I Have a Dream Foundation. Over the past few decades, a number of extraordinary people have initiated programs that have made very significant differences for low-income children. For example, in 1987 George Weiss, interested in Lang's example, founded Say Yes To Education. Like the I Have a Dream program, Weiss' program provides a range of supports and services to inner-city children who face the kinds of hefty challenges that often obstruct a young person's success in school. Unlike the I Have a Dream projects, each Say Yes initiative rests on a solid school-university partnership. But like Lang, Weiss promises higher education to his children when they finish high school. And Mr. Weiss has been the exclusive funder for each project. He has had a profound impact on the lives of many children. Because I Have a Dream has allowed me to gather data from a varied group of engaged philanthropists, I've been able to construct a kind of case study that lets us reflect generally about the meaning of personal engagement over time—not specifically for those less fortunate than ourselves but for those who decide to "do good" up front and in person. We have an opportunity to better understand the consequences of such decisions—not on the object of the impulse, but on the agent.

To describe the sponsoring experience as simply a kind of "giving" is crude and inaccurate. Engaged philanthropy is much more complex and intimate than this word implies. Sponsoring, it turns out, is not only standing but walking in another's shoes. It is not only "being there" but growing along with people and institutions as they change. It is not always a matter of "knowing best" but of being ready to "learn along with" others in many different contexts. It is being ready for adventure. As one sponsor quoted on IHAD's website has said,

> The most important thing is relationship. . . . When you're
> involved in the hearts and homes of these children and they
> accept you and you accept them, anything can happen.
> That's the most important thing.

Today we live in a world where the distance between those with resources and those without is greater than it has ever been. The greatest percentage of the world's wealth is in the hands of a tiny proportion of its people. In the course of this inquiry, I have heard many times about sponsors' friends and acquaintances who "have more money than they know what to do with," or who are "looking for a higher purpose in their lives." What might happen, I wonder, if we all began to understand the deep rewards of moving beyond what is familiar and instead engaging with people in other worlds? What might happen if everyone understood that, far from being a one-way experience, personal social investment has astounding and immeasurable rewards for all concerned? Might an account of IHAD sponsor experiences encourage other good, energetic philanthropists to get personally involved in the lives of people whose futures they may now only dream of improving from a distance?

One lesson I have learned from this inquiry is that by taking action we change ourselves. May this book itself be a javelin: it is directed at all of us who need to know that immeasurable, unexpected rewards come from reaching out to people in different worlds and from staying connected, over time, with others who need us. There is so much we can do.

CHAPTER 2

OVERVIEWS AND CLOSE-UPS

Personalized philanthropy has the potential to
transform relationships structured around "gifts" to
relationships embodying care. . . . It requires a meaningful
relationship—giving does not.
                —Joseph Kahne, "Personalized Philanthropy"

Given the privileges of choice and efficacy that money affords, philanthropists have precious opportunities. They can contribute to the development of nations and institutions, the advancement of scholars and scientists, the prevention of disease, the resolution of international conflict, the alleviation of poverty. They can create and support new initiatives dedicated to their strongest passions. By intentionally supporting endowments, interventions, or inquiry, philanthropists can have measurable impact on public problems about which they care deeply. They can make a mark on the world.

Of course no philanthropic act is thoroughly unilateral, something that only benefits the recipient. There is great personal satisfaction in being able to give money for a new hospital or theater, a special scholarship program, a new research initiative. And before they became involved with IHAD, many of the sponsors I interviewed had followed fairly conventional, more remote models of philanthropic giving. Some had served from a distance as board or advisory committee members, as fund-raisers, or as advocates for a range of large and small community institutions, including, for example, hospitals, symphonies, schools, faith-based organizations, museums, community music schools, settlement houses. Some had run family foundations, been involved at times with hiring staff, soliciting proposals, discovering promising programs, reviewing proposals, and awarding grants. But all of these kinds of philanthropic acts are discrete and bounded. They do not expose the donor to the kinds of unpredictable ups and downs that happen during a period of many years when one is in direct relationship with the people who are the ultimate recipients of the gift. When sponsors step into IHAD, they are committing themselves to a different, more personalized kind of giving. They will be caring for children who live in worlds far removed from their own. In choosing to become engaged philanthropists, IHAD sponsors are deciding to be more than finite, financial givers, to move beyond one-way forms of generosity. And they are taking action in a way that may change their lives dramatically.

SPONSORS AND THEIR DREAMERS

What do IHAD sponsors actually do? First of all, sponsors begin by raising funds and creating a financial structure for managing them. IHAD programs are run as independent, non-profit organizations—501 C (3)s. When there is more than one IHAD project running in a given city, it is common to fold the initiatives together into one local IHAD foundation. This foundation, governed by a community board, functions as the administrative umbrella for all local projects.

At the start, sponsors choose the age group and site for their programs. Though Lang adopted a class of sixth-grade children when they graduated from elementary school, many sponsors now begin with younger children. Whatever group they choose, sponsors must hire a project coordinator (PC) and establish memoranda of agreement with partnering schools and/or community-based organizations. Many also draft contracts for students and parents to sign. Once they've made their public commitment to their chosen dreamers, sponsors work with their project coordinators and their community partners as managers, in a way. They begin by designing a structure of regular, age-appropriate activities that bring additional attentive adults into the children's lives. Activities may include individual and group mentoring, tutoring, afterschool programs, summer schools and summer camps, cultural enrichment trips, career exploration and college guidance, and home visits. Over the years, as sponsors get to know their dreamers and the youngsters' needs change, they may set up additional interventions in response to particular developmental issues that come up—for example, activities focusing on pregnancy prevention, peer counseling, public speaking, self-esteem, study skills, violence prevention, anger management, and grief counseling.

Managing the logistics of their projects is one way that IHAD sponsors are actively and regularly engaged with their dreamers and the community. But IHAD sponsors are also involved through active investment in personal relationships with their dreamers over a long period of time. Lang's fundamental conviction about the central importance of consistent, caring relationships in children's lives is the engine that drives the IHAD model. The projects are all built around activities that give kids meaningful relationships with adults, including the sponsors themselves.

Because every IHAD project is shaped by the individual vision and temperament of its sponsor or sponsors, each is distinct. Sponsors may decide to meet with their dreamers weekly, bi-weekly, or monthly in their schools, in the project office, at their own workplace, or in a community setting. One sponsor chose to have birthday groups so she could gather together all the dreamers whose birthdays occur during a particular month for a pizza party and conversation. Others choose to be a more frequent presence in the children's lives. Lou Irving, for example.

> Our school was two stories tall and my kids—the sixth graders—were up on the second floor. I made it a point—every day that was possible—to go to school at 2:30 or 3:00. We didn't live all that far. And I would stand at the bottom of the stairs. And watch my kids come down. I wanted them to see me. Because I wanted them to know there was a presence—that we were with them. I didn't say, "Hey, come talk to me." I just wanted them to know I was there, that there was someone—if they wanted to—someone they could talk to, ask questions. Joe, our PC, used to call me "the guy at the bottom of the stairs." And then I'd stick around the school, and some of the kids would come into the PC's office.

Who are the dreamers? As IHAD explanatory materials note, they are "children from low-income areas," from "some of the most disadvantaged neighborhoods," from "schools that generally have low achievement scores, high dropout rates, and low projections of college attendance." Many—but not all—dreamers match current descriptions of children who are considered to be "at risk." That is, they are youngsters whose prospects for healthy development and success are threatened by a variety of chronic challenges including poverty, family unemployment or illness, inadequate housing, poor nutrition, lack of access to health care.

Most dreamers attend severely under-resourced schools. Most have parents who work—often at more than one job. Dreamer families may find it hard to be actively involved in their children's education. Many dreamers' parents left school themselves before they were eighteen; few have had any experience with higher education. And many feel uncomfortable with their children's teachers. In fact, a lot of dreamer families eagerly anticipate their children's eighth-grade graduations, saving money to buy special dresses and jackets for what they expect may be their son's or daughter's only commencement. And parents aren't the only ones with modest expectations for these children. As Lang's interaction with the principal at his old elementary school illustrates, many teachers and administrators in under-resourced schools don't expect many of their students to finish high school either.

"Once a dreamer, always a dreamer." This tenet is central to the commitment that most IHAD sponsors make to their kids. It means that if for any reason a child drops out of school, moves, or doesn't graduate, he or she can still turn to the sponsor for guidance and support. Not all dreamers want to stay in touch—and some sponsors have a more robust commitment to this feature of the contract than others. But most of those who choose to become IHAD sponsors do so because they are in it for the long haul. They want these young kids to know that they are earnest about wanting to help them through life.

Of course, this means there will be lots of surprises along the way—and sponsors are surprised many times. Some examples? Most dreamers qualify for hot breakfasts and/or free or reduced-price lunches at school during the week, and some sponsors have found themselves bringing those kids meals during school vacations, to take up the slack. At times they take dreamers to optometrists, orthodontists, and lawyers. From time to time they may have to pick up groceries for a family, buy clean clothes, help locate a new prosthetic device. They make trips to emergency rooms and arrange for medical evaluations or family counseling. Sometimes they find themselves helping a family look for housing, paying an occasional gas or electric bill, searching for foster homes or emergency shelters. One sponsor I spoke with had donated a washing machine and dryer to a school so her students could wear clean uniforms.

Some sponsors have worked side-by-side with their dreamers in community service projects. One such project involved building a playground in an abandoned city park. The activity garnered so much attention and respect in its community that the city's mayor decided to replicate the initiative by incorporating it into a summer youth project. Now there are twenty-three play spaces throughout the city that have been built by kids. Sponsors may write newsletters, spend time in classrooms, have weekly rap sessions with their dreamers at different stages of their school careers. One sponsor stayed in regular touch with a dreamer struggling through the difficult first months of US Marine Corps basic training. Another recalled supporting a youngster in a residential treatment center.

Above all, sponsors play and explore with the kids. They take them bowling and fishing, skiing and ice-skating, to climb mountains and pick apples; they fund field trips, celebrate birthdays, host cookouts, set up visits to colleges and local businesses, organize public speaking programs; they take kids to baseball games, to the symphony, to the beach. They bake Christmas cookies, host holiday parties, find summer jobs, send kids postcards from their travels.

Clearly a commitment to this kind of giving involves responsibilities that have an enormous impact on the engaged philanthropist's life. We will meet several more IHAD sponsors in the second half of this chapter, but first I think a brief review of some past and current observations and research about mentoring programs, philanthropy, and human development through the lifespan will help explain the context in which they and others have made such active, long-term commitments.

MENTORING, PHILANTHROPY, AND GENERATIVITY

MENTORING

At its heart, IHAD is a mentoring program and, over the past twenty years, there has been a great increase in such initiatives. The earliest ones aimed to enhance productivity in the workplace by providing new or stressed workers with supportive, collegial relationships. Business people, novice teachers, and health care professionals, for instance, received ongoing guidance and support from experienced peers, and this kind of personalized coaching was seen to improve workplace performance and morale.

Descriptions of mentoring programs for children and youth often begin by referring to the character of Mentor, the Greek elder who protected Telemachus during the long absence of his father, Odysseus, and they have often been shaped by traditional psychological assumptions that equate maturity with autonomy. Good mentors, counselors, coaches, or advisors, it is proposed, help young people grow up by encouraging them to move toward competent self-sufficiency and "stand on their own two feet."

Programs involving the mentoring of children and adolescents grew significantly during the 1980s and early 1990s—just as the public was becoming more familiar with the challenges that confront at risk children and youth. Bill Shore, author of *The Cathedral Within*, cites the Carnegie Council's recommendations, which advise that at risk kids are more likely to beat the multiple odds stacked against them if certain conditions are met:

> They must be in sustained, caring relationships with adults; receive guidance in facing serious challenges; become valued members of a constructive peer group; feel a sense of worth as a person; become socially competent; . . . find expression for the curiosity and exploration that strongly characterizes their age; believe in a promising future with real opportunities; and find ways of being useful to others.[3]

Data from the well established Big Brother/Big Sister program bear this out, helping researchers to show that well run, longitudinal mentoring programs that create "caring relationships between adults and youth . . . yield a wide range of tangible benefits," which include improving academic performance and delaying young people's first use of drugs and alcohol.[4]

In his book, *The Kindness of Strangers*, Mark Freedman describes specific ways that mentoring can make a big difference for urban youth: by giving them information they might not otherwise have, by helping them cope with a great variety of pressures, and by bringing nurturant, supportive relationships into their lives.[5] In addition to reviewing some of the social factors that have contributed to heightened interest in mentoring and considering the basic psychological processes that inform good mentoring relationships, Jean Rhodes analyzes findings from program evaluations and looks clearly at the challenges of implementing strong mentoring programs. According to Rhodes, these initiatives give mentors important perspectives on poverty that they would not otherwise have, and good mentoring relationships can stimulate civic participation in young people who might otherwise not see the value of social engagement.[6]

One reason that mentoring is so attractive is that the process itself seems so accessible and familiar. We know—or think we know in our hearts—what mentoring is, what it takes, what it can mean. We feel we have had, or maybe we have missed, an idealized relationship with a protector who could make us feel special, cared for, and confident in the future. As Freedman says, mentoring has six straightforward appeals: it is simple, direct, sympathetic, legitimate, bounded, and plastic. It satisfies an individual's desire to be of direct assistance to young people in a way that is both defined and "accommodating" to a variety of perspectives.[7] Advocates for mentoring programs note that these programs reflect

> a quintessentially American outlook: optimistic, individualistic, anti-institutional, anchored in the belief that we can reinvent ourselves—even the most disadvantaged among us—and overcome the odds, no matter how daunting . . . [Mentoring implies] a heroic conception of social policy.[8]

In reality, of course, mentoring is not a quick or easy fix for the personal loneliness, isolation, and alienation that many young people experience today. When it's done well, mentoring centers around a nurturing relationship that endures over time—in spite of a large range of obstacles, including logistical changes, difference, and discomfort. But structuring these programs so that mentors are really constant and continuous in their relationships with children—especially ones who have been frequently abandoned and disappointed—can be difficult. Good training is a critical component of strong programs and, sadly, it is common to hear of service initiatives that don't have enough resources to provide ongoing, consistent training of mentors.

Most mentoring programs have relied heavily on private sector funding. And it is not a coincidence that many of these programs began during the 1980s, a decade in which what remained of a fifty-year-old safety net of supportive social services for the neediest among us was shredded.[9] As public funding for organizations that had been created to address social problems decreased, new approaches were developed to help meet society's most serious needs. The needs were growing, but so were perspectives about the interrelated consequences of poverty and social neglect.

PHILANTHROPY

In her book *Why the Wealthy Give*, sociologist Francie Ostrower explores "the culture of elite philanthropy." In their habits of giving as in their lives, she reports, the elite have traditionally tended to remain apart. Until the last few decades of the twentieth century, the kind of philanthropy most often practiced by wealthy people had been the anonymous, "arm's length" kind of giving, This tends to reinforce a separate, privileged way of life. Serving on boards, for example, offers donors a trustee role that usually keeps them at some distance from the rest of the world. It also confirms their identity as members of a special cohort. In the nineteen-eighties, however, a number of changing social factors began to influence the demographics of philanthropy. The boundaries delineating the old elite from those with "new money" shifted and new donors emerged. At first,

> the newly wealthy and the formerly excluded shared the priorities of previously established elites and valued similar organizations. . . . [M]ore entrenched members of the elite were willing to open up the doors to "outsiders" in order to preserve the organizations they valued.[10]

At the same time, these new donors brought with them new perspectives and goals.

Meanwhile, as the private sector—including a burgeoning number of nonprofit organizations—has begun to play an increasingly important role in addressing public sector problems, new studies have focused on emerging patterns of philanthropic behavior. Using a large data set, researchers Russ Prince and Karen File, for example, developed a "Seven Faces" approach to describe "donor segmentation," shaped around seven distinctive donor profiles: the Communitarian, the Devout, the Investor, the Socialite, the Altruist, the Repayer, and the Dynast.[11] They address the intentions of donors systematically, categorizing and quantifying specific aspects of giving behaviors with reference to demography, motivation, strategy, and personal expectation. While this study helps fund seekers, grant writers, and nonprofit institutions to understand patterns of giving and advance strategic developmental planning, it also documents new approaches to philanthropy.

These new approaches have a variety of names, but whether they are called "engaged," "venture," "social," or "moral" philanthropy they have in common a personalization of the process of giving. As Joseph Kahne writes,

> Personalized philanthropy might build bridges of understanding, trust and respect. It aims to forge relationships that bridge social class as well as racial and ethnic divides. When such bridges are built, proponents argue, the impact on both those who receive support and those who provide it can be substantial.[12]

In personalizing the relationship between donor and beneficiary, these new approaches are changing the traditional structure of the charitable relationship. Venture philanthropists, for example, invest not only their own money but also their talents, time, and expertise to direct projects, design evaluations for the initiatives they are funding, and sometimes involve themselves directly in program implementation.[13] Bill Shore notes that most of the new philanthropists are experienced entrepreneurs. As such, they are people who are willing to take risks others would not take, by exposing themselves to greater potential loss than would others or, perhaps, than common sense dictates. Such rule-breaking is for a purpose, of course ... getting to a desired outcome.... Entrepreneurs seize opportunities ... break rules by thinking outside of them, not because they are rebellious or ornery, but because their own lives have not followed a linear path.[14]

Like "jaywalkers," Shore says, who are "too impatient to wait for the light to change," entrepreneurial philanthropists feel empowered by understanding their strengths and putting them to work on behalf of others.[15]

When entrepreneurs become philanthropists, they may assume a wide range of roles and responsibilities in the projects in which they get involved. Applying techniques practiced in their successful businesses, they help shape initiatives that are aligned with their values. Often drawing on their own experiences in overcoming adversity, these people, Shore finds,

are redefining not only what it means to give back to society, but also what it will take to solve society's most pressing problems, whether in education, poverty, health care, child development, or other critical areas of need. Pioneering strategies of personal engagement and leverage, the moral entrepreneurs have the potential to unleash and mobilize the talents and resources of society's most successful individuals to address our most pressing needs. The product at the core of their business ... is the transformed conscience of their fellow human beings.[16]

When all this happens, the philanthropists have crossed the traditional divide between giver and beneficiary. This doesn't mean that they don't still carry the burden of power in the relationship—they *are* paying to sustain the process, after all. But it does open up a large range of possibilities for relationships between the giver and the beneficiary.

In several large studies of wealth and philanthropy, Paul Schervish and his colleagues at Boston College's Social Welfare Research Institute have done research about a subset of millionaires engaged in the kind of "adoption philanthropy" that IHAD exemplifies. Adoption philanthropy, they find, differs from other kinds of giving because it is a "personal and often unmediated relation between philanthropists and the individual or collective beneficiaries of their assistance."[17] Adoption philanthropists are particularly eager to do something individualized and personal. They want to have an impact on the reality of their beneficiaries' lives. In some way they identify with certain aspects of the recipients' lives and derive a tremendous sense of gratification from making a difference in a relationship characterized by both their caring and their power.[18]

"Hyperagency" is a trait that Schervish says distinguishes the very wealthy from others. It means having an "ability to construct rather than merely live (even well) within one's social environment."[19] That is, unlike most of us who dream about what we could do if we had more resources, the very wealthy actually can make their dreams come true. But, as Schervish points out in relation to adoption philanthropy, "Transforming the destiny of others is a delicate moral enterprise."[20] Within each philanthropist, he reminds us, are contradictory impulses both to care and to control. Because of the intimate contact that can develop between donor and donee in adoption philanthropy, there is always the potential for the philanthropist to cross that delicate boundary that can distinguish care from control. While pointing out the delicacy of the adoptive philanthropic relationship, Schervish also emphasizes that this model is one that realizes an ideal form of giving.

> [It] embodies the crucial attributes that transpose philanthropy from a distanced and sometimes faceless practice of monetary contributions to an empathetic social relation engaging the donor's time and effort. As such, adoption philanthropy . . . can be considered the prototype of ethical charity. Although it would be neither practical nor advantageous for adoption philanthropy to become the only valid strategy, it would prove fruitful if its positive relational elements were to become incorporated into the various other strategies.[21]

GENERATIVITY

In his book *Prime Time*, Marc Freedman describes a number of promising community service initiatives that are engaging older people in particular—"third agers"—in a range of community service and mentoring programs. This opens up another perspective on IHAD and similar programs. As Freedman says,

> We are on the verge of a doubling of people in the stage of life when the principal developmental task will be coming to terms with what it means to be generative, to pass on to the younger generations what we have learned from life.[22]

Freedman reports that seniors who take part in these programs say they get back much more than they give, that they find great value in having the chance to "leave good memories of yourself, to leave something behind that's worthwhile."[23]

This kind of participation in community life represents what Erik Erikson, the pioneering psychologist and stage theorist, called generativity. Usually a feature of the later years, generativity unites an "interest in establishing and guiding the next generation" with a degree of "emotional integration which permits participation by followership as well as acceptance of the responsibility of leadership."[24]

Since the 1980s, studies of human development have devoted increasing attention to the complex ways that psychosocial development continues throughout the human lifespan. Approaching development from a diversity of perspectives, some researchers focus on the broad ecology of our lives—where and when we live. Stage theorists propose that development proceeds along a continuum that reflects the increasingly complex mastery of age- and stage-appropriate tasks. (Erikson's enormously influential *Childhood and Society*, published in 1963, remains a classic example of this approach.) Some developmentalists emphasize transitional events as the principle determinants of growth; others map the process of development through in-depth analyses of the kinds of meaning people make of their lives, at different ages, in relation to core themes like career, family, intimacy, and family life.[25]

Some lifespan theorists suggest that development can be seen as a scaffold structured around core themes that anchor people's identity during different decades of their lives. For example, the twenties are seen as a time to master intimacy and the thirties a decade centering around career issues. Middle adulthood—from forty to fifty—is a time of reorganization and renewal: people's primary preoccupations may now center on self-reliance, self-analysis, and a new sense of independence. Then, when people begin their fifties, they are readier to become more interdependent again, more connected with others. This includes a new willingness to assume leadership roles—so they can put into practice what they have learned during the preceding decades of their lives.[26]

A recent study by Warren Bennis and Robert Thompson explores how the capacity for leadership reflects both personal and societal history. The authors, who hold that leaders develop when personal and social history coincide with transforming events in their lives, summarize the attributes of two disparate generations of leaders, one born in 1925 (the "geezers") and the other born in 1975 (the "geeks"). Geezers lived through the Great Depression and the Second World War. They grew up worried, aware of their own vulnerability and the fallibility of their parents, and wanting stability and security. For them, entrepreneurship often became a way to put themselves in charge of their own destinies. Geeks, on the other hand, came of age during the 1990s, a decade the authors call an "era of options." Geek behaviors reflect a comfort with abundance, technology, globalization, and large-scale growth.

> Geezers and Geeks did not stand for opposed or contradictory things at the same age as much as they were trying to find their bearings in very different times. Geezers felt themselves reaching for a stable handhold after a period of instability and scrabbling. Geeks, on the other hand, looked to be reaching for higher limbs in the tree with an innate assurance that either they wouldn't fall or that someone or something would be there to catch them if they did. An interesting paradox, in other words. Geezers at roughly age 30 were striving to put instability behind them, while geeks were impatient to shake things up.[27]

Both geeks and geezers share certain characteristics with the IHAD sponsors I interviewed in the course of my own inquiry. These include high energy, optimism, an ability to communicate very well, and a highly developed capacity to observe and understand both the bold and the subtle aspects of context.

Bennis and Thomas identify two more characteristics that are particularly relevant to the topic of this book. One is what they call the leader's "adaptive capacity," which fosters curiosity and confidence and turns what others might experience as anxiety into attractive feelings of challenge and stimulation. Like most IHAD sponsors, the leaders in their study

> believe that if they leap, a net will appear—or, if it doesn't, they will be able to find or fashion one in time. Where others see only chaos and confusion, they see opportunity.[28]

Bennis and Thomas call the second relevant characteristic "neoteny," after "a zoological term [defined] as 'the retention of youthful qualities by adults.'"

> Neoteny is the retention of all those wonderful qualities that we associate with youth: curiosity, playfulness, eagerness, fearlessness, warmth, energy. Unlike those defeated by time and age, our geezers have remained much like our geeks—open, willing to take risks, hungry for knowledge and experience, courageous, eager to see what the new day brings. Time and loss steal the zest from the unlucky and leave them looking longingly at the past. Neoteny is a metaphor for the quality—the gift—that keeps the fortunate of whatever age focused on all the marvelous undiscovered things to come.[29]

It would seem that, taken together, their adaptive and neotenous attributes reinforce what for the leaders Bennis and Thomas studied may be an almost instinctive attraction to risk. Most IHAD sponsors are people who define themselves as risk-takers and entrepreneurs. While they may not all think of themselves as leaders, they certainly direct their projects and, in fact, because of their public commitments, many become important members of their communities.

After a four-decade study of adult development building in part on Erikson's authoritative work, researcher George Vaillant has found that once people master the tasks of identity, intimacy, and career, generativity often manifests itself in "community building."

> Depending on the opportunities that the society makes available, generativity can mean serving as consultant, guide, mentor or coach to young adults in the larger society. Research reveals that between the ages of 30 and 45 the need for achievement declines and our need for community and affiliation increases. We may view deans, matriarchs, and business magnates as the products of crass ambition and infantile narcissism. But in so doing we ignore the psychosocial skills necessary to allow one individual to assume sensitive responsibility for other adults. Empathic leadership only looks like self-aggrandizement until one tries to do it.[30]

Vaillant shares with Erikson a deep understanding of the relational component of human development and a central interest in generativity and what Erikson called "integrity"—a mature experience of satisfaction and acceptance with what one's life has been. Today these achievements, widely acknowledged as important components of lifelong health and well-being, are increasingly seen in relation to one's connectedness with others.[31]

It is not surprising that caring for others is a critical component of healthy maturity. It has profound rewards—not the least of which is a feeling of power for those who may too often be thought of simplistically as "altruistic." In fact, it is enormously gratifying to feel one's life coming into alignment with one's beliefs.[32] A deep sense of gratitude for the opportunities one has been given can fuel an impulse to contribute, to serve.

And in serving, through connection, one discovers what another seminal theorist, Eric Fromm, spoke of as love and sometimes even as faith. In *The Art of Loving*, Fromm connects love with giving and describes its intimate joys in ways that coincide with the satisfactions that many people say they experience from engaged philanthropy:

> [W]hoever is capable of giving of himself ... experiences himself as one who can confer of himself to others. . . .
> In giving he cannot help bringing something to life in the

other person and this which is brought to life reflects back to him.[33]

As we shall see, many of the experiences described by the IHAD sponsors interviewed for this book coincide with Fromm's reflections on the relationship between love and action.

> Love is an act of faith, and whoever is of little faith is also of little love. . . . [And] activity is an indispensable feature of love. To be fully awake is the condition for not being bored, or being boring—and indeed, not to be bored or boring is one of the main conditions for loving. To be active in thought, feeling, with one's eyes and ears, throughout the day, to avoid inner laziness, be it in the form of being receptive, hoarding, or plain wasting one's time, is an indispensable condition for the practice of the art of loving. It is an illusion to believe that one can separate life in such a way that one is productive in the sphere of love and unproductive in all other spheres. Productiveness does not permit of such a division of labor. The capacity to love demands a state of intensity, awakeness, enhanced vitality, which can only be the result of a productive and active orientation in many other spheres of life. If one is not productive in other spheres, one is not productive in love either.[34]

One of the rewards of becoming engaged in the world, then, is what Fromm calls "the enhanced vitality" of a life that connects us to one another.

MEETING THE SPONSORS

Over a period of three years (2001–2004), I talked with thirty-eight people, including Eugene Lang, about their long-term relationships with IHAD and the impact their involvement with the program has had on their lives. I think of those who followed most immediately in Lang's footsteps—who became affiliated with IHAD in the 1980s—as "first generation" sponsors, and those who began in 1990 or later as belonging to a "second generation." Some demographic patterns distinguish the two groups. Of first generation sponsors, many—though

not all—were in their fifties and sixties when they adopted their first
IHAD class, and most—though not all—were people who are now
described as "high net worth" individuals. They tended to bear full
financial responsibility for their programs themselves. Although some
second generation sponsors have also borne all project costs by themselves, as a group they are more likely to have structured and sustained
their IHAD projects through various kinds of consortium funding.[35]

Among the first generation sponsors with whom I've spoken,
most were themselves the products of public elementary and secondary schools. Among the second generation, some sponsors had
attended private or parochial elementary or secondary schools. All
but four of the first generation sponsors I interviewed were married at
the time they adopted their classes; only two second generation sponsors were single when they began their projects. (I hasten to add that
being married does not mean that sponsors and their spouses shared
equal responsibilities for IHAD projects. As we shall see, some IHAD
sponsors went into their projects very plan-fully; others, particularly
among the first generation, had almost tumbled into the experience,
as Lang had done, with few ideas about what lay ahead. Especially in
the latter case, project adoption could, of course, mean unexpected
changes for sponsors' spouses.)

This book is structured around the voices of the sponsors. We
have already begun to learn something about Lang's story, in his own
words. Now I want to introduce four other sponsors, representing
three IHAD projects. I have chosen these individuals to give readers
a sense of the different stories that sponsors have to tell. (Again, to
protect their privacy, names have been changed and certain details
blurred.) These brief portraits are intended to introduce the reader
to the appeal of these individual stories, invite them to experience the
power of what sponsors describe as engaged philanthropy, and help
orient them before we examine other sponsors' narratives in a more
thematic way.

LAURA AND RICHARD:
TAKING CARE OF "OUR KIDS"

Laura and Richard Joseph met at one of the country's oldest Ivy League universities, located some distance from where each had grown up. Richard's family lived in a poor Southern state—one that was second to the lowest, nationally, in terms of educational achievement in the year that he graduated, at the age of sixteen, from his town's public high school. His father, a butcher who owned several small meat markets, was too preoccupied with the details of supporting his family to spend any time talking with his children about the importance of community service. But both of Richard's parents stressed how necessary it was for their children to get more education than they themselves had had.

Laura, on the other hand, went to university-affiliated schools, "lab" schools steeped in John Dewey's experiential approach to learning and life, in the large Midwestern city where she grew up. Her father, a general practitioner, often took her with him when he visited patients and made it very clear that what he was doing was the kind of work she would one day do as well.

When Richard graduated from the university in 1955, Laura left her own studies to marry him, and Richard joined the Navy. After his military service was complete, the two stayed on the West Coast while Laura supported her husband, who went back to school to get an M.B.A. Three daughters came along, and after a year of work in the Southwest, the family settled in a large city in the East, where Richard moved directly into the world of finance. By the late 1960s he had done well enough to start his own investment company. When their youngest daughter was ready for first grade, Laura started back to school to finish her bachelor's degree and get a master's degree and a doctorate in developmental psychology. In the meantime, she spent the next ten or fifteen years as an interior designer, volunteering actively at her children's schools, and working most intensively with hearing impaired children. Following a special interest in literacy, she eventually became the director of a school for the deaf.

Richard's company was very successful, and by the late 1980s, when it went public, he had decided it was time to leave. He'd read about IHAD in *Fortune* magazine and had the thought that he would like to create a fund to educate children in the low-income Southern community where he had grown up. But when he approached Eugene Lang, Lang pointed out to him that this was not the program's intention: he, Richard, no longer lived in that place, and direct sponsor engagement with the kids was always at the center of the model.

Richard, then fifty-three, and Laura, fifty-two, had sent their children to independent schools. Although they knew nothing about the problems of under-funded public schools in "the big city," he was intrigued by the challenge. And, he said, "it seemed to me that maybe after thirty-five years of marriage we should get a common interest." They would start, he suggested, with sixth graders. "That will never work," Laura said, insisting that her training made her confident that this was much too late to turn things around for kids. But Richard, not easily daunted, assured her that, with his background of success in business, it would be no problem.

And so, with their own three daughters grown, Richard and Laura became IHAD sponsors in a school that was located in a seriously under-served neighborhood in the city that was now their home. The district superintendent had expressed real concerns about the large numbers of under-performing Latino children at this school; he had also said he did not want do-gooders coming into the neighborhood, even if they said they were going to try to get the kids into college. This challenge only cemented their resolve: they began the program promptly, in September of 1987.

One year later Richard and Laura both realized that if they were really to make a difference for the children they now thought of as "our kids," they would have to start at the very beginning. Almost every business Richard had been involved in was a small one that he had either helped to expand or had created himself. So, while they continued to sponsor their dreamers, they also began negotiating with the city to open a new school. By the time their original dreamers were in tenth grade, they had navigated through the school system's minefields of bureaucratic and political obstacles to create the first of two new schools, both of which now begin with the youngest children and function as charter schools in the same neighborhood.

IHAD sponsoring, Laura and Richard discovered, "took a great deal more than we had imagined it would to keep the kids on track and going in positive directions." It was, Laura says, almost like setting up a "mini social-service organization," and often more about keeping kids alive than getting them into college. But the experience led them both into new lives, for they established a foundation that is dedicated to improving urban children's educational opportunities by creating autonomous, high-performing public schools. Running the foundation has become a way for them to develop and nurture the schools, and this work continues to absorb them as intensely as any other jobs they have had. Along the way, they've seen some of their original IHAD dreamers come back to the community to work in their charter schools.

When Richard thinks about his former colleagues, most of whom are still plugging away at the same work they've been doing for forty years, he feels they're missing a great deal. Now, he says, he has a passion for what he is doing: it is valuable work, it is new, and it is tremendously energizing. He and Laura have always had a strong partnership. When Richard struggled with business dilemmas, Laura, listening intently, would help him thread his way through interpersonal challenges. And Richard's keen analytic skills, in turn, helped Laura solve the organizational nightmares she encountered in her own work. They both feel terribly lucky for their marriage of fifty years, and for their three daughters, who have all turned into people whose lives combine entrepreneurship and philanthropy. And when she watches her grandchildren play, Laura notices that they too have begun to reflect the culture of community commitment and engagement that she and her husband and their daughters have modeled for years.

Laura acknowledges that neither she nor Richard ever really knew anything about the effects of true poverty until they began working with inner-city children. They have learned more than they ever dreamed they would. But they never feel "hopelessly stuck," she says. Richard has shown Laura that one can always find money for a good idea; and Laura believes in the immeasurable value of connection between people and, she says, in the universe's only constant—the law of change.

TESSA: DOING MORE

Tessa Bloom was born and raised in South Africa, the youngest of three girls. Her father owned a small supermarket in a tiny village of two hundred families where, one generation earlier, her Lithuanian grandparents had decided to stop their wagon. Her father and mother worked together at the store until, when Tessa was nine, the family moved into a larger town about twenty minutes away. Her father traveled daily to keep his market running, but in the city the girls began attending a bigger school. Here the teachers who made the strongest impression on Tessa were the mean ones. Corporal punishment was a regular feature of South African education, and she has vivid memories of "boys being caned and girls smacked." "They got you to behave!" But the South African public education system, she says with some distress, worked well enough for white children. She majored in speech, drama, and English, and got a master's degree in education. Her husband majored in accountancy and got a master's degree in economics.

Tessa's family was a traditional, but not Orthodox, Jewish family. They observed the Sabbath weekly and went to services on all the Jewish holidays. And when the family moved into the larger town, the Jewish community there seemed a lot like the little village where she had spent her first nine years—tight and cohesive, with everyone knowing everyone else. Part of the Jewish religion is its tradition of *tzedakah*, or giving back. "Charity is the most important thing you can do," Tessa says. And one thing she and her husband have always loved about IHAD is that it is not a handout: instead of giving people fish, as the saying goes, it teaches them how to fish, prepares them to provide for themselves all their lives.

When Tessa and her husband, Josh, married and decided to start their own family, they rejected the idea of bringing their children up in an apartheid system and moved to a large city in the eastern United States. Her husband's family had a department store in South Africa and the entrepreneurial gene was strong: he and his brother began a successful retail business. The brothers did very well, focusing primarily on retail and real estate development and expanding to several other cities in different parts of the country. Tessa was very involved with volunteer activities at her children's Jewish day school when they were young. At the same time, she worked part-time with her husband. In 1990 the family resettled permanently in a large southeastern coastal city and Tessa began to work full-time for the family business. Tessa's two sisters live in Israel and South Africa. One of her two daughters lives in Israel and the other two are in the northeast.

In 1986, Tessa and her husband saw the *60 Minutes* program about Gene Lang. If they were ever in a position to do this, they said to each other then, they would like to start an IHAD project, because "this was something that really makes a difference!" Nearly a decade later, in 1995, when she was forty-eight and her husband fifty-one, they began a project. Tessa has always had a keen appreciation for the way environment influences children's learning—perhaps from seeing the impact of the apartheid system on the lives of South African children. While she knew there would be real limits to what one single IHAD sponsor could accomplish, she had big dreams from the beginning. Why shouldn't every child in the system have the chance her dreamers would get, she asked? But of course she would have to start small.

She found herself a school board administrator and told him that she was looking for a school where at least 75 percent of the students were eligible for free lunch and where the principal would welcome IHAD into the building. They found a school and from the beginning Tessa chafed at the limitations of the model, which, in its original form, instructs sponsors to adopt one single classroom of children. When Tessa saw that there were eighty-two children in the second grade she went home to her husband and said,

> "You know, we have a problem here. There are eighty-two children." And he said, "You're crazy. You said forty-five children." And I said, "Fine. You go and line up all the children and just tap them on the heads and say, 'You've got the chance of a lifetime, but I'm sorry, you don't.'" So he said, "OK. OK. We can't do that." Because how can you do that? You can't just take a grade and halve the people. So we took all eighty-two. And then there was a rush on enrollment!

So the project began. Tessa threw herself into it with the same determination and confidence that she had used with her own children. She developed all kinds of adjunct programs and activities for the dreamers and the Blooms' project coordinator became a fixture in the school—someone to whom teachers and administrators turned for occasional help with special workshops and difficult situations. Though they began with eighty-two children, they opened the invitation to additional children and families when their first cohort reached second grade, and the total number of dreamers grew to a hundred and seven. Within a few years ten had been lost because they had moved. But in 2004, Tessa's dreamers were in their senior year and Tessa expected *all* of them to finish high school. This is an extraordinary statistic: in the city where she lives, in the year 2000, less than 30 percent of those between the ages of eighteen and twenty-four are high school graduates. And when you measure success, Tessa insists, college must not be the indicator either for individual children or for the program as a whole. "College is not right for everyone," she says. What matters is that dreamers become "proud and productive citizens," and this is what she is seeing as her dreamers now come to her home, in small groups, for weekly dinners. "They are meticulous, they enjoy talking to adults—wonderful—and they feel good about themselves!"

Together, Tessa Bloom and Gene Lang are developing a kind of balance sheet that can show how IHAD success correlates with savings for taxpayers. From a strictly financial point of view, when you calculate the cost to society of abandoning young people in inner cities—including the annual expenses of juvenile incarceration (in her state, it's $40,000 per child) and the down-the-road costs of limited access to health care, just to cite two examples—the value of an IHAD program on the other side of the ledger per year is huge. Such programs represent an investment for states and cities, as she sees it, because ultimately they save taxpayer dollars for city and state residents. And the best thing is that children who finish high school will begin in jobs that pay at least several dollars above the minimum wage. This means that these young people have jobs, they have purchasing power, they are contributing to the tax pool, and their children will be educated too.

Tessa says she always wanted to try and make a difference to society. Her good fortune includes being married to a man who, like her, has big ideas. During their long marriage of thirty-five years, Josh has never told her any idea she had was "silly." Never, she says, was she told to "think little." And she thinks much of her determination is connected to coming to America: "It's so big, so wide open, so inviting of people to be creative, to come up with ideas, to do things." Deeply thankful and busy as she can be, Tessa's greatest gratification is knowing that "you really can change the life of the child and the family."

Five new projects are beginning in her community and Tessa has played an important role in mentoring prospective sponsors, though she wishes there were more. She has her sights set on the school system as a whole now and looks forward to working with the new superintendent, who, she thinks, understands a great deal about the complex problems that are dogging urban schools. For Tessa, being an engaged philanthropist has "made everything fall into place" in her life; there is a perfect alignment between the way IHAD works and her own life-long determination to make a difference. Knowing now how to make a second project even better than their first, the Blooms have joined forces with another family to begin again with a new group of dreamers who are now second graders. She can't imagine not carrying on, not having another group of wonderful children in her life. There will be no stopping her.

TAD: A REAL JOB

Tad Johnson had been working for five years at a Fortune 500 global science and technology company when he became an IHAD sponsor. At work, he was participating in a school-business partnership, one that contributed employee volunteers and an annual donation of $1,000 to a local school. But he was struck with how inadequate the corporate effort was: "All little stuff, just a hit here and a hit there. And think about it! The education system and the social ills of the inner-city—it's something everybody's always crabbing about. Somebody ought to be doing something!" Back then, Tad says, he was "just like everyone else." He'd sit around watching public service announcements and mutter to himself about why nothing was getting better for poor kids. But as he turned forty he found himself re-evaluating his life. He had a decent home, a good job, a nice car. And he started feeling that "all the rest is gravy." He'd look at his friends and say to himself, "How many cars, boats, houses, ex-wives do these guys need? Don't they want to do something significant? It's nice they drive a Lexus, but what does it all mean?"

At the time, Ken Robinson was well known in the big Eastern city where Tad lives, as a man who had had great success in real estate and become deeply involved in charity. A born-again Christian and a first generation IHAD sponsor, Ken had become passionate about the importance of IHAD and, in a variation on the ancient church tradition of tithing, he'd already recruited nine other people to start their own projects. Now, as his own first project was winding down, he decided to seed a second one. He'd provide the core funding, but he was looking for someone else to act as "the real arms and legs" of the project—to take on the responsibility for primary sponsorship and raise whatever additional funds might be needed.

Tad had been hearing about Ken and IHAD, and he'd been impressed by the program's track record. When you consider the norms, he began to think, this was a comprehensive program that was helping more kids graduate from high school and decreasing the numbers of kids who got pregnant, or incarcerated, or shot. Results matter to Tad—even though, as a consultant, he spent most of his work time thinking, not doing, and he'd become very conscious of the fact that his colleagues were always more conceptual than pragmatic. So, when he and Ken met, and the older man invited Tad to come along with him to a few local IHAD meetings, one of the things the younger man loved was seeing that sponsors are people who see a problem and take action to do something about it. "They want to make things happen." As he listened to people talking about their IHAD projects, he was "jazzed by their personalities," and he loved the fact that IHAD was cutting across differences to focus everyone's attention on urgent common problems. "These are the people I want to run with," he remembers thinking.

Tad grew up in the mid-Atlantic states, the only child of an immigrant, blue-collar family whose hard-working parents were determined to see him have advantages they'd never had and would have mortgaged their modest home or given up their car to see their only son get to college. Tad says he was one of his parents' "top missions in life—like their own personal dream class." He remembers being a happy kid. The only mentor he had when he was young was the guy next door, who played the accordion and taught him to love music. Tad plays saxophone, clarinet, and keyboard. He fondly recalls having "all that time for creativity, imagination," in his teenage years, "the chance to noodle along by yourself, learn, stumble, fall and accomplish something." He majored in civil and environmental engineering at a state technical college and, as he was thinking about what to do next, a friend told him, "If you want something you have to ask for it." So he applied for admission to a graduate program at a prestigious Ivy League school and was accepted. And then he asked for financial aid and got a generous scholarship. His parents were elated when Tad got his master's degree in science.

One good job followed another. Tad has held executive leadership and management positions with major public, nonprofit, and private sector organizations. He has developed extensive consulting skills and broad technical knowledge of systems. And whether he was working at nonprofits, public agencies, or Fortune 500 companies, Tad had always been one of the employees who participated in whatever community-business partnerships the organization offered. He tutored, coached, offered technical assistance to schools, and helped youngsters with science fair projects. And while he had also managed many of these outreach initiatives, the feeling had grown that he wanted to do more. Then he met Ken.

In 1996, in association with Ken, Tad became what he calls "a pocket philanthropist." Drawing on his management expertise, he developed a business plan and started a second generation IHAD project. Tad and his experienced project coordinator, inherited from another first generation sponsor in town, began their project with sixty third graders at the same well run local elementary school where Tad and his corporate colleagues had been volunteering.

While Tad has been very excited to watch his dreamers grow up, he's also been very eager to find ways to strengthen IHAD as an organization. For two years after our first phone interview he sent me periodic messages about how he hoped to expand the program as a whole. In addition to serving as chairman of the local IHAD board, he has also headed up the national program's marketing and public relations task force.

Over the past eight years, Tad has became infused with the excitement of "doing something." Realizing how handicapped his dreamers were by their inadequate communication skills, he has now created a new business to develop a communication, public speaking, and life skills program for first through twelfth graders that is currently being taught in schools and youth organizations in four states. The now-retired principal of his dreamers' elementary school and his project coordinator serve as vice presidents of the new company. Together they have designed a full curriculum, aligned with the district's educational standards, which they train and pay teachers to deliver to students in an afterschool format. The company has contracted with an evaluator who is helping to assess and strengthen the program's design while its managers focus on developing new ways to foster kids' public speaking and leadership skills.

In choosing teachers, Tad and his vice presidents look for people who are not just good teachers but also know the school, the system, the kids, and the parents. Perhaps most importantly, they must be good communicators because, as Tad says, they will be role models for the kids.

> I wish somebody had told me about mentoring. I wish somebody told me about networking. I wish somebody had told me about the importance of good communication skills. I see a need for these kids to be speaking properly and learning how to be prepared for opportunity. That is one of the secrets of success in life. I see a need for this. So I'm just doing it myself. That's the typical sponsor mentality. IHAD started me on a career I couldn't have figured out otherwise.

Tad is grateful and energized. He's stunned by how fast time goes, how grown his dreamers are, and how "eloquent" they've become. And he knows that he's beating the odds: between 90 and 95 percent of his dreamers—as compared to about 50 percent in the district as a whole—will graduate from high school. But he's also impatient; he still can't understand why more people aren't paying attention to the "early warning system."

> They could see the tsunami coming if they went into these poor inner-city schools once in a while. What's going to happen when this next block of kids hits society? If people went into these schools sometime, aside from being occasionally terrified, they'd see that these places are breeding grounds for bad stuff. Sometimes I look at these anti-abortion stickers and wonder what people really mean. Would they rather kill kids after they've grown up and committed crimes? It's incredible. This is the time when you could prevent, intervene. If you don't nurture a kid, what do people think is going to happen? This is not brain science. And nobody's doing anything!

That's not true, of course. Tad and many other people—from teachers and principals and social workers to cops and judges and philanthropists (both traditional and engaged)—are trying. And he's not simply talking. IHAD and the communication program he's created mean more to him than anything else now. "If I had more money," he says, "I'd be running more projects."

Tad has heard many IHAD sponsors talk about sponsoring as a way for them "to give something back." But his perspective is a bit different.

> I don't really do this to give back. I need a real job on this planet, while I'm here. The jobs I've had have all been interesting, well paying and reflective of what I studied for, but nothing comes close to this. I've found a niche I truly believe in. And I'm doing it because somebody's got to do it and I have the skills. Let's get moving! There's a Goethe quote I'm fond of: "Knowing is not enough: we must apply. Willing is not enough: we must do." There are so many talkers, so few doers in the world. You mustn't end up in the coulda-shoulda-woulda club. Do something real!

Tad draws on his creativity, his skills, and his experience to develop projects that have great meaning for him and that give young people the kinds of supports and advantages that his parents gave him. Long after his dreamers finish high school Tad will surely keep searching passionately for solutions to the "real" problems that he used to think other people should solve.

QUESTIONS COME UP

Like other narratives to follow throughout this book, these "close-ups" raise questions. One wonders, for example, how Richard and Laura's combined confidence drove them to tackle big city bureaucracies and create whole new schools? Why does someone like Tessa, whose life is so full of family and friends, become so enamored with IHAD that she dreams of transforming not only the lives of one whole grade level of kids but also the entire school in a troubled inner-city district? And what, one might ask, is the meaning of doing good deeds for scores of kids to Tad, who was himself an only child and is not married? What moved him from simply admiring a group of powerful philanthropists with more money than he had to completely refocusing his own life around the futures of low-income children?

These are some of the questions that have occurred to me, but I hope that as you read this book you will look for answers to your own questions. This is an inquiry rather than a sociological, anthropological, or psychological study. It's designed to raise questions.

Among the very diverse group of people I interviewed, certain sponsors may seem to you more like old friends than others. People are very different. Some sponsors grow increasingly determined to change public systems. Others focus sharply on individualizing opportunities for some kids. Some have strong convictions about the importance of strengthening public solutions to challenges that, in the long run, impact all of us. Others feel increasingly frustrated by government programs and insist that the only way public institutions will be improved is through intense competition and private sector innovation. Some feel their hearts bursting with new empathy for the kinds of interconnected obstacles that low-income families face every day. Others sometimes find themselves angered by the powerlessness of these same families—by the way their helplessness limits options for their children. In the end, though, sponsors are so involved with their dreamers that they want to pursue any option that can let them reach their goal: helping these kids grow up well.

As you read on, you'll hear the sponsors you've already met— and many others—talk about how they decided to become involved with IHAD, where they come from, what they actually did with dreamers, and what it has all meant to them. I hope you will start asking yourself quietly, "Where do I fit on the continuum of givers?" Everything is a matter of degree. Few of us may have the wherewithal to sponsor a whole class of children—or a neighborhood clinic, or an afterschool program—but some of us do, and more of us can than are. In fact, there are all kinds of ways to contribute, from the heart, to these and other efforts. I hope you will ask yourself if you are doing enough—and I hope you will stay interested to see what the next chapter of your own life may bring.

CHAPTER 3

TAKING THE LEAP

Part of wisdom is knowing that the pool will fill up before you hit the ground. You just have to leap.
—Mike O'Donnell

What prompts people to make sudden moves in new directions? No decision happens in a vacuum. Our choices reflect a great variety of things going on in our lives at the time we make them. What was going on in sponsors' lives at the moment when they decided to commit a great deal of money—and, even more importantly, time and emotional involvement—to a program like IHAD? For many it was as if something had "seized" them, propelling them into new and uncertain worlds. Put differently, what kinds of contextual factors may have prompted them to take a chance on engaged philanthropy?

Risk-taking is a fascinating subject, one that psychologists and economists, epidemiologists and sociologists, historians and novelists have all approached in their own ways. For the purposes of this inquiry, let's start with the hypothesis that a propensity for risk-taking may well be a character trait of many who choose the world of business as the arena for their life's work. If you focus your life around profit and loss, you are inevitably preoccupied with assessing risk and reward. Perhaps successful business people can be expected to approach philanthropy in the way they have gone about their work: evaluating opportunities while remaining open to inspiration. After all, though the nature of the dividend may be uncertain at the beginning, all philanthropy represents an investment.

Before he created the I Have a Dream Foundation, one of Eugene Lang's favorite ways to invest in people was by contributing to higher education. Objectively this is sensible. Higher Education is one of the philanthropic realms in which the prospects for reward are most favorable, because most young people who have made it to college have already developed many of the skills they will need to become productive, responsible citizens. And in his case, college had changed Lang's life. "Fortuitous and defining things" had happened to him there, he says, and these experiences had everything to do with his ability to have made a successful life for himself.

After graduating from high school when he was just fourteen, Lang took a job waiting on tables. A customer who came into the restaurant regularly got to know the boy, recognized his potential, and one evening asked Gene if he'd ever thought about going to college. "Yes," he said, "in the abstract. But it's not for me. I can't afford the tuition." The man gave him an application to Swarthmore and, at barely fifteen, with the support of his "sponsor," he began his studies there.

At college Lang found he was different from most of his fellow students in many ways. He was younger, shorter, and poorer. During one of our first interviews he told me the following story.

> During orientation week, they took us all on busses to see Philadelphia, show us the historic sites. Before we finished, they showed us a settlement house, the Guild, in the slummiest slum I had ever seen. We had a tour, and at the end the tour director asked if any of us would volunteer to lead their youth group. I was the only one who volunteered. I knew I could intimately become a part of that place, even though the kids were bigger, older, all black. It didn't make any difference to me: I had grown up having contact with kids from all kinds of backgrounds.

> This led to my Monday evening groups, the most serendipitous experience of my life. I didn't know ahead of time what we would do each week. I'd go in, trying to find something that would interest them and want to come back each week with something new.

It was kind of an odd pairing. The kids didn't know how inadequate I felt, and I didn't know how minimal I was in their lives. At the same time I was taking required biology as a freshman, not because of any particular interest in science—I was interested in economics, political science, social action. But we had to take an introductory science course and this one had a lab component. We each had to dissect a dogfish. The class was very structured. We had scalpels and guidebooks and every day we came into the lab and did exercises from a book, making drawings and following instructions. I thought it would be a great thing for us to do in a Guild group. We wouldn't do a complete job scientifically, but it would be an interesting activity in which kids could be engaged. So I begged an extra dogfish, extra scalpels and guidebooks, wrapping the fish in a big brown paper bag.

When I got there, I passed out the scalpels and told them to move the table into the center of the room and put the chairs around it. I put the brown bag in the middle of the table and unwrapped it. There was the dead fish in all its glory. I told the kids we would dissect it, and I had organized the whole sequence, so we began with the head. I don't remember all the wonders we covered—not with much scientific finesse, technically, but so everyone could have the experience. It seemed to me that right or wrong wasn't the point here.

Each kid took a turn with the scalpel. A "surgical team" was organized to open up the stomach and I can still remember seeing the kids cut open the abdomen. Inside we found two little fish that had been in the process of being digested when the big fish was killed. This wasn't the moment for a long parable, but we did talk about how big fish swallow little fish. And how the clever ones survive.

It was a terrific evening. I couldn't have anticipated its ultimate, defining significance to me, but five or six years later, after I'd graduated, the college forwarded a letter to me. "Dear Gene. I don't know if you remember me. I was in your group at the Guild. You told me I ought to go back to school. You remember the night you dissected the dogfish? And we talked about big fish and little fish? After that evening I kept thinking about it and decided I wanted to be a doctor. I have just been admitted to Howard University as a pre-med student."

You never know where things are going, or how one person, without intention, can have meaning for another. This is about my own sense of purpose: it makes everything worthwhile.

Gene Lang certainly didn't know, when he was waiting on tables, where things were going. Nor could he have dreamed how that regular customer would change his life. It was a variation on the kind of attentive gift this man bestowed on him that Lang transferred to the kids he worked with at the Guild—and now passes on, directly and indirectly, to thousands of others. Years later, when he saw the children looking up at him from their auditorium seats at P.S. 121, Lang wanted them to have access to the kinds of opportunities he'd known. Lang says his move was impulsive, but it was also rooted in his own history.

About 40 percent of the IHAD sponsors interviewed for this inquiry expressed surprise at having stumbled almost spontaneously into their new identity as engaged philanthropists. Like Lang, they say that when the moment came they didn't think carefully about what they were doing: it was a startling move. Others—especially second generation sponsors, who had more information about the program—proceeded in a more careful, systematic fashion. Either way, their retrospective reflections about how they began can give us some insight about the kinds of things that motivate people to reorient their lives in such a profound way.

SUDDEN MOVES

For many sponsors what first got their attention was the spellbinding television interview with Lang on 60 Minutes, an interview that was straightforward, direct, and lasted less than ten minutes. As Lang describes how he began, the viewer is watching film footage shot at the original P.S. 121 sixth grade graduation ceremony. It's grainy, like an old home movie, and one listens to Lang talk about how he felt looking out at the kids, and what happened after he made the offer.

> There was literally a gasp. And as I stood there and heard that gasp I thought, "Today I am a man!" It felt so good! I had come out. They were there. We had met. And we were together!

He is joyful as he recalls the power of feeling connected to the kids. The rest of the interview focuses on the kids themselves: how shocked they were by the offer and what it came to mean to them—not only that Lang was paying $500 towards their college expenses for every year they stayed in school but, even more importantly, that he was paying attention to them. The viewer listens and then watches as excited young people who surely face tough odds sit in Lang's office and articulate very specific dreams for their futures. This was hopeful and compelling journalism.

The program was followed by several articles in prominent newspapers and magazines. As one first generation sponsor recalls, there was a sudden, "enchanting blaze of publicity." From all over the country, people began to phone Lang. They flew to New York to meet with him and invited him to come speak in their communities. Another woman from the same cohort said she and her husband had been watching *60 Minutes* and she had commented quite simply that the program was "interesting." She and her husband thought of themselves as very methodical people, and she had no idea that her innocuous remark would prompt him to contact Lang. At the time her husband was preparing for retirement, after decades of devotion to business and golf. Although he had never seemed very interested in children, his wife told me, he'd been a loyal supporter of a summer camp that meant the world to him when he was young. And now, suddenly, instead of thinking about moving to a warm climate, they both found themselves totally immersed in IHAD.

One couple told me that they'd been reading the newspaper over breakfast one morning when they came across an article that was stimulated by the *60 Minutes* program. They called Lang the next day.

> We had always been interested in education and disadvantaged people. The IHAD commitment fit in with what we'd

done. But nothing we had done entailed the kind of financial commitment or time that this took. The two major components of our responsibility with which we had had no experience were the money and the time. In fact with IHAD, it was always more important that we were willing to invest ourselves than our money.

Most of the people who first responded to Lang's ideas so quickly were in their forties or fifties, but not all. One was a young financial manager who'd become very successful at an early age—perhaps somewhat sooner than he'd expected. But he was similarly decisive:

> I saw Gene Lang on *60 Minutes*, picked up the phone next day, called him, and told him I wanted to do the same thing. Let's see: it was 1986, I was thirty-two, and I wanted to make a difference.

Once he went to the neighborhood where he went on to adopt a class, he said, he immediately grasped the extent of need in the community around him. He hated the fact that a part of the big city he loved was so distressed. And he saw IHAD as a way to work for change.

Of the original group of sponsors, one recalls,

> Everyone in NYC got involved in 1986 because of the *New York Times* article. When the first eight groups were adopted, there was a great deal of publicity because of the high visibility of the first eight sponsors. But nobody had a clue about what they were doing. We were a high-powered bunch of people from the business world who thought that if you had a plan, you would get things done. The program took off quickly. Gene was flying all over the country. It was an idea whose time had come: everybody was thinking about the lost generation. And, in four years, there were twenty-three projects in this city. But what were we thinking? That you could just go in there and make changes? We were sophisticated and incredibly naïve!

If it was "an idea whose time had come," these sponsors were also a group of people who thought they could do almost anything. They were self-confident and daring. In fact, to listen to them, the move into what would become engaged philanthropy sometimes seemed to be rooted as much in their cocky certainty that they could "make changes" as it was in any lofty sentiments about helping the poor.

Each start-up story is distinctive, but many of the people I interviewed seem to have taken the leap into IHAD when something in their personal lives was shifting: their personal fortunes, their work situations, their relationships with their families, or their responsibilities in the institutions with which they were involved. Almost all were attracted to Lang's program because its hands-on, results-oriented assumptions were well aligned with certain aspects of their temperament, personal histories, and values. But whatever the personal impetus may have been, when they look back the spontaneity of their initial decision—a move that would change their lives—still surprises many of them.

The following three narratives help us understand these decisions in more detail. Let's first consider Hal Davies. Having worked in a variety of businesses and banks, "troubleshooting small, underperforming companies" and doing investment consultation, he was used to being fairly autonomous on the job. As a young man, he'd always been interested in business but, he says, he "fought education every step of the way: it wasn't till my junior year in college that I figured out that the people there really wanted me to succeed!" When he first heard about Lang's program, Hal was in his mid-forties, married, with two children, and looking around for new challenges at work.

> I saw *60 Minutes* and three weeks later I was in Lang's office. That was the single biggest catalyst. Nobody knows what it was about that piece that hit them, but it hit. And if you'd ever told me I would do this, I'd have told you you were crazy! The idea of taking on fifty or sixty kids when I couldn't control my own two? Why would I do that? I'd always been civic minded—but never crazy!

> There was nothing in my past that would lead you to any logical or emotional conclusion about why I did this. I was up to my ass in things, married with two kids who were twelve and fourteen, and rebuilding the zoo here in town,

which was keeping me plenty busy—with a day job on top of all that.

Why did I do IHAD? I don't know why. The simplicity of it, and the high success of it—you could look at the successes Lang had—and there was the program's relatively low cost. These were three things I remember being impressed by when I saw the *60 Minutes* show. It seemed like the most efficient move, with the least amount of bureaucracy and the most amount of touch. It was the personal involvement. It wasn't just creating a system and an operation. You had to get in there and touch and feel and really get involved. Anything that I get involved with I like to really be involved in it, be very hands-on. If I can't be very involved, I don't much care to mess with it. Because if I can't feel like I'm really making a difference, feel like I'm really making a contribution, then I don't want to do it. When you start an I Have a Dream program, you're it. By definition, you're making a contribution. If you don't get up in the morning, *it* doesn't get up in the morning.

Hal has a perfectly reasoned explanation for his decision to chose this particular program: it's an efficient model. But he also acknowledges that taking on this commitment reflected his need at the time to make an important contribution, to be "it." He would be central to his own project's impact. If he didn't get up in the morning, neither would it. Like Lang, who felt the joy of connection after that first gasp in the auditorium, Hal wanted the hands-on contact, the opportunity for personal involvement "with the most amount of touch."

Pamela Marconi was also in her mid-forties when she made the initial move into IHAD. Unmarried at the time, she had spent several decades building up a very successful track record in real estate.

I had made some money as a real estate developer and, assuming my parents would predecease me, I was trying to figure out what to do [with it]. Then I remembered seeing *60 Minutes* and thinking, "Gee, that's a nice program because it's not another give-away. These kids obviously have to do something, stay in school and keep their grades up. If they do that, money shouldn't stand in the way of going to college." So I got the number for the foundation office in New York, explained what I wanted to do, said, "Just give me the name and address. I am going to name IHAD as a beneficiary." I did all this, and a week later Gene called me back, saying, "I understand that you did this." I was touched that he had taken the time to call. He said, "Do you ever get into New York?" I said, "Of course, I'm nearby." So we made a date to meet.

As Gene tells the story, he was expecting a doddering old lady of ninety-five to show up, somebody about to kick the bucket and leave the foundation a lot of money. In I walked, at forty-five, with a lot of energy. Now, Gene and I are very different financially. But he talked about what he was doing with the kids, and I saw so many pictures of him with these kids and their reactions. I knew that a lot of people in New York were stepping up to the plate, basically putting their money where their mouth was. They were not just complaining about the poor school system. They were actually trying to do something about it. Within two hours of talking to him I said, "I want to do more than just put this in my will."

At the time we were talking about $400,000, and I was still earning my estate. So I said, "Look, at this time I don't have that amount of money. But I can raise it. I've been raising money all my adult life to build buildings, and I can raise the money." And it was that easy. I went back, thought about it for a minute probably, on the train ride back, put together a coffee and pastry breakfast at my office, drew up a list of twenty-five people, made the pitch, and twenty-three of them signed up before they left the room. Of course, this was in 1987, when people were making money, particularly in the real estate business. But I made the commitment to Gene that I would be the visible sponsor and I think the key to this program is having the consistent face, the same face, over and over and over again. I started it that spring, in 1988.

Pamela's account of the decision-making process has an energizing kind of naiveté about it. She easily acknowledges the power of Gene's compelling interpersonal style. Like Tad Johnson, who we heard from in Chapter 2, she liked the idea of being associated with people who were really "putting their money where their mouth was." In only a matter of hours, Pamela decided to refocus her life, drawing on what she knew she had always been good at: getting people together. She quickly assembled a funding collaborative that she would lead *and* made a commitment that she would be the "visible," "consistent face" of the project—that is, that she would be involved personally as well as financially.

Spontaneous in a different way, Rob Mitchell's move into IHAD was a reflection, he says, of "the contrarian" in him. Education had not previously been a focus of his philanthropy. By his own admission, he was "not a great student" himself—in fact, he had dropped out of college for a while before going back to get a bachelor's degree in philosophy. After that, he took a variety of "odd jobs" and was teaching tennis when serious troubles struck his family at home. First his mother, then his grandmother became very ill, and the family's real estate business ran into major difficulties. Rob went home to help take care of things, settled into his community, married, and had two boys, both of whom were very young when he became an IHAD sponsor, right in the midst of another cycle of hard business times and while one of his sons was struggling with a serious medical problem. As he tells it,

> Business was really bad at the time. I had a young son whose health was not good. And I just thought I was always going to make excuses. The contrarian in me said, "The time to do it is when it looks like it doesn't make any sense to do." That's the only way I can make any sense out of it. If you wait till you feel you're absolutely comfortable financially, you can always think, "Well, maybe I'll never have enough." So I just woke up and said, "I'm going to do it."
>
> Maybe the underlying thing was that I was starting not to believe in myself. I kept saying, "Well, it's a good thing to do," and "I'm going to do it someday." And then finally I said, "Well, are you really going to do it? Or aren't you?

Time to put up or shut up, and stop making excuses!" My wife is still resentful that I did it, that I picked the wrong time. When she said, "Why can't it wait?" I said, "It can't. I'll do it all." But in order to be true to my inner self I had to finally commit. Otherwise I was full of soup. I talked a good game but I was going to be like the folks who are very big on causes unless it's a little inconvenient, you know? Like the people who don't believe in wearing furs unless it's cold out. There are people who have convenient beliefs, convenient philosophies, until they become inconvenient. When it becomes hard to have those beliefs, then they're suddenly not so important, not as dearly held.

There are a lot of things about IHAD that appeal to me. One is that you can put your arms around it. You can have a personal relationship with the children and hopefully make a difference. It was a model that seemed to work: Gene had gotten impressive numbers that demonstrated its success. I'd love to be creative and invent the wheel, but if I'm gonna spend a lot of time and resources, it's nice to know that I have a good shot at success. Gene's model was encouraging in that regard. And as for me, I like to be involved. I want to be hands-on. I want to make sure that all the dollars I contribute go for what's intended. That's not true in some organizations, where ninety percent of what you give ends up going towards fund-raising or administrative overhead. It feels good to know that my money goes only for the kids. No one else pays rent, buys the paper clips, donates the scotch tape, charges for copies. Within some pretty fixed parameters I get to make decisions, hire the project coordinator, decide about the curriculum, the number of trips we'll take, how many tutors we'll get and what we should pay them. I'm in control.

Rob sounds a lot like Hal Davies when he talks about how much he likes the prospect of calling the shots. A fiercely independent guy who will later tell me he's a life-long risk-taker, Rob characterizes himself as a "contrarian"—by which he seems to mean someone who does things when they don't make sense. At the moment, though, he had an acute sense of time passing, and he seems to have experienced an almost physiological urge to line his life up with his belief system, no matter what else was going on. One of the worst aspects of serious childhood illness for the child's parents is feeling helpless. Perhaps Rob's move into engaged philanthropy was motivated in part by a need for the opportunity to be in charge of everything, on his own terms.

Each of these three narratives—Hal's, Pamela's, and Rob's—confirms that the hands-on, engaged aspect of IHAD is at the heart of its special appeal. None of these three individuals had strong previous commitments to schools. None would have predicted they would devote a significant portion of their lives to education. They were all experienced, successful business people who seized on Lang's model because of what they saw as its relative simplicity, efficiency, and interpersonal connectedness. And they all seem to be people with temperamental preferences for action and adventure, individuals who like to get personally involved in what they do and who want to make a difference.

Media reports—especially those that followed the first 60 Minutes show—had a powerful impact on many who became IHAD sponsors. But at the same time various internal prompters were also pushing these individuals to take action. Hal, Pamela, and Rob have all come to understand that their initial commitment to engaged philanthropy reflected a combination of situational and temperamental dynamics. Like Rob, Hal made his decision to become a sponsor at a time when much was complicated in his work and home situations.

> You know, I can always give you eight or ten reasons not to do something. But at some point, you just dive off and do it. There was a lot of change going on around the same time. I had been a banker for eighteen years when I got interested in this thing. Right after I started IHAD, my life changed so much you wouldn't even know I was the same person.

> Within a year, I was helping with a new business merger. The company wanted me to move, and I remember bringing it up at the dinner table one night. You would have thought I had asked everybody to cut off an appendage. I barely escaped with my life. The family had no interest in moving.

But the firm was asking me to do something I didn't much want to do either. So I started looking around for other stuff to do, and I set up the U.S. office for an overseas company. This took me into all different kinds of businesses, doing so many new kinds of things.

In 1990 I filed for divorce. My wife was not even a little bit interested in IHAD and my kids, twelve and fourteen, were pretty self-absorbed as well, as are all at that age. So I was just sort of doing it. All this stuff that was coming together.

As with Rob, shifts at work and at home coincided with Hal's tendency to "dive off," and in a time of some chaos he made a decision that would put him in charge of his own ship, no matter what else was going on. When he called Lang, Hal was at a point in his life when he was experiencing a personal need to feel more effective, to have more impact than he was experiencing at work or at home. Over time he's come to understand that his uncharacteristic move into education was partly an effort to give others an opportunity that he himself had squandered. But his most conscious feeling at the time was that things were a bit out of control both in his personal and his professional life, and at the intersection of the two. Maybe, to keep everything humming along in a familiar way, he turned to IHAD because he believed that by sponsoring a project he could use his talents to do something that he believed was simple, effective, *and* relational.

Pamela was born and raised in a close-knit, Catholic, blue-collar world. With an ethos of service embedded in her family and the parochial schools she attended, she had long wanted to give back to the community where she was born. What she heard about Eugene Lang's philosophy and program coincided with her moral conviction that good deeds, to be effective, should not be "give-aways." Thus, guided by her own values and the temperamentally satisfying, action-oriented feel of IHAD, she'd felt right at home with this new commitment.

At the time, this was a project, and I'm very project-oriented. I'm not very reflective in terms of why I do things. My husband doesn't always understand why I don't think about things first. He always says to me, "It's in your mind, on your lips—*done!*" That's probably true. I don't really give a lot of thought to planning my life. I kind of wake up and say, "What's happening next?" And I tend to be someone who likes to fix things, to get things done. So for me it was an easy jump, a very short trip from thinking about leaving a bequest to actually sponsoring a program. The need was there. I guess I like to think that there's more equality in the world than there is.

But I'm just the kind of a person who rolls up my sleeves and does things. And if I make a commitment, I do it 110 percent. So it isn't like I would have made the commitment and then two years into it said, "Gee, why did I do this?" So, you know, it appeals to my sense of making things right, or fixing something.

Values matter to philanthropists—but for engaged philanthropists so does grabbing an external opportunity to get busy and *do* something, no matter how long a project will take.

As Rob thought back about what motivated him, he reframed what he first constructed as a kind of problematic personal obstreperousness into a positive single-mindedness, a drive to invest in the future.

[I was] pretty non-conforming when I was younger. In some good ways and in some maybe not good ways. I never did drugs—maybe because everybody else was doing them. And I never did destructive things. But I always marched to the beat of my own drummer.

My wife fights with me about spending so much time in one school. She says there are so many hungry people in the world that I shouldn't concentrate everything on one small group of kids. But there's that old axiom, you know? If you give someone a fish, they can eat it, but if you teach them to fish, they can catch the fish themselves. In effect, you're giving them the tools they'll need, you're enabling them to become drop-ins instead of dropouts, taxpayers instead of tax-takers. Those things molded my thinking. If you look at some other statistics—for instance, the fact that two-thirds of welfare recipients don't have a high school education—all of a sudden you see that education is an important way to deal with all this. The problems in the schools are major, not minor, these days. You can even make the economic argument that the cost of the program is the same as it might cost taxpayers to keep one or two people in jail for ten or fifteen years. I always like to tell people that for me IHAD was a way of investing in some young people.

In our interviews, Hal, Pamela, and Rob all talked rationally about specific ways that IHAD appealed to their business sense: it seemed simple, straightforward, and efficient. If engaged philanthropy gave them each a sense of being in control when other aspects of their lives were in transition, the structure and rationale of the program also appealed to them as people accustomed to thinking about the bottom line. And if theirs was a decision that seemed to be made in the moment, it also reflected the temperamental predilections and moral values that had shaped their lives.

STARTING WITH A PLAN

For many IHAD sponsors, the decision to become an engaged philanthropist grew in part from a sense of restlessness, a readiness to change their lives. It may have reflected the fact that they were finding themselves with more money or more free time than they'd had before. Some had been preparing for retirement, others were transitioning into or taking on new jobs that gave them more flexibility or the chance to reevaluate their long-term financial planning. And some individuals moved into IHAD sponsorship because they'd had prior relationships with established organizations—corporations, churches, community agencies, or family foundations—but were now looking for new ways to strengthen their commitments to action at a local level.

In the case of the Hulls, for example, their established family foundation was poised to invest new money in different ways, and Sam and Ann Hull had given their grown children, now professionally educated adults in their twenties, the opportunity to research potential candidates for new foundation projects. Certain that they wanted to help low-income children in their own community, they met with Lang. After that, it was easy to persuade their parents that IHAD was where their foundation should make its new commitment.

One of the most methodical sponsors I interviewed, Mara Emerson had known about IHAD for years and long planned to get involved as soon as she was ready. This happened when she found herself in a financial position that enabled her to retire in her early fifties. From the beginning, she was careful and systematic.

> I started in January 1994, said "I'm going to do it," got in touch with IHAD national. I picked my school, my class, my grade, and the school district. I set up my foundation, hired a project coordinator, and did all the legal work. I wrote my own articles of incorporation and corporate bylaws and application to the IRS for tax-exempt incorporation. I hadn't worked that hard in a long time. I was putting in twelve-hour days for about six months, but I was up and running in September. And I always knew it was just meant to be.

Mara had actually served on the board of a settlement house that was the home base for two IHAD programs in her city. She had met the people who were involved with IHAD, gotten to know how the program was working, and promised herself that "if I ever have the wherewithal, that's what I want to do." So when she was not only "mentally ready" but also "financially capable," she made her commitment. And one of the reasons she thinks that her sponsorship was "meant to be" was that everything went so smoothly. Soon after she began, she was asked to talk to prospective sponsors about how she had negotiated the challenges of starting up her project. She declined because, she said, she'd had no difficulties at all.

> I mean, if you don't have any snags, and you have nothing plaguing you, if nothing gets in your way and you just glide through everything, it was meant to be!

As it happened, when she had the resources to become a sponsor, Mara left the East Coast to start a new life in the West, where her commitment to engaged philanthropy anchored her squarely in the new community. But her belief that taking this step was in some way predestined echoes the conviction that other sponsors expressed when they told me that no matter how and when they made the decision, they now couldn't imagine what their lives would have meant without it.

In the previous chapter we listened to Tad Johnson describe how he was primed for engaged philanthropy by participating in his company's school-business partnerships. During the past decade, faith-based organizations, like corporations, have been increasingly interested in strengthening their commitments to under-served, local communities. At one sponsor's church, for example, a decision was made to establish "a Christian education center." But as he explained to me, "St. John's has always said that if we do something for ourselves, we should do something for the community," and he was one of a group of ten church members who were elected by the congregation to find a project. The committee settled on IHAD for two principal reasons. First, it would give them an opportunity to establish a long-term partnership with another church in a low-income area of their large mid-Atlantic city. The two churches shared the project from the beginning, which meant that congregants of each would get to know people from another part of town. Secondly, they wanted to find a project that would get people involved in ways that went beyond the one-way act of giving money. The committee intended to do something that would allow them to "build relationships in more than a band-aid way, and to change lives." Connecting—always a program priority for Gene Lang—was a primary motivation.

Another man with a strong commitment to his church, Frank Matthews, like Hal Davies, became an IHAD sponsor when his personal life became unsettled. For years he'd been a faithful churchgoer in a Southwestern state, and distress about his divorce made him feel strongly obligated to take good actions that were directly aligned with the basic principles of his strong faith. But Frank was frustrated with the ordinary committee work he'd been doing for years.

> Our church was ingrown, as most suburban churches are. Taking care of their own people and their own needs, and spending an awful a lot of time taking care of people who really were not nearly in the shape of a lot of other people in the city. While the city was falling apart, our people were prospering.

> The Christian world today is a bunch of pew-sitters, mostly. They love to go to church and they love to be with their friends. The fellowship is wonderful and the support is

wonderful when they get sick themselves. But you know, it's just a warm place to be. Basically I think what we have in the United States today is a bunch of greedy, greedy, greedy people who could care less about anybody else except themselves. But what we did and are doing and can be doing is about the only way that a neighborhood can be changed.

So while some of the IHAD sponsors who agreed to talk with me described themselves as having acted impulsively, others maintain that they moved into engaged philanthropy very deliberately, being driven intentionally by conscious, explicit values.

Frank and Tad were not the only people I spoke with who talked about feeling discouraged about the limited impact of traditional outreach efforts. Mike and Meg O'Donnell, whom we met in Chapter 1, had worked very actively to bring about change in their community for years. Before attending law school, Mike, who became an activist lawyer, spent formative years in the military service and in the Peace Corps. Meg was a passionate painter who spent years working in her own children's public schools, serving on the board of a local foundation, and running for public office. But Mike and Meg had become disheartened.

> We had run or had supported candidates for so many years that were going to change the world. We thought we might change it ourselves when we were elected to town committee. But we didn't win. We put all our energy into this. We'd go from town to town, door to door, with our kids and we were going to change the universe. In fact, our kids were talking about us as people who thought we could save the world. But about 1985 we looked at each other and said, "You know, I don't think so. It's not going to happen." And we said to ourselves, "Forget this political stuff! We've got to start doing something that really impacts, that means something, one to one."

> That's the big reason we got involved with this project and with the dreamers. Because we had to do something that's relevant, something that really meant something. All the energy it takes to dance around election campaigns and then,

> even if we worked for someone else, it would backfire. You
> have to just go get real people, dedicate your life and move!

For Mike and Meg, becoming sponsors meant that they could transfer their energies from political action, which in their case seemed to have little effect, into more direct social engagement.

Like the O'Donnells, Chuck Peterson was something of a political activist before becoming an IHAD sponsor. He'd been extremely involved in good work far from home, offering legal support to activists struggling against apartheid in South Africa. But when he was in his late twenties, members of his family began to insist that if he was so eager to make a difference, there were lots of people that needed his energy closer to home. Now, in Chuck's family there was a long history of political tension and disagreement. Some were staunch Republicans, others were equally committed Democrats. Some held firmly to the familiar bootstrap conviction: anyone who really wants to make it can do so. Others, believing in the idea of a level playing field, insisted that life is not always fair and that government is the institution that can equalize opportunity so that everyone has a good shot at a decent life. But everyone in the family agreed on one thing—no matter how you get there, individual success takes hard work. For Chuck, IHAD became a way for him to unite family members around common convictions. His original intention was "to start the program and get other people to fund it." As it happens,

> IHAD has allowed several generations and people with a
> wide range of political views to get involved. In my fam-
> ily, nobody agrees about anything. But here, everyone can
> find something to do. Ideology within my family is no small
> matter. I Have a Dream, as an organization and a motto,
> was one thing that I could come up with, as the crusading
> family liberal, that actually appealed to both sides.

This wasn't always easy, as we'll hear in subsequent chapters.

In the meantime, as our final example here, let's consider Will Christopher, who was in his fifties, with two grown children, when he took on IHAD sponsorship. The product of public schools and a liberal arts education, Will had crafted a great variety of jobs for himself as a young man. He played jazz and learned all about hotel management from the ground up, finding places to work where there was also great music to hear. Will describes himself as someone who always wanted to find a way to do what he loved. Eventually he started his own successful event-planning business; his sons are in the business with him today. Though Will moved into engaged philanthropy somewhat more methodically than Hal, Pamela, and Rob, his decision to choose IHAD was, in some ways, serendipitous, like theirs. He and his wife, Carol, had been at a cousin's graduation in a West Coast town when they saw the front page of the local newspaper, which happened to have an article about a very successful IHAD program that had been started by one of the nearby university's business school classes a year before. They had already been thinking about wanting to get more involved in their own community.

> We had made that decision approximately when I turned fifty. Carol's a couple of years younger than me. Life's been good to us, business is good, this is our home. We're comfortable and we both have a very, very strong passion and commitment to social issues. So we made a decision. "We're here," we said to each other. "We've been here a long time. It's a goofy city, but we're not moving and it's time to give back." We opted to give something to inner-city education as opposed to camps or medical causes because public education here is awful and we've got to step forward and do something. But to simplify, it was really making the decision that it's time to give back to the community.

> We were thinking about our age bracket. I don't know whether it's the chronological age, you know, or having had a certain success in business. There was a touch of boredom, too, in the prospect of continuing to do what you are doing strictly in the business world. Maybe it was that, and maybe you have to be certain chronological age before an interest in others really kicks in. For us it was the right time. Come to think of it, neither Carol nor I had any kind of a history of philanthropy like this: we were no different from my sons, I guess, in giving back.

> This is a fluid city, but we just knew that we probably weren't going to leave. This is home. There are a lot of prob-

lems here, and, you know, it was just the two of us. We'd sit down to eat every night and complain and bitch about all the social ills, nationally and locally. There certainly were plenty locally. But after you complain to each other for long enough, you find yourselves saying, "Well, let's try to do something about one of the problems." Otherwise you would get bored talking to each other.

Part of it is, if you don't do something, I think guilt and selfishness play in. You know, I've spent a good chunk of my life going to nice places all over the world, and I couldn't live that way my entire life. I just couldn't. The greed in the news really gets to me. But we're not crazy in our advocacy. We're both very hands-on—business people. We look for results more than other people who approach these kinds of things from a political point of view or an ego point of view. That's not us. We're very bottom-line: that's how we've approached everything we've gotten involved in. So I just did what came naturally. And that's also my frustration with people who just give me lip service, saying, "That's wonderful what you're doing," and then they don't do anything. They have the financial wherewithal to do a lot. I have to really control myself when I'm around people like that.

When Will got home after that graduation he searched out local IHAD sponsors, who invited him to join their regular meetings. He spent several years raising the money he would need and becoming familiar with the program. But his narrative captures several constants from other sponsors' stories, including the turning point triggered by age, a shift in business, and a new acceptance of one's stage of life. Will's resolve to give back, to apply his values to his personal life, coincided with the "bottom-line" mindset that characterizes so many sponsors. The IHAD model has been a way for many people to do something concrete in their communities and, at the same time, to see what kind of difference they can actually make. And now, more than a decade later, Will talks about how the rightness of his decision makes him very impatient with bystanders, more certain than ever that engaged social investment has great value and rewards.

So what do we conclude about first steps into engaged philanthropy? There are moments in lives, perhaps transitional times, when people need to bite off big challenges. They fall for new adventures the way, at other times, they might fall in love with new people, places, languages, music. Engaged philanthropists acknowledge that they are particularly drawn to IHAD because of its "hands-on," "bottom-line," results orientation. And they have arrived at a time in life when they want to do something with tangible impact, something that makes a difference. And now—perhaps because they are mature and comfortable with themselves in the world—they believe that the way to accomplish this is through relationships. The fact that IHAD combines concrete financial support with a direct commitment to young people is particularly appealing. And, as we shall continue to hear, once they begin connecting with young people their new relationships intensify the meaning of the present in ways they had never dreamed.

When Gene Lang is searching for a way to describe the precious personal rewards he gets from relationships with his dreamers, he thinks of individuals like Raquel, for example, who came for a recent Saturday morning visit. It's now nearly twenty years since he first met her, when she was a sixth grader at P.S. 121. In the course of her visit with her husband and young baby, Raquel asked Lang if he would write a letter to help establish her eligibility for a new apartment. His response to her request was simply to be grateful. He felt honored that she would ask, because, as he puts it,

> I'm spending time with people because I can, and if I can, it's the right thing to do. I get such pleasure from it. The fact that my young friend will ask me for a reference is an indication of a relationship. There are a lot of people you wouldn't ask for a favor. But it's really a tribute when someone asks you for something. It's a recognition that you have worth. Because I know that if I needed something, if I were in serious trouble, I could turn to that person and they would come to help me. That is very special.

Connections, Lang insists, bring unpredictable and incomparable rewards.

CHAPTER 4

WHERE WE COME FROM

A lot of people had helped him along the way and he had always wanted to do more than write checks. The magic of this program is involvement.

— an IHAD sponsor, about her husband

There are many ways to think about how our history shapes our lives. History, with a capital "H," certainly matters. It's relevant to this inquiry that the 1980s were a time when the "newly wealthy"—even when their fortunes theoretically qualified them for acceptance into the old, established circles of traditional philanthropy—began creating original foundations and new charitable initiatives. For some who had amassed considerable amounts of money during the second half of the twentieth century, traditional ways of giving—donating to established charities or institutions, providing money for a new wing at a hospital or a new college science building—were satisfying enough. For others, Eugene Lang among them, they were not. Lang and others like him wanted to do more than donate from afar—they wanted to be directly involved in the projects they funded. And some of the programs and institutions that he and other pioneers of engaged philanthropy created allowed them to cross the class boundaries that had kept them confined, for most of their adult lives and no matter how hard-working they were, to the world of the affluent. In other words, the demographics of philanthropy were changing, as were patterns of giving.

This is where personal history with a small "h" comes in. Lang's own experience at Swarthmore, we know, was central to his lifelong interest in higher education. Coming from another direction,

Hal Davies has come to realize that committing to IHAD was for him a reactive move. Partly it is his own regrets about having squandered educational opportunities that have made him so passionate about this particular program.

> A lot of my motivation may have been that, as I learned later in life, I had been given every benefit of a quality education that any child anywhere in the world could want. I went to good boarding schools, private schools when I was in elementary school, and then the University of Virginia on top of that. But, by God, I fought the system the whole time! I realized much later that I had been given an amazing gift and had wasted most of it. Maybe this was my way of helping others not make the same mistake I had made.

Development is not a straight path. As Robert Frost so eloquently reminds us, we have choices to make when the roads open to us diverge, and the one we do not take can make "all the difference."

How do we choose a road? The role models in our families, the ways that we are loved and accepted by those to whom we are closest, the hard times and the joys we experience as children have much to do with the values we hold and the decisions we make as adults. It was because of their own or their family's experiences with hardship that many IHAD sponsors found themselves drawn to support children whose lives are also fraught with difficulties. Others were strongly attracted to the program because of a family ethos of direct community service that surrounded them as they were growing up. This chapter explores some of the ways that personal history can predispose people to being open to the attractions of engaged philanthropy.

THE LEGACY OF HARDSHIP

A number of the IHAD sponsors I interviewed spoke of personal and familial experiences with adversity, Even when they did not say so directly, I think it's fair to assume that these experiences made them particularly eager to help kids for whom childhood is difficult. Immigration and the Great Depression of the 1930s, in particular, were recurrent themes.

Immigration, of course, has a powerful impact on families. Though it may imply above-average capacities for courage and resilience, whether the elders have chosen to come to a new land to better their chances in life or to escape persecution at home, that decision wrenches people away from everything with which they are familiar. Several sponsors whose parents or grandparents came to America in the twentieth century spoke to me about growing up in homes where hard-working adults wanted their children to know that while life could be very difficult, education opened the way to a better future. "Education is one thing they can't take away from you," Lang and others remember hearing. He was lucky, he says, because his parents were literate.

> Though they were immigrants, they made learning part of my regimen. Knowing how to do things for myself was my father's philosophy. He taught me how to make my own toys. I learned to use tools at a very young age because my father always said, "So long as you know how to use tools, you will never go hungry."

Sponsors who grew up in immigrant households recalled parents working long hours to bring both bread and stability to their homes. They talked about single-minded, purposeful role models who were completely "involved with the struggles of daily life." A couple of the people I interviewed remembered fathers unable to speak a word of English who left home early each morning and came home exhausted, falling asleep in their chairs before their kids were ready for bed—that is, on the nights when they weren't participating in a settlement house program, English language classes, or other efforts to better their lot. One man, who helped to translate for his father, recalled,

> He may not have been able to speak English, but he was always active in the union. They had meetings in our own kitchen. We didn't have a living room, but I remember those meetings. He was a tailor. Many of the boys I knew in high school never graduated. My father was so excited when I won a spelling prize: they gave me a copy of Mark Twain to read and he was thrilled. After two years at City College, I went to work. This is a great country.

His wife believes that her husband's enthusiasm for IHAD

> came in part out of his own identification with under-class
> kids who are seen as not having a chance to succeed or being
> expected to succeed. He was a child of immigrants, and
> everything was based on the expectation that they would
> stay here, make a home here, and go to school. He remem-
> bers his father going to the neighborhood settlement house
> to learn how to speak English and become a citizen. And the
> Jewish culture always put a strong emphasis on education.
> His parents remembered their early life sadly. They didn't
> want to go back there and they didn't want to be on welfare.

Children of immigrants often see their parents make great sacrifices for their families. This is a complicated business because, on one
level, children may resent the fact that their parents are not as present
in their lives as other children's are. But once they grow into mature,
engaged philanthropists, parental sacrifice seems to have instilled deep
feelings of gratitude and pride. For them, their parents became models
of courage and, in the end, hope. As Lou Irving explains,

> My father woke up at six in the morning, went to work at
> seven, came home at seven at night. He was whipped. He
> worked hard—in scrap iron, a junkyard. He was outside all
> day and he would come home, have dinner, read the paper,
> go to sleep. You know, I'm a very traditional guy. My par-
> ents were immigrants from Poland. I'm a first generation
> guy. First kid in my family to go to college. But I've always
> been so proud of the country. And I always wanted to give
> something back. I felt I had to. When I was overseas [in
> World War II], I used to tell my mother, "If I die, don't
> feel bad. It's not too much of a price to pay for what this
> country's given our family." I meant it.

Another sponsor still marvels at her father's spirit.

> He used to say, "Every day, if there's something you can do
> to make the sun shine for somebody, do it." He worked very
> hard, came to this country at the age of fourteen, and didn't

have anyone to go to. He was an educated man, even at the age of fourteen, and his values were right.

No matter how hard he worked, he always was on committees, he always had time to go to meetings at night. I would think he would be so tired. But he was not just involved with his own problems, even though they were legion, especially when he started his own business. After he got on sort of a firm footing, the factory burned down. Everyone advised him to declare bankruptcy. He refused. He wouldn't do it. And he came back. He was a highly respected member of the community. I wish I knew what happened in his early life because I wonder how he got to be such a smart, educated person in such a short time.

She is still amazed when she thinks about her father's strength and his determination—as we all must be today when we think about the kind of energy and optimism required for a fourteen-year-old to start a new life on his own in a new land. There's a way in which these family histories engender pride and, in turn, a deeply felt gratitude that can nurture habits of civic engagement, habits which can be passed from one generation to the next. Another sponsor, a second-generation American, remembers his grandfather, who emigrated from Ireland without a penny to his name but "made it very clear that we had an obligation to make society better. He never ceased to remind us how extraordinarily blessed we were. That's true and that's right."

A much younger sponsor reiterated this message.

I'm first generation; my father and mother came from Lebanon forty years ago. My father had got his M.D. degree there but he did his real medical training here and then went into private practice. One of the things he always talked about was this sense of taking care of people and giving back. He did that through his work—but that was something that all of us kids got inculcated with. That we were fortunate, you know, and that you should try and give back.

Like immigration, the Great Depression had transformational effects on families. Many of the original, first group of IHAD sponsors talked about parents and grandparents barely scraping by through the

1930s. These people inherited a different but equally memorable legacy of firsthand experience with want, often coupled with feelings of obligation toward those less fortunate. Some sponsors remembered how determined their fathers were to protect their families against disasters and how zealously they husbanded their resources. Mara Emerson and Meg O'Donnell both said that surviving the Depression seemed to inspire their parents and grandparents to throw themselves into community volunteer work when they retired—through local churches, schools, and civic organizations. Mara recalls that her mother learned Braille in order to type books for the blind and, as she explains,

> When my father retired, he did a huge amount of volunteer work through the Rotary Club. He would spend three or four days a week driving sick children to their hospital appointments. That kind of thing. Being a child of the Depression, someone who had gone to school with scholarship help and all that, he was not financially giving. At the same time, he was concerned because he had kids he wanted to leave his money to.

Meg's grandfather, an Irish immigrant, was a grocer during the Depression. Though he died the year she was born, stories kept him very much alive in the family.

> He ran a meat market. When the Depression came, he was the local savior to people who were starving. He would not send bills out if he knew the family couldn't pay and he would make sure there was food in their homes. . . . After my father died, and we had a gathering at a local restaurant, my mother asked the restaurant for a bill. But they said "There will be no bill." My mother said, "Excuse me, but why?" And they said, "Your husband's father took care of us during the Depression. We will take care of him now."

Misfortune has many faces. Immigration and the Depression were common themes in the sponsors' stories, but there were others too. Some sponsors lost their parents when they were very young, leaving them with significant care-taking responsibilities within the family. Others had had to cope with parents or other relatives with serious health problems or addictions. A few, like Rob Mitchell, had stepped in to rescue a family business or support their relatives financially.

It's interesting that personal experiences with immigration, economic depression, and family crises—all of which involve significant change and loss—can apparently, in some instances, accentuate the importance of connectedness to one's community. This is not inevitable. It's easy to imagine people in similar circumstances whose character would be shaped more by anxiety about their unmet needs than by an impulse to share and connect. But one legacy of hardship can be a heightened awareness of the welfare of others. As Chuck Peterson explains,

> My father was a small businessman who worked his tail off in a series of unsuccessful ventures. Ultimately he went bankrupt and left us when I was about eleven or twelve. A series of experiences I had as a young man in that period later opened my heart to the importance of individual caring, adult role models, and the value of education. That is part of why this model, which is really about mentoring, appealed to me. Because of my own family experience.

I found it equally interesting that virtually all the IHAD sponsors I spoke with would agree that the magnitude of multiple troubles that poor, inner-city kids face today far surpasses whatever trials they themselves may have endured as children. In fact, when they began sponsoring few had any idea how powerfully the deck would be stacked against their dreamers.

Visiting the neighborhood where the Hull family was to begin their project, Sam Hull was horrified to discover his future dreamers living in "unbelievable conditions." Lou Irving told me that he quickly came to understand that, while his own family had made great sacrifices for education, this was barely an option in his dreamers' homes because parents "need their kids to go out, get a job, and start contributing to the family when they get to be fifteen or sixteen." For Lou, this particular expectation hearkened back to his parents' generation. They too had had to strike out to build new lives for themselves at an early age, but they'd also managed to study hard to better their prospects.

The question of personal resolve aside, for most sponsors the level of violence in the lives of the inner-city kids they wanted to help was appalling. As Mike O'Donnell recalls,

We asked one of the dreamers, "How many people do you know who have been shot?" Now remember: this is not Kosovo. This was when she was fourteen years old. She starts counting on her fingers, saying aloud, "Seven, eight, nine. You said 'shot.' What about stabbed?" I said, "Count that too." She got to nine. Then she said, "You said, 'People you know.' What about the ones I just saw get killed? Like the man coming out of the package store that got blasted with a shotgun in the chest and got killed? Does he count?" And then she said, "Of course, my uncle died of an overdose on his birthday. My aunt found him in the bathroom. Should I count that? And what about people I know who died of AIDS?" She gets up to thirteen quickly. Remember: this is a fourteen-year-old kid.

The magnitude of need in the lives of the low-income inner-city children these sponsors encountered differs in degree from the adversity they had personally experienced. But it is very likely that their recognition of the potential for resilience—especially in young children—intensified their empathy and solidified their determination to help their dreamers.

One last theme. For some sponsors, the chance to participate in IHAD was a way to make up for hardships they felt they'd inflicted on others. Chuck Peterson, who spent a few years working for the national IHAD organization before going home to marry and become a sponsor himself, said,

In conversation after conversation, when you really talked to these guys you began to understand that half of why they were doing it was because they screwed up their own families. They had been too busy. Now they're looking back at their life, finding they've got more money, power, or influence than they know what to do with. And they are helpless to make their own children like them. They want to be admirable. They want to have done something that matters in their life. They go to charity balls and sign checks and think, "This is stupid! This is not what I'm about! I'm about action, I'm an entrepreneur, I create big businesses, I move stuff! I don't just write stupid checks." When they hear about IHAD as a model they say, "That's it! That's the thing I'm going to do! I'm going to get in there, wrap my arms around these kids, shake them up! I'm going to make a difference!"

Driven as they had been when they were younger to create security and safety for their own families, some of the sponsors Chuck had gotten to know had not taken time for their own children, the ones they loved the most. Whether or not philanthropy in later life can compensate for absence when one's own children are young, an urge to keep trying to reach out to children is often part of the motivation of some engaged philanthropists. Hal Davies admits this obliquely when he speaks of how much it meant to him when one of his alumni dreamers, whom he'd invited to talk to a new middle school group, said to the kids,

> "Don't forget your sponsors. They're a great asset." Pointing to me he said, "This guy is better than anything I ever thought I could have for a father."

> Now where do you get that kind of feedback in life? Maybe one day from your grandchildren, but not from your own kids. You know you did good with them—but you may not have done well.

THE FAMILY ETHOS

Often the habit of giving is acquired early, passed on by either precept or example. Laura Joseph, as we mentioned in Chapter 2, has vivid memories of making house calls with her doctor father when she was very young and of hearing him say that this kind of work would also be her job when she was older. Another sponsor, one of several who grew up with comfort (or, as she says, "the benefits of largesse"), told me, in speaking of her family of origin,

> You always knew there was something to be returned. It isn't religious, particularly. It's just a feeling that if you had the benefits that society has offered, you should be willing to give back.

Other sponsors told me about energetic and devoted mothers who ran community organizations, worked as teachers, organized and staffed local libraries; one recounted how her mother, recovering from major surgery, wrote a manual about how to survive a heart bypass operation.

Pamela Marconi, whose father was a sheet metal worker, "blue collar, union," said that, because of her parents' example, she grew up assuming that life was about giving.

> My mother was president of the PTA, my father was at the church, at the school all the time. I just assumed everybody was like that. I didn't go to private school, I didn't go to camp every summer, I didn't have lessons and everything under the sun. But I had a very warm, loving, stable environment. If my parents saw that something needed to be done and they were able to do it, they just did it!

> I remember little things. Our family all lived within a ten-to-fifteen mile radius of each other, and as various uncles would die off my father would take it upon himself to drive by that aunt's house every night on the way home, just to make sure the car was in the driveway and she was okay. He became the man of the house in terms of fixing the screen door, building this or that. I always saw that. And I saw my mother constantly baking and cooking and bringing food to people. They were just very generous people, within their means. Generous with time more than money. What they gave was their ability and their time because they didn't have a lot of money to give. It just all happened, you know? I was growing up in that environment. If you have something you can share, you just really didn't think twice about it. You just shared it.

Another sponsor told me,

> I spent a lot of summers with my grandparents on the farm. We lived in town, but my mom and my sister and I would go to the farm for the summer. And what you do on a farm is help people, or get involved in whatever is going on to do your part.

My mother grew up in a very small town in a farming community. With farm life you all help each other. You have to. In the cold hard winters up north, you help each other. The church is a part of the community, the school, all of this. Everybody just supports each other and helps each other. Our state has a long, long history of education being extremely important and having very good schools. That's just a part of what we learned: that you go to school, do your work, and work hard. To be a farmer is a very difficult small business to run. You have to do all of it.

Her family, like many farm families, nurtured the habit of helping as if it were another crop they depended upon. Giving of their own time and effort, as all of these people did, is, of course, a template for engaged philanthropy.

It's also a basic premise of learning theory that meaningful education takes place both formally and informally. In situations where parents are absent or work long hours to support their families, grandparents often play an important role. Many IHAD sponsors—both "first generation" and those that followed—describe how important the influence of their grandparents was to them.

Frank Matthews's father was a lawyer who worked for the state department of agriculture. The family never had any money—didn't even own their own house. Frank remembers that his parents always wanted their children to "do better than they had done," and he also remembers that he used to sit on the swing on the front porch and wait a long time for his grandfather to finish doing the crossword puzzle so he could talk with him. "He was a very, very smart man. Read a lot and talked with me a lot about history and economics, and just lots of subjects." Lou Irving told me,

I was in love with my grandfather! He was an old bearded guy, but he was really a scholar: he was never meant to be a businessman. Though he and my father and my uncle were partners in a business, my grandfather would just sit and talk with me. He knew I was a bad kid and doing things I shouldn't be doing as the good son in a devout family. But he never said, "Don't!" He would just sit and explain to me why we do this, and why we do that. And he was a very holy guy. A wonderful guy. I learned more from him than from my father.

Perhaps because it is less fraught with the intensity of the parent-child connection, this kind of interaction with an elder can remain imprinted within us as an experience of acceptance and love.

Another sponsor told me a story about another grandfather, one who ultimately became an esteemed fund-raiser for a major institution. (In some ways, she has followed in his footsteps, becoming not only an IHAD sponsor but also the director of a regional IHAD chapter.) This story, which the grandfather told often, was about a summer evening when he was young farmer and his barn caught fire. At the time he was keeping cows, and many were killed in the fire. The sponsor described the aftermath, as they were dragging the carcasses of the animals out of the barn.

> There was a sixth-grade boy standing there, looking kind of shocked at the goriness of what had happened. There was a volunteer fire department in town and the boy's father was the chief who only made money when there was a fire. His father had told him he couldn't have a bicycle because they didn't have enough money to buy him one. It turned out that the boy had been going around lighting fires to try to get himself a bicycle.

> I know how much my grandfather cared about his cows: he always used to say that the day he had to finally sell them all, in the mid-sixties, was the saddest day of his life. To have his barn burn to the ground and lose a lot of the livestock was very, very upsetting. When they figured out that the fire was set by the fire chief's son, my grandfather's reaction was not to prosecute him. He went around to all the people in town and said, "This kid needs a better education than what he's getting." They raised money and sent him off to a private school. When I was a little a girl I met this man on several occasions. He would come back once every couple of years to visit my grandfather—who lived to be ninety-seven—to thank him for being so generous and changing his life.

Though a few first generation IHAD sponsors grew up in families where financial want was not an issue, more came from humble homes with no inherited wealth. After their last year of formal education, these individuals struck out on their own, beginning their work lives on the lowest rungs of large institutional ladders with no particular advantages over anyone else. Eventually, they all found themselves established in productive careers that enabled them to provide adequate material security for their own families—as their parents and grandparents did for them. And it seems that the experiences that they had when they were young have something to do with their determination to see that at least some poor children will be able to grow up the way they did, with adults in their lives who stand by them, have faith in them, and expect them to succeed.

RELIGION AND CULTURE

For some IHAD sponsors, the patterns of their own civic engagement were established within the context of their family's faith and cultural background. One told me,

> Being raised in the church and being raised a Christian had a lot to do with [my philanthropy]. One was always taught to be very loving and giving. I think that's the most exciting aspect of the Christian faith: the fact that it teaches you to love and give at every opportunity.

Another, a second generation American whose grandfather came from Ireland, was raised in a devoutly Catholic home. His very successful father often talked to his family about how blessed they were, and, in turn, how obligated to make the world a better place. This man served on the boards of many Catholic service organizations and, in fact, eventually decided to move many of his dreamers from public to parochial schools, where he was convinced that they would do better.

For Ken Robinson, the born-again Christian we met in Chapter 2, his dedication to Christ is absolutely central to his sponsorship. Though he achieved extraordinary material success in his adult life, he grew up in poverty and had one negative experience after another with education. When he was still a teenager, he got into sales. He was so good at this, in fact, that he sometimes wonders if it was his success in business that distracted him from schoolwork.

> I grew up so dirt poor that I thought I'd never have a car, or have two bedrooms and a bath. My father's top pay was $250 month when he retired as a master sergeant. He wasn't religious, but my mother was a wonderful Irish lady who was a little avid. She read the bible every Sunday night and went to church every Sunday and gave her little tithe. She was a strong believer.

> Did I have important school experiences? No! All negative! I was asked to leave college. I was asked to leave military school. I was asked to leave Catholic school. A college professor told me I was wasting my time in college. I should learn to drive a truck.

> But I did well. I went into sales when I was young. And finally, in my forties, in 1981, I turned my life over to the Lord. I was a success, according to the secular world. I had an airplane, two or three homes, and boats. But my life was an empty shell. Everything was going through the cracks. I decided to put Jesus in charge of my life, rather than me. I told him he could do a lot better with my life than I had done. And I promised God that I was going to give him ten percent of everything I made, from that day forth. I set up a bank account and dedicated it to good works, mainly oriented around children. And when you ask God into your life, he opens up territories that you never knew existed.

Though Sam Hull speaks of the influence of religion in his life less dramatically, he comes from a long line of ministers that includes a grandfather whose "mission was to have his church give away more money to those who needed it than it would spend on its own church building and congregation." Sara Hull, one of Sam's three daughters thinks a "deep-seated faith" has always driven her parents' "sense of obligation to the larger community and connection with it." Sam himself said,

For me it's less connected with the church, per se, than it is with the fact that this is just a big, complex society, we're all connected through it, we all have advantages and opportunities. Others are struggling. How do you find ways to leave things a little better than you found them? What's always impressed me is how ecumenical the whole thing is. I think each of us is motivated by our conception of faith, a belief in the almighty, and a desire to give back, but not in the sense of any specific theological dogma.

"How ecumenical the whole thing is"—by which Sam means, of course, that both hardship and the obligation to care for others are non-denominational.

The culture in which one grows up can be just as influential as the daily practice of a faith. When Tessa Bloom explained *tzedakah*— "giving back"—she was speaking more of Jewish tradition than devout religious practice per se. Another sponsor, who grew up in a Jewish neighborhood but a non-observant home, told me that although he's proud of being Jewish, he has no use for religion at all:

> Religion is a disaster. I think we'll end up blowing each other off the face of the earth in the name of religion. But you know, if you live the kind of life that we live, you should be obligated to give back because God has been good to us. That's kind of how I see philanthropy. For those of us who have been blessed with good health and money and family: you owe it. You should give back. Because you're just lucky. If you look at your life, there are so many things that are just pure luck. I don't know why but I always kind of felt sorry for the underdog. I grew up in a Jewish ghetto, and from early on I always had a liberal view of the world. I always felt poor people were getting the shaft, you know? Getting the shaft.

Although he rejects religion, he nonetheless explains his philanthropy using phrases like "God has been good to us" and "those of us who have been blessed," and he identifies strongly with people who, like his ancestors, have gotten "the shaft."

Feeling compassion for others is, of course, what philanthropy is all about. Whether or not one becomes an engaged philanthropist who steps into the fray and interacts directly with the less fortunate may have less to do with the doctrines to which one has been exposed as a child than it does with the degree of gratitude one feels for good things in one's life, along with attendant feelings of obligation to share with those less fortunate.

COMMON DENOMINATORS

One thing our inquiry reveals is that people who are drawn to engaged philanthropy represent a continuum in terms of several variables, rather than a type. They take on the commitment at different ages: some are in their thirties or forties, many others begin in their fifties. Their childhood histories vary enormously: some grew up in comfort, while others knew scarcity and want firsthand. Some are proud to associate themselves with an organized religion; others are just as proud to declare their independence from the dogma of any particular faith. Some are Republicans; others are Democrats. Some are more educated or have traveled more widely or become more prosperous than others. But no matter where they come from, there is one feature of engaged philanthropy, as illustrated by IHAD, that particularly appeals to them all: it is designed to be empowering.

No matter what their political preference, many sponsors used the familiar fishing metaphor to explain what hooked them on IHAD—that it's not simply "a handout." "We're not liberals," one told me emphatically.

> Sponsors are very conservative, in general. We teach people to fish, we don't give them fish. We want to help kids do better for themselves. We are very comfortable with the other sponsors—who are not just a lot of idealistic liberals.

This man might be interested to know that some IHAD sponsors who comfortably identify themselves as idealistic liberals use the same precept to explain what *they* love about engaged philanthropy. Would he be momentarily startled to think that there is an idealist hidden in his conservative self? Would the rather liberal Tessa Bloom be disturbed to find herself quite in agreement with a self-identified conservative?

I think not. Because no matter what kinds of simplifying generalizations people may use to label others, they can in fact share a common passion—in this case to see less fortunate children and families grow into self-sufficient, productive citizens by dint of their own efforts.

George Norman was young when he became a sponsor—and even younger when he went into business. Work and personal values have long been braided together in his life, as he explains.

> I went into business, for a couple of reasons, while I was still in college. One was to provide a challenge for myself. One was, obviously, to provide for me and for my family at some point in the future. And the third was to use that company as an instrument to give back to the community. I didn't view myself at that time as somebody who wanted to be a social worker. And I loved business. But I always saw a connection between the role you can have in business [and] in shaping a community. . . . [And] the importance of community is in our company's values statement. It's part of what we're known for.
>
> A few years ago we were forced into bankruptcy, a nightmare I wouldn't wish on my worst enemy. So our near casualty was driven by a customer who didn't pay us. They ended up having to pay us, but it was a harrowing three years at a time when the manufacturing industry in this country, and in this state, had collapsed. But a group of people in my business fought their way though operating a business in bankruptcy, which, in a manufacturing firm, is amazingly insane, incredibly pressure-ridden. For me it was equally hard because what I love doing is giving away money, and all of a sudden, after twenty years of being able to do that, I couldn't do it. At the same time, what kept me sane was that I still could be connected to the things I was doing in the community.
>
> At the time this all happened, I was chairing the United Way board. And I could go chair one of those meetings or go to a campaign meeting or spend time with my dreamers and focus on something other than myself or our problems.

> It was that community involvement that, in large part, got
> me through the worst time in my life, you know? And part
> of our survival in the bankruptcy was because people knew
> who I was, what I stood for, what I believed in. Everybody
> was pulling for the company, 'cause we stood for what people
> want companies to stand for. Everybody was saying, "How
> do we not let this happen? How do we keep this company
> and what it stands for going?"

Loving doing business never diminished George's passion for giving,
and he made sure that the culture of his company reflected his own
personal values. This connection has sustained him during tough
times, even as it has nurtured the community around him.

Chuck Peterson's story illustrates how people of different
political preferences have found common value and meaning in
engaged philanthropy. To recap and update his personal history,
when his mother remarried after her divorce from his father, he was
sent to an excellent private school and college, during which time he
spent a transforming semester in Africa. After graduation he worked
for several years in South Africa before coming home to get degrees
in law and divinity and eventually take a job in his stepfather's well-
established business.

> I have met and know a lot of very conservative people. Some
> of them are my relatives. Please understand. I came out of
> the Reagan years feeling embittered and angry about con-
> servatism and what I saw as the fraud of claiming that volun-
> teerism and faith-based programs should do what I believe
> is our society's obligation, which can only realistically be
> funded and organized through the federal government. But
> in my heart of hearts, my very conservative grandparents
> from Boston still speak to me.
>
> On her deathbed, my grandmother begged me to return to
> the Republican Party. It was the last conversation we ever
> had. She said to me that she was so bitterly disappointed
> that I had turned away from the true party and that I didn't
> understand that the Democrats were enslaving people
> through welfare and dependency.

My grandparents were ideologues. I said, "You know, Grandma, I will spend my life trying to listen to you. I value freedom. I understand the importance of the individual. I understand the importance of responsibility. But you just can't abandon millions of children who have no responsibility for what's happened to them. You can blame parents. You can hold people responsible for criminal acts. We can even argue about treatment versus jail for substance abuse and drug crimes. But I've gotta tell you: if you're a two-year-old and you're growing up in the streets, in a Christian nation, just in a decent nation, a minimally civilized nation has a responsibility to provide for that child—housing, health-care, and education. The Republicans, by damn, will never do this. It's all just an excuse to give a tax break to their friends so they can sail around in their yachts!"

Of course I didn't say all that to her: it would have been a little meaner than I was in that moment. But we had had pretty direct conversation! The day I came home from Africa and told her I was going to vote for Walter Mondale, she went to the mantelpiece and took the big framed portrait of me that she had off [it], put it in her drawer, and said, in her best Yankee clipped accent, "Now that's all we're ever going to say about that!"

We'll hear more about Chuck's arguments with other members of his family about how best to help those less fortunate. For now let's just say that certainly his grandmother's voice is still quite robust today, when debate about public and private solutions to common challenges is alive and well.

But both Chuck and his grandmother were, like others whom we've met and will meet in this book, profoundly grateful for their good fortune. This gratitude—whether framed as a sense of being blessed or a duty to give back—pushes engaged philanthropists to take risks, to learn from new opportunities, to share their "fortunes." In gratitude, they have built their lives in part around moral commitments—though they would never frame it in such lofty tones. But their lives do integrate their personal sense of who they are with their beliefs. They are materially secure enough to feel they will be provided for and consequently they have money and energy to spend on others. There is passion in Chuck's voice—and in his grandmother's. On both sides one hears a common determination to help others achieve independence and individual success. Across major differences, engaged philanthropy pulls people together to make the world better for all of us.

CHAPTER 5

WHAT'S IT LIKE TO BE A SPONSOR?

Long-term mentoring is not a task for timid souls.
                    —*The Washingtonian*, February 1998

Imagine that you suddenly find yourself with fifty or sixty new children in your life. You've committed yourself to them for at least six years—in fact, it's more likely they'll figure in your daily life for twelve to fifteen years, and you'll probably stay in contact for decades. As you begin, you know that over such a long period of time a host of unexpected developments will mean taking actions, making decisions that you cannot anticipate. Your eye is on the future—and that's where you want your dreamers to set their sights. But any given day may bring unforeseeable events. The experience of engaged philanthropy IHAD-style is a voyage between the predictable and the unexpected.

To help new sponsors know what's ahead, Ann Hull wrote some moving notes.

> What's it like to be a sponsor? It's getting to know a bunch of kids who have never had a single advantage in life, making it extremely difficult to personally identify with their problems.

> It's batting your head against the wall, talking through problems, cleaning out your closets, getting a card in the mail thanking you, getting a phone call at night, having a teacher who couldn't find anything good to say about them

notice a difference in dreamers, learning a mother didn't send her dreamer to school the first week because she didn't have any money for school clothes, not knowing what we should be doing next, having your entire family involved, knowing that some of your dreamers are being abused, watching your husband become totally involved about something other than business, watching the absentee rate drop, seeing test scores go up, realizing how spoiled you've been all your life, wondering why you ever got involved in what you cannot really be in charge of. . . .

It's knowing that this is the best thing you could ever do with your time or your money, and that it makes you feel better than anything you've ever done.

Eugene Lang's impromptu offer in 1981 plunged him into the unanticipated task of designing a complex, six-year scaffold of support for his dreamers. By 1990, however, I Have a Dream sponsors were beginning to understand that their dreamers' chances for success would be greatly improved if they began when the kids were younger, even before they graduated from elementary school. As we know, at heart sponsors are entrepreneurs and they do everything they can to maximize the likelihood of successful returns on their investments. Thus many IHAD projects now begin when children are in the early grades. And each is based on a premise that's also a promise: once a dreamer, always a dreamer. So even when it takes some kids longer than others to finish high school, most sponsors will stand by them for many years, ready to support them in post-secondary education or in training programs that will lead them into responsible, productive adulthoods.

START-UP AND STRUCTURE

One of the first things new sponsors must do is to choose a site for their project. While the site selection process is usually fairly systematic, there's plenty of room for choice. Sponsors work with school superintendents, housing authorities, or church leaders, for example, to help them find sites aligned with their priorities. Some might look for a school with a large number of "at risk" students, or a high percentage of kids eligible for free lunches, or one that is situated in a neighborhood with significant rates of drug use or teenage pregnancy. Others look for the school with the best academic track record in the poorest neighborhood, or for a low-performing school with a "strong" principal, or for a school whose principal is very enthusiastic about bringing IHAD into his or her building. Some sponsors look for sites in neighborhoods where the "feeding patterns" that move children from elementary to middle to high school are not too disruptive geographically, so their dreamers will be able to stay together throughout their school years.

Every project needs to enlist a partnering community-based organization, a home-base agency that will help to house and coordinate services and supports for dreamers. Sometimes sponsors set up their programs in schools or housing developments that are close to community-based organizations with which they are familiar. Preexisting relationships may also be a deciding factor: sometimes knowing a principal or a principal's spouse personally has made a site feel particularly appropriate. And some sponsors have chosen schools they or their own kids had attended, or where they themselves had once been teachers, or where they had previous connections as volunteer mentors or tutors.

In Chapter 2 we heard Tessa Bloom begin to talk about what the start-up process was like for her. As she said, she started with twice as many children as she and her husband had initially anticipated—one big surprise right from the beginning. But in many ways, Tessa's description of the steps she took to set up her program is fairly typical. She wanted to find a school that was no more than thirty minutes from her home and, as she told us, one in a neighborhood with a high poverty rate and where the principal was eager to have the program.

> My school is in the area you read about in the headlines, where tourists are murdered. I had called the school board up, said I wanted to do a program and asked to be introduced to someone from the school system. Actually in my district someone else had promised to do a similar program but within six months he disappeared, leaving some very heartbroken people behind. So when I came along they said, "Oh God, here we go again; we don't want to deal with this lady." But they sent someone to help me, a wonder-

ful man who's been with me all along and become my best friend in the system. . . . He took me to a school on Liberty Hill. We met the principal and looked around. The school, from all appearances, seems like it's got everything it could possibly need. But when you start to look closely you see that a lot of it is window-dressing. It's a very distressed neighborhood. . . .

We started in the second grade. Many people try to take the whole grade in a school and some do housing projects. I didn't like the idea of a housing project. And I felt that choosing a whole grade would have more influence on the whole school. You know, with peer pressure, when you've got everyone in a grade as part of your program it's much easier. But we did cut it off. Any children enrolled by the end of third grade could be part of the program, but in fourth grade they couldn't. We went up to one hundred and seven very quickly. And then we lost ten children just because they moved out of town and the parents didn't respond to us. We sent them a certified letter saying, "Look, if you're not going to keep in contact with us, you need to know that your child will no longer be a dreamer." And ten of them we never heard from. This could be because, you know, they move around so much. But now we have ninety-seven kids! I would say for 75 percent of our children, their parents are on welfare. And at least as many are single parents, always moms.

Many sponsors use contracts to help establish the kinds of relationships they want to have with dreamers and their families. This is one way to ensure that all children and parents agree to meet the specific expectations that will structure the sponsor-dreamer connection. Some contracts have "a little more muscle" than others, as one sponsor put it. And some sponsors revise these agreements as dreamers get older in order to formally address new challenges that come along as young children become teenagers. Middle and high school versions, for example, may include promises not to use drugs, alcohol, or firearms. Mara Emerson, whom we met in Chapter 3, told me,

I have two contracts: one with the children, one with the parents. And we have our own very explicit one about what we do, which is educational enrichment. It details our scholarship promise, which is that for any advanced learning institution up to our state university's resident rate, I will pay tuition. I draw the line at clown school. But I will pay for technical college. I will pay for culinary arts school and probably cosmetology, because some of my girls are really talented and if that's where they want to go and what they want to do, I think I should support that.

In the parents' contract there's an agreement that "I will do my best to send a clean, fed, appropriately clothed, rested child to school every day. I will provide a quiet reasonable place where the child can do homework every night. I will ask the child if he has done his homework every night. I will do my best to make sure my child has a safe environment." The kids have their contract, too, which says, "I'll do my homework and I'll be responsible and I'm going to learn how to learn and do my homework and pay attention in class and accept the fact that my job is getting the grades so I can get accepted into college."

Some IHAD programs, with whom I disagree violently, kick a kid out of the program if they move away. But does that mean that if a kid's dad gets a great job in Georgia, he might not go just so the kid can stay in this program? Time out! That's backwards! My kids will not be dropped. They cannot be kicked out. They can go to jail and come back; they can join a gang and drop out for a long time and come back. It's quite all right with me; they've known that from day one. It's part of our contract.

As Mara explains, renewing contracts every year guarantees that sponsors have regular contact with dreamer families even if many find it difficult to support their children actively in IHAD. Low-income parents often work several jobs and sometimes feel intimidated by their children's schools. It can be hard for them to become engaged with IHAD activities and services, even when these are individualized. In the experience of most of the sponsors I interviewed, only a small core group of parents became regularly and actively engaged with the program. And although a few told inspiring stories about parents who, when their kids become dreamers, took themselves back to school and made significant advances in their own jobs, more often than not sponsors find that, day to day, dreamers are mostly "on their own." In fact, while the relative scarcity of supportive, caring adults in these kids' lives is something that surprises most sponsors, this is one of the central issues that the mentoring component of the program is designed to address.

Though Lang originally conceived of I Have a Dream as a school-based initiative, some IHAD projects are now sited in housing projects. This means that sponsors adopt a group of children on the basis of where they live rather than grade level. Children's ages may range from early childhood to adolescence. In choosing these sites sponsors often work closely with housing authorities to find a complex that is correlated with high dropout rates or perhaps one that is located in a community where the sponsor has other commitments. The housing development model of intervention may require a longer term of commitment than the school-based one does. It also requires that a greater variety of services be provided simultaneously.

While Lang and many of the first generation of sponsors began on their own, many current IHAD projects have been initiated by small groups of lead sponsors who share the financial burden. After she met with Lang, you'll recall, Pamela Marconi went home to raise money from a number of colleagues and friends to start her project. Chuck Peterson turned to various family members to help him create the fiscal infrastructure for his project. In some communities, churches pair up to share the labor and funding for IHAD. Similar kinds of funding collaborations have taken place under the auspices of two universities. In one instance, as its alumni newsletter reports, Yale's graduating class of 1956 decided to "find the most diverse and well run elementary school in the city and raise as much money as possible, in order to offer an [IHAD] program to an entire fourth grade class at that school." In this project a local businessman became the primary sponsor to the group. Under the direction of an alumnus with many years of experience in schools, class members contributed funding. At Stanford Business School, two graduate students developed a program of mentoring and tutoring services that are provided by business school students to children in the local school district, and they turned to various friends of the university to establish college funds for its dreamers. When the business school class turns over, every two years, the dreamers get new mentors. A strong project coordinator provides continuity. Many new graduate students are enthusiastic about the opportunity to do direct community service for two years. As one says, "This is definitely a way you can reach out and see your impact."

When responsibilities for support and program implementation are shared among several sponsors, co-sponsoring can foster the development of a wider array of services for dreamers. In one case, for example, while the project's founder bears the lion's share of its running costs, and meets with groups of dreamers for dinner once a month, one co-sponsor is a trained psychologist who has helped develop other aspects of the program. First she hired a half-time social worker. Then, with the help of students from local universities who need internships, they set up a host of services, including individual and group counseling, a sex education program, and computer access with some training for dreamers. This part of the project is located at a community-based organization that has become a regular drop-in center. Other services—including mentoring, tutoring, special interest groups, job procurement, college prep, and a music program—are administered by the project coordinator and other staff at the project's home base, while the second sponsor runs weekly meetings for staff from both locations to coordinate their efforts. In this particular IHAD project, when dreamers finish high school a third co-sponsor will pick up the financial burden for college.

In many ways, project coordinators are the critical links, the glue that holds dreamers to the project. Usually closer in age to the dreamers than the sponsors themselves, the PCs strengthen all kinds of vital connections—between kids and sponsors, kids and teachers, and dreamer families and schools. They act as intermediaries who can move tactfully between different worlds, helping children learn to navigate between cultures and contexts. Good PCs are empathic and eager to help, as determined to be good role models as to build their own repertoire of skills as effective youth workers. Many have had some previous experience and/or training in education or human services. Above all, they need to be energetic people who can make a long-term commitment to a challenging job. Over time, some sponsors make dreamer-like commitments to their PCs as well, supporting them in furthering their own education. The philanthropists who have done this describe it as another kind of investment that has borne rich fruit in their own communities.

ADJUSTING TO REALITIES

Most IHAD sponsors have been fairly naïve about the realities of under-resourced schools before they begin. What they learn as they go along naturally influences the development of their projects. For example, sometimes sponsors find that in spite of an initial enthusiasm for IHAD, overworked school principals and teachers begin to resent the special attention that the project confers on a randomly chosen group of students. Staff can feel threatened by outsiders who are determined to do "better." And many thorny issues influence inner-city children's success in school these days. For example, in some districts it's common for at least 40 percent of the students to change schools every year. Of course this can have daunting practical implications for the structure of an IHAD project. And even in the best situations, children rarely stay together as a cohesive community of learners all the way from elementary through high school. Sponsors have to cope with what happens when a city's school assignment process breaks up a group of dreamers, when immigrant families take their children out of the country for weeks at a time, or when housing troubles or unemployment force families to move. Over time, many sponsors, project coordinators, and staff have found themselves facing daunting geographical challenges, traveling from school to school or back and forth from schools to community-based organizations in order to stay in touch with their dreamers.

Most will also encounter the welter of factors that complicate learning for students with special needs and for children whose primary language is not English. They'll see how bureaucratic routines may limit a teacher's ability to connect with a student, and what happens as maturing young people move through the turbulent middle school years into high school, where the pressures on adolescents intensify, both to succeed and to fail. Some will see young people being influenced by friends and families to drop out of school.

Sponsors are a diverse group, as we've learned, and they respond to these challenges in many different ways. Some added more intensive outreach services. Some choose to "stay under the radar screen," working to resolve difficulties quietly without attracting too much public attention to the interventions they offer. Some decide to place certain dreamers in parochial or alternative school settings. As we know, in response to what they learned as IHAD sponsors in the public system, Richard and Laura Joseph started two independent charter schools.

> We have thought about what we're doing as the last civil rights issue. The *Brown* versus *Board of Education* decision eliminated legal segregation. But what we've had is *de facto* segregation. These kids don't have a chance. In the Washington, D.C. school system, when they tried to put vouchers in there three or four years ago, Bill Clinton and Al Gore and all the Democratic senators blocked it. But these people all send their kids to private schools.

> No matter where you come down on the voucher issue, it does seem a little wrong that if you have the economic wherewithal to either move or send your kid to private school, you don't have to put up with the public school system. But if you're poor, you not only have to put up with the public school system but you have to put up with a failing school that's been failing for twenty or twenty-five years and nothing is being done about it. That's criminal. This is a civil rights issue because the people who are in this position are largely urban minorities.

Lang himself objects when sponsors decide to take their dreamers out of the public system. In so doing, he maintains, they leave schools even more bankrupt than they are. Personally, he's always hoped that his model—taking good care of a randomly chosen group of children—might demonstrate to the establishment just how easily one might in fact reform the public schools.[36]

But IHAD projects all function autonomously, and most sponsors maintain that the program's strength lies in the freedom it gives each of them to shape projects as they want. Some, like Frank Matthews, whom we met in Chapter 3, believe that only large-scale change can make a difference. Frank lives in a Southwestern city that busses its pupils from their neighborhoods to schools all over the community, so he has based his efforts in housing developments rather than schools, and he has started with a thousand children. From the beginning he admitted that this would mean that a thousand dreamers would get less personalized attention than hoped for in Lang's original vision. But he firmly believes that this approach is the only way to bring about significant change.

> Gene felt that we took on too much, that we didn't do the job individually with each child as well as we should have. I'm sure he's right, but I wouldn't change it for anything. We've got a lot more kids graduating from college. Our percentages may not be quite as good as his, but it's like throwing those starfish in the water. The ones we've helped have appreciated it. You just cannot have a neighborhood with a 75 percent dropout rate improve. It just can't. If most of the kids are dropping out of school, that whole neighborhood is doomed. And until we change that I just don't believe that anything is going to happen. . . .
>
> It's all about the greater community, not just the one where the kids live. It has to do with crime statistics, illegitimate pregnancy statistics, the whole thing. You better start when the children are young, because if you don't they'll soon be pregnant or on dope, or dropping out of school. And it works better at home because when they come home to a housing project, then we had a study hall for them right there and then. They came. I think housing project-based programs are better than school-based programs because of the logistics. When they walk in that door they sit down and they have a tutor right there.

Frank's is one of several faith-based IHAD initiatives, each of which has a distinctive life of its own. In his own community, where Frank has now overseen three IHAD projects, the third one takes a different approach from the first two. It's entirely staffed by people from a consortium of churches who believe, as Frank does, that the

Lord is their "most important mentor." As he explains, the projects have become increasingly evangelical.

> Last time we had lots of civic clubs and corporations with us, and I'd do that again. But this time our group all comes from churches and we're going to emphasize the importance of spiritual life along with everything else.

> You know, it's not that the churches aren't down there in that neighborhood: they've got one on every corner. But there are also an awful lot of people down there that do not go to church, and even when they go, they don't get the view that they ought to have of the gospel. I don't mean by that that I know what it is, and that no one else knows the gospel like I do. But I think everybody needs to know that there are rules to follow. They are good rules, rules that were established thousands of years ago. And what they need to hold on to, really, is the Lord, and what He taught, and what He was, and who He is. You know, He said, "Be holy because I'm holy." I think that needs to be taught to kids.

> I just think sometimes that the deep spiritual relationship people can have with the Lord needs to be explained to them, taught to them. That's the way a church can move into a neighborhood and do something. They're not going to do much good by going down there and painting the houses. It may be a nice expression of Christian love, but it won't change a neighborhood. In three years, the houses will need painting again and nobody will have changed because of it. If you don't see changed lives, you don't see anything happen. And that's what's got to happen.

While Frank feels a need to be explicit about the role of faith in life, other faith-based projects, like the one we described in Chapter 3, are quite different. That one is structured as an inclusive partnership between two churches, one suburban and one in the inner-city, and the members of its guiding committee believe that the "spiritual" aspect of the work consists of "setting an example, not preaching."

However sponsors decide to run their projects, Hal Davies is one of those who are absolutely certain that the autonomy that I Have a Dream confers on sponsors is at the heart of its success. He's been on the national board for many years and knows that "sponsors are broad thinkers." They hate being bogged down by lots of regulations and protocols and are grateful for the openness of the basic design. In fact, only funding and imagination limit what these engaged philanthropists can do. "These people don't take no for an answer, in life: they just want to get things done." So they forge ahead, thriving on the challenges that their commitments bring.

STAYING FLEXIBLE AND STRONG

Challenges bring frustrations, and most sponsors acknowledge their initial naiveté. Like Lang, at the beginning many believed that promising money for college would lead to a happily-ever-after ending for good kids in poor communities. As one recalls, "In 1986, we all began with soft, squishy ideas about how to make a difference. Everyone was just pretty much a seventies-style do-gooder."

But as they come to appreciate the obstacles inner-city kids are up against, sponsors begin to frame new goals for their dreamers. Without for an instant diluting their high-beam focus on the importance of education, many begin to see that, as Lou Irving said, for some dreamer families, higher education feels like an imposed, irrelevant priority; in fact, it can even be perceived as a goal that threatens family values and culture. So sponsors start identifying a range of different kinds of objectives. In the end, they hope such adjustments will enable dreamers to take many paths to reach the ultimate goal of becoming responsible citizens who are in charge of their lives. As Hal Davies said,

> We worked hard with each of our dreamers, in groups and with individuals, to help them to see the importance of accepting individual responsibilities and to understand why this is something they want to do for themselves, not just to please us or their parents.

> We fought tooth and nail, to the death, to break the welfare mentality, and talked openly about it. It was part of almost every conversation we ever had. And the kids came to understand that though their families may have had the welfare mindset instilled in them, they couldn't come to our

table with that mentality. I'd give us a mark of 80 on that. It was hard work, first getting them to understand what it was, and then to admit they had it, that it had been instilled in them. But I feel we added a lot to their life in doing that.

By identifying "welfare mentality" as a problem, Hal is arguing against a passive, entitled mindset that keeps kids resigned and unable to see ahead. To beat this, some sponsors told me, they tended to toughen up over time. More and more they felt a need to make it clear that they expected kids to be accountable for their own successes and failures, to take responsibility for what happens to them. While acknowledging the simplicity of their earliest hopes for their dreamers, they nonetheless refuse to let the young people off the hook, to excuse mediocrity, or to compromise their firm expectations that these kids will succeed.

Goals change. Instead of dreaming of college for every youngster, sponsors may instead focus on ensuring that each student will graduate from high school. And to encourage self-reliance, some, like Frank Matthews, begin to emphasize

> *getting* scholarships as much as giving them. We do still give scholarships, but we also attempt to get that twenty-five-year-old dreamer scholarship supports [from other sources]. Almost all colleges have PELL grants now, and we start with that so we can get them into a community college—even when they're older. We suggest that someone who's been in prison, maybe, or who may have been out of the public system for a while, take the community college route too. Often this is the best place to start anyway.

Sponsors also identify new objectives that incorporate what they are learning about some of the pressures that can derail the brightest of youth: teenage pregnancy, dropping out of school, and petty crime, each of which takes a serious toll. And, like Chuck Peterson, sponsors start thinking about individualizing success. Chuck has formalized these expectations by defining long-term goals for his dreamers in new ways: they will become ready, willing, and able to succeed—socially and vocationally as well as academically.

There are many stories about how sponsors and dreamers choose new stars to steer by so children can reach their *own* goals and, as Mike O'Donnell says, "find themselves succeeding in ways they have never succeeded before." But fundamentally, what's been most astonishing to me is that no matter how their dreamers change, sponsors do not let go. Their tenacity has enormous impact.

Mike and Meg O'Donnell tell a vivid story about Manny, a boy who had experienced many losses and troubles in his family and had a terrible time controlling his temper. One year they set up a special summer tutoring program for their dreamers. They promised the teachers they would have control over the program: if they found any child too difficult to teach, they could dismiss him or her from the program. Mike remembers how Manny resisted his sponsors' hopes, going only with great reluctance into the summer program. One day the boy lost his temper.

He took off his shirt and started screaming at the tutor. The teachers kicked him out of the class. They were going to suspend him from the program: you can't allow violence against the teacher.

So he comes to see me, and I say to him, "Now we're going to meet with the teachers, and you can make the case about what you want to do. You ought to apologize, tell them it won't happen again, explain the reasons why you did it, and say it won't happen again." Then, in the meeting, he started to talk. He hit all the points that we talked about: you look them straight in the eye; you don't make excuses for what you did; don't try to wiggle out of it. Tell them how sorry you are, what your plans are, what you'd like to do. He went through them all. But they still kicked him out. After he got kicked out he comes up to me and he says, "I don't want to be a dreamer anymore."

I said, "Nope! It just doesn't work like that. It just doesn't! We gotcha! We're just like your parents. You can't get rid of your parents. And you can't get rid of us! You're always going to be a dreamer, no matter what you do! No matter what you do, no matter what happens to you, we have you and we love you. Because we want you to make something of yourself! You're always going to be a dreamer!" He said, "Well, okay."

It's possible that on some level Manny knew he wouldn't be able to contain himself well enough to succeed in this summer program. Hence his resistance. But one thing he discovered was that failure did not cost him the care and consistency of people who would stay by his side as he pushed himself to try for new achievements.

Sponsors have many stories to tell about their dreamers. They describe children with special needs or limitations whom IHAD helped to become attached to the regular structure that school provided in their lives in spite of their disabilities. They talk about kids who, upon completing high school, have gotten good jobs that match their skills and enable them to live self-sufficient, independent lives. They describe children who have experienced horrific kinds of devastation in their lives—seeing a parent beaten or killed, or becoming pregnant because of an abusive, incestuous relationship, to cite just two examples—and who have responded wonderfully to the structure and supports that IHAD brings into their lives.

Sponsors also acknowledge that there are some dreamers who are probably not changed dramatically by IHAD. At one end of the spectrum, this includes the kids who come from strong families and whose parents were always determined to see that they got through high school and onto a career track. On the other it includes those for whom not even a long-term, comprehensive intervention like IHAD could have helped them move purposefully onto a path toward "success," as conventionally defined. Sponsors talk about their failures as well as their successes—those kids whom no amount of outreach could hold, the kids they've lost.

RIPPLES AND EDDIES: NOTICING IMPACT

Because sponsors make long-term promises to their dreamers, they maintain active relationships with them over time, and many talk about seeing the young people they supported became parents who have much higher expectations for their own children than their families ever had for them. One sponsor recalls a young guy named Ernesto, "who now drives a truck for a florist."

> He never graduated from high school and he was one of
> our dreamers. But he's married, he has a kid, he's driving

a truck, he's taking care of the kid. I can remember taking him out with a group for a birthday dinner. He said, "Well, you know, my dad never made me go to school, so I'd roll over in the morning and go back to sleep." I asked him if he thought that was right or wrong, and he said, "It was wrong. I should have gone."

So I said, "So what are you going to do about it?" And he said, "Well, I'm going to make sure that my child goes to school."

This is an example of the collateral influence of engaged philanthropy. As one second generation sponsor told me, the program has a "big impact on siblings" in particular.

In families where kids went to college, where that had never happened before, the youngest kids draw strength from the older kids. It has impacted lots of families in positive ways.

Extending that observation, another sponsor says,

This program doesn't affect just one person. It affects their siblings and their parents. A dreamer will usually marry a college person. Dreamers' children will probably be college kids. Their children's children will probably go to college. So it's not just one shot for one person: you're not only affecting one person's life. It goes on and on, for generation after generation.

Not only is the broader family impact of engaged philanthropy impressive but so are its contextual implications. One of the first sponsors I met used the image of ripples in a pond to describe the many ways that IHAD affects a variety of people. Project coordinators who worked with him have rearranged their lives to pursue advanced degrees and become human service professionals. Principals at other schools in his district, hearing about what he was doing, began to ask him for suggestions about how to develop more individualized mentoring and tutoring programs at their schools. A local university was so impressed by the gains in academic performance among his dreamers that it established a scholarship fund for any high school graduate in the community. "You can't say enough about the impact of this on people," he told me.

One of Tessa Bloom's dreams has been to eventually gather enough sponsors to bring IHAD to every class in her school. While this has not yet been realized, she told me about the ways in which her project is already making a difference to that school as a whole.

> We have really told the children that we have high expectations of them. But the school has expectations too, and so do the teachers. My project coordinator is always interfacing with the teachers. He now has permission to walk into a classroom whenever he wants to.
>
> In fact, the school actually uses our PC for disciplining. If any one of our dreamers is in trouble, they know that they will probably have a harder time with our PC than with anybody else. . . . And if something comes up at the school, like a general need for some conflict resolution, he will be asked to talk about it to all the students, not just our dreamers. The school relies on him very heavily because he's a very sound, stable person and they see the strong relationship that he has with the kids. And he hasn't confined himself to only our dreamers. If he sees a kid doing something inappropriate, it doesn't matter who the kid is, he'll stop the kid and say, "Wait a minute, what are you doing?"

A lengthy magazine article on the partnership between the suburban church and one in the inner-city that we described earlier particularly emphasizes the way that engagement affected the lives of the mentors.

> Long-term mentoring is not a task for timid souls. Yet virtually every participant in the [suburban church's] program described it as one of the most rewarding experiences of their lives. "The Dreamers changed our lives," says one of the church leaders who spearheaded the original IHAD commitment. "It started off as a program—an effort to fix something that was broken. But looking back, it's about individuals—it's about Edward, Gary, Kermit, Sheina, Abeni, Jason, and all the children we got to know. And it's about the friends we made in our own church and at [the city church] because of the time we spent together doing things we cared deeply about."[37]

Among the many who became committed to long-term mentoring because of this partnership were the daughter and son-in-law of one of its leaders. After years of legal wrangling, the young couple finally became eligible to adopt two of the dreamers into their own family.

Engaged philanthropy sets off a swirl of currents all around. And seeing the broad impact of what they have done gives sponsors confirmation that they can make a difference. As Mark Thompson has seen,

> There are eddying effects. Three of our first dreamer group's parents have gone back to school. Then you have the volunteers themselves, who are really changed by working with the kids. Once we decided to start the second group with kindergartners, we got a broader group of volunteers to help us and some of these people have children the same age as the dreamers. They often bring along their whole families when they come once a week to read, tutor, mentor.
>
> The cultural enrichment on both sides has been great. As you know, some of the first IHAD sponsors, the "founding fathers" themselves, have started a charter school. Another example? After joining with one of our local projects, the major airline company in this town began a program on its own to give college students frequent flier miles in exchange for mentoring young people. This particular corporation also energized a lot of their own employees to be mentors. It's all a win-win situation. A local foundation whose director participated in the first IHAD programs here developed a similar kind of outreach program for dreamer siblings. In fact, the guy who headed that foundation went on to become superintendent of schools and is now using some of what he learned to shape his policy for the whole school district.
>
> Other things keep happening too. When our mentors take the kids to ball games and to concerts at our symphony's summer home, more people get excited about what we're doing. We've rehabbed a temporary space and our state senator is helping us get a Twenty-first-century Community Learning Center grant. This will let us expand the

space. Now two child-serving agencies in the neighborhood are very interested in collaborating with us. If we can raise the additional funds this initiative will become a lasting contribution to the community. It will house future IHAD programs and also become the central community-based organization in this town, which really doesn't have a community center of any kind.

The Hulls' project too has had extraordinary collateral influence. As their original dreamers finished up, the family foundation was growing, but the Hulls knew they wanted to keep "doing something in a personalized and comprehensive way with people." They chose a single neighborhood on which to focus—one that was characterized in a local paper as "America's millstone. It has some of the worst statistics you can imagine in terms of poverty, unemployment, single mothers, et cetera." With a 75 percent school dropout rate, the community was described as a "war zone, fought over by gangs and ruled by drug lords." Here the Hulls and several other families founded a charter school that is heavily influenced by lessons the Hulls learned as IHAD sponsors. For example, all the young people have student advocates who stay with them all the way through school, just the way each dreamer has a significant relationship with a supportive adult for years. And within the neighborhood the Hulls have established a school-to-school network that allows all the schools to share resources and tap into new supports that the local initiative makes available. They have developed an employment and training program that offers job placement and counseling to residents, and they have started an IDA (individual development account) program that rewards kids for building financial assets for their futures.

In addition, the family foundation's small grant program builds lots of good will in the community by making a modest amount of money available for small neighborhood projects—clean-ups, community gardens, newsletters. Because of the Hull's connections with public agencies, they've helped the neighborhood get grants that have brought in new childcare slots and early learning-disability screening for young children. New businesses have started to move in and neighborhood banks are concentrating more of their annual giving on local initiatives. Large foundations and corporations are contributing in new ways and there are now vibrant partnerships between the neighborhood and the city's symphony orchestra, botanical gardens, and art museums. Finally, a new master teacher program at the high school, directed by a local university, pairs new and experienced teachers in order to strengthen teacher training and retention. "The people in the community are in charge now," Sara Hull says. Her father Sam adds,

> We have been able to extend our influence well beyond what our immediate efforts have been to get more people exposed to what the issues are and understanding how they can get involved.

Over the years, many dreamers have gone on to complete vocational training programs, or to public and private colleges and prestigious graduate schools. Some are now professional athletes, teachers, accountants, lawyers, personnel officers in large corporations, social workers. Like a proud parent, Pamela Marconi talks about some ways that she's seen the impact of her project endure.

> My kids are mostly turning twenty-six years old this summer. I had dinner with four of my girls who graduated from college about a month ago. It was so rewarding. They have jobs, they have apartments, they're paying rent, they're paying off a car and car insurance, they're twenty-five years old and they have never been pregnant. These are girls whose mothers were fifteen or sixteen when they were born. So already the cycle stops! It's broken!
>
> I don't know how you put a value on that, but that's incredible to me. The interesting thing, too, is that they're doing jobs where they're giving back. One girl is a counselor for teenage runaways. She's terrific. This is a young girl whose mother was a druggie. Her father, thank goodness, was stable. She went off to school, graduated, and now works in town for an agency, which is a home for teenage runaways. We talked about how I was so proud of her and she said to me, "You know, Miss [Marconi], my dad keeps telling me I could be making more money because I have a college degree." "But," she said, "Somebody reached out to me and I want to reach back." She called me last week to tell me she

just got engaged; they're waiting a year until they get their finances organized! This kid has made a remarkable change in her life! It's incredible.

From the other side of the equation, one young woman wrote about how both kids and their sponsors change over time, insightfully applying the word "dreamer" to both.

The dreamer that has learned and grown the most is Mr. King. I have had a chance to get to know this man on a level that many individuals do not get a chance to. To me at first he was just a rich guy from the next town who wanted to do something good for kids. In sixth grade I did not understand why. But I think that his objective changed as he realized he was changing lives; he was giving kids an opportunity that was unfamiliar to their ears. He realized how unfortunate some of us were and how much we had been missing out on. He introduced summer camps, art, drama, so that we learn and have fun. He has spent an amazing amount of money on special schools for those that need that extra help.... He spent money on some of our personal problems.

His reward is knowing that his dreamers are doing well and that's what we have become, his dreamers. A group of kids that will never be forgotten. How can he grow away from the memories and differences he has witnessed? This man did not have any reason for investing time, money, and concern. We are not from the same town, we are not in the same social and monetary status, we are not even of the same race. But he did. He invested all he could to provide for our success.

And the biggest success he has had is not seeing those kids who he knew from the beginning would make it. It was seeing those who had the least chance come out of the "gutter" and succeed. Once a Dreamer, always a Dreamer, that is how much the program has affected me. I have made the program a part of my life and it has not been for the financial ideal of the program, but more for what became of the objective. The relationships I have made, the people I have met, and the experiences I have been through will always be in my memory.

As that testimony confirms, in many instances the influence of a project on a dreamer plays itself out over time. Several of the young people who came through Laura and Richard Joseph's program are now themselves working with inner-city children. "Having people that believe in me," says one, was crucial to the choices she made later. Laura thinks it's the continuity of the program and the steadfastness of staff and sponsors that makes the biggest difference to young people.

Actually, they called us "I Have A Nightmare." When we asked them why, they said it was because we never went away: we were always in their faces. It's the constancy that matters.

Maybe no single factor alone explains what means the most to all the youngsters about their dreamer status. Children respond differently, depending on their histories, their capacities, and their needs. At IHAD's twentieth anniversary celebration, in 2001, two dreamers read essays submitted for the event. An eleven-year-old spoke about how the IHAD program has given her confidence that she can, in fact, achieve her dream to become a lawyer because she is learning that the key to her success is in her own hands. And a sixteen-year-old who spoke about her dream to go to college and become an undercover agent for the FBI also talked about taking responsibility for one's own life. She acknowledged the struggles she'd had and the mistakes she'd made, but, she said, her IHAD friends

gave me the support I needed to be strong, reminded me of the good things that I've done, and showed me that the one bad choice I made is not so bad after all.

Each day I remind myself of what my goals are and remember what makes me want to achieve those goals so much. I remember all that I have accomplished and think about how I can work towards achieving my dreams. Being proactive when times get rough gets me closer every day to achieving my dream. . . . I believe the only way I will achieve my dreams is to surround myself with a positive and healthy lifestyle and always remember to be strong no matter what comes up in life. Throughout my whole life the "I Have a Dream" program has been there to reinforce that belief.

THE QUESTION OF PROJECT EVALUATION

This book intentionally focuses on sponsor experiences. Thus the evidence submitted so far about IHAD's effectiveness comes almost exclusively from sponsor descriptions. And data about the impact of the program on the youngsters come mostly from sponsors too. But the issue of more complete and objective evaluation becomes important to sponsors as they begin to understand the range of challenges in kids' lives and want to know what kind of difference they are really making. Subjectively they have no doubt about the positive impact of their projects on the lives of the dreamers and their families. In fact, the more certain they are, the more they wish they could quantify the process in some way, so that it would be easier to persuade the world about the value of this kind of engaged philanthropy. And because as a group sponsors are always concerned about the impact of their investments, many begin to wonder how they can more accurately measure the results of what they're doing.

Project evaluation is a thorny matter in many ways. First of all, sponsors never approach the schools or housing developments that they choose as researchers. In fact, they work hard to cultivate very different kinds of bonds—relationships with their local schools, community-based organizations, and housing authorities that are collaborative, reciprocal, and personally engaged. Moreover, they pointedly do not want to be seen as outside experts who are trying to demonstrate that they can out-perform the local authorities simply because they have more money to invest. Their focus is on building real bridges, not creating artificial laboratory situations.

One might assume that to demonstrate the value of the IHAD approach it would be fairly easy to obtain quantitative information about dreamers as a group, and about control groups from the relevant school districts and housing authorities—easy enough, one would think, to compare the development of a group of dreamers with another demographically comparable, non-IHAD group of children from the same school or the same housing development. But several sponsors report that it's been difficult to gain access to data about achievement, attendance, grade retention, and promotion rates for non-dreamers. Issues of privacy, politics, and protecting institutional reputations arise. Schools, some of which are chosen by sponsors particularly because of their documented failures to educate children well, are not eager to share dropout and discipline data. Another complication occurs when IHAD sponsors adopt a cohort of children in a housing development, since these dreamers' ages may range from elementary to high school, and, as one such sponsor says, "The kids are going through different things at the same time."

While they acknowledge these difficulties, several IHAD sponsors and groups are trying to develop guidelines for evaluating their projects. When Mark Thompson began overseeing the development of a second IHAD project in his community, his board felt the need to define clear goals and outcome measures for this initiative. More careful documentation, they hope, will not only allow them to assess their project's impact and refine their approach, it will also provide evidence for others about what works best. The group aims to track changes among dreamers and their families in relation to certain specific benchmarks:

1) Dreamer Progress
   a) Attain individualized behavioral goals during Dreamer activities.
   b) Regular attendance at Dreamer activities.
   c) Improved school performance as measured by report cards and verbal teacher reports.
   d) Improved behavior at home, as reported by parents.

2) Parent Participation
   a) Participation in consultations with P.C. in person and/or by phone.
   b) Service contributions to IHAD.
   c) Active participation in Dreamer progress through learning support at home.
   d) Steps taken to further education, job skills improvement.

A constructive template for Mark's group, this should promote valuable record-keeping and ongoing evaluation. But their other goal—to be able to compare how Mark's second dreamers do with the progress of children in other IHAD programs—won't be achieved unless other sponsors agree to adopt the same indices.

At the same time, among—and within—IHAD sponsors there's some tension between the desire to find ways to measure the results of a project and the need for such measures to be flexible and subject to change. As noted earlier, the goals of individual sponsors may shift over time as their appreciation of the many variables that affect young people's development and growth increases. And, as they become more attached and involved with the kids, they find themselves less and less interested, personally, in simple "counting" as a way to measure impact. They become more and more convinced that easy record-keeping—tracking school grades and attendance, for example—doesn't begin to capture the kinds of transformations they see or the nuances of personal engagement that they experience directly. Lang himself, who began with the specific goal of college for his children, explains.

> My biggest achievement was not the kids I sent to college but the few dropouts whose lives I helped develop so that they have not become welfare cases but good citizens. If we were to make a profit/loss statement, I'd see profit in the number of boys who will marry the pregnant teenage mothers of their children, get jobs, maintain support for their families, vote, and appreciate education. Several kids have actually said to me, "I dropped out but my kids won't!" And nothing could make me feel any better! I can quote percentages of kids who finish high school, for example. But it's easy to do that. The value of what we're doing is not reflected by setting up a good statistical design. To me the value is each child: each child represents 100 percent of a problem.

> Dreamers are not statistics. And success is a relational thing. The question is: in relation to what do you want to measure success? In relation to what they have come from? Or in relation to the limits of glory these children may grow up to? Which way do you measure it? From the ground level up? Where is the bottom? Where is up?

You can measure certain differences that are associated with "socially significant" shifts. But, in terms of our catalogue of anecdotes, the dreamer who graduated from a prestigious law school and is now an attorney with a major accounting firm, while a great success, may be less significant in terms of cost and benefit to society as a whole than the kid who dropped out [of school], maintained contact with the program, and, as a result of the program, got a job which enabled him to give up the only other work he could get: being a courier for a drug dealer. He kept the job we got for him and married the teenage mother he created a child with because of the relationship we created for him over time. Now, fifteen years later, he still has the job we got for him, along with three children from the same teenage mother. He's not on welfare. He admits he missed an opportunity when he dropped out. But he says, "My children will go to college!" And this is a boy who never had a parent who said, "My son will go to college." When you consider all the ramifications of his experience, it all adds up to a very important total.

So, when you're thinking about success, there is no standard formula for judging. The value of what we do is the value we have for each child. Each child benefits, more or less, but you never really know how much "more" is. Moreness is not visible. And it makes no difference to us. We are not measuring one against the other. It's each dreamer.

Everything Lang says is true. Nonetheless, many sponsors continue to feel that there are important reasons to keep thinking about formal means of evaluation. They want to disseminate the model, and know that efforts to do so will be more persuasive if they're backed up with hard data. Others just want a way to take stock themselves, to try to "understand what it has taken to make them 'really glad' that they've gotten involved in this thing." Most sponsors collect data: grade point averages, test scores, records of contacts, up-to-date addresses, grade promotions, for example. They use this information over the years to refine and sharpen their approaches to advising, tutoring, and mentoring. Keeping good records, even of simple statistics, is a beginning.

For instance, everyone involved knows that something real has been achieved when more than 80 percent of the dreamers graduate from high school and most go on to post-secondary studies. This is the case for dreamers in the Yale IHAD project, funded by over a hundred alumni of the class of 1956 and scores of local donors. An article in the 2003 alumni association newsletter reports,

> The results are becoming clear and dramatic. [The project coordinator] reports that 46 of the original 56 Dreamers are on pace to graduate on time and 100% of these have prepared applications for college, technical school, or have chosen a military career. He expects another 10% of the Dreamers to complete high school in 2004 (making 91% of the original 56). This figure contrasts with a graduation rate of less than 40% in [the district], the seventh poorest community in the U.S.[38]

At Stanford, where IHAD sponsors have now begun their third project, the figures are also promising. In the fall before their high school graduation, 94 percent of the second group of dreamers were on track to graduate, with all slated to go to college. A third program has begun there, this time with first graders.

To help formally assess their project, one couple hired an evaluator, who reported the following comparison.

> Eighty-five percent of the students graduated from high school and 60% went on to college. In the previous year for which information [was] available, only 40% of the students from [the same high school] had graduated, . . . and only 4 had gone on to college.

By these measures, these particular projects were successful. But some sponsors want more rigorous assessments and are wary of leaping to conclusions.

Walter and Barbara King, for instance, wrestled continually with the issues of ongoing evaluation and the "measurement of success" in the real-life world of their project. Walter kept careful records all the way along—despite the familiar problem that as children travel from one school to another (as many of theirs did), their records sometimes get lost—but, to his frustration, he was unable to get comparative data about graduation rates and teenage pregnancy from the district. Moreover, he felt that comparisons with district averages might be misleading because of markedly different family, cultural, and linguistic variables, and he was unable to find out if the high percentage of "special needs" children in his group was representative of their peers as a whole in the district. At the same time, he was struck by the diversity of cognitive skills among his dreamers and acutely aware of the fact that a high school diploma represents a different kind of achievement for different kids. (He and Barbara placed a number of their young people in private secondary schools, and this further complicated the picture with regard to this variable.) In a piece he wrote for a local newspaper, describing their project and its outcomes, he was very reluctant to take credit for the fact that only five of their young women had become teenage mothers within a year after they graduated from high school—another index of "success" sometimes cited by IHAD sponsors. Rather, he felt,

> This is more likely to be a statistical anomaly. If we were to take credit for this relatively low figure, the largest share of such credit should probably be placed on the fact that many of our DREAMERS felt that they had a future, and that parenting would preempt their progress toward that future. Other supplementary thoughts to discourage teenage parenting seemed to "fall on deaf ears." We did not feel that a child who has little self-esteem and no real belief in their future is influenced by any program which attempts to reduce teenage parenting.
>
> At best, statistics do not provide a full evaluation of a project and can only point to what might be further reflected upon, and not used as the end judgment. The measure of success which may be more reflective is to appreciate the accomplishments of individual DREAMERS.

Many sponsors, including Lang, agree with Walter that the most important things dreamers get from IHAD are very difficult to measure. Good evaluations are as useful as the questions they are designed to answer. Thus if sponsors' goals are, as some say, "to do whatever is in the best interest of our kids, as if they were my own," or to invest in a relationship that is "like when you have children, it's never over," it is complicated to agree on a research design. Lives change.

As projects evolve, sponsors talk to each other and compare notes about their IHAD experiences and their attempts to assess them. Some, like George Norman, argue,

> The real evaluation that we gauge the success of the program on is really two pieces: A) do they graduate? and B) are they able either to go into post-secondary education or a career that's not an entry-level paying job? College is not for every kid, but every kid should have a good career. And you can have a great career with some post-secondary education, not necessarily a four-year degree. That's kind of how we measure it.

> Two or three years ago I was concerned about getting to an 80 to 90 percent graduation rate; I think we're already there. Hopefully we'll close out with an 80 to 85 percent graduation rate. That's the best evaluation on the surface that I can think of without doing a full study.

Indeed, we've seen that IHAD high school graduation rates are impressive, particularly when compared to overall district rates. But, like Lang himself, other sponsors point to the less easily captured details, things that, to many of them, are more important than school grades. As Mike O'Donnell says, it's a triumph when nobody is shot by the time they reach high school, "a miracle" that they are all still alive. And Tessa Bloom insists that just having "no run-ins with the cops by eighth grade" is significant.

> When you talk about people wanting a return on their investment, the saddest part of all this is that we shouldn't just be asking what the kids' school grades are. It should be all those other things we talk about: no dropouts, no crimes, no pregnancies. Those are the statistics that matter.

> Yes, it's important that 99 percent of these kids probably go through high school. But it's important what they are when they leave, what they think of themselves, what they've become. And if all you're doing is counting grades and

dropouts, the numbers don't tell you anything. There are kids who drop out and come back. Some kids drop out and don't end up in jail but go on to do something else. I agree with Gene: one can only measure a kid against himself.

Defining success is one issue, but there are others. Sponsors often find themselves wondering which of all the things they are doing is making the biggest difference for their kids. This, one might say, is an evaluation question that might be answered if posed when a project begins. But heartfelt involvement with one child after another, all of whom are different, makes it hard to frame the question, let alone pinpoint an answer, as illustrated by this memory of Mike's.

> It's all subjective. With Larry, for example, we took him out to dinner after he graduated *summa cum laude* from [a private university] three weeks ago. He was a street kid, a ward of the state. They had removed [him from] his mother and he went from one institution to another. He left town for a few years and then he came back. But once a dreamer, always a dreamer, you know?
>
> At dinner, we said to him, "Larry, a lot of people are going to want to take credit for you, you know? But basically it was you! It was you who achieved, you who succeeded."
>
> And he said, "Well, you just don't know. Remember the time you drove me to the airport so I could go to [the university] for that interview? You just arrived at my house and made sure I got out of bed. Do you remember that?" And then he cited other things that I had forgotten completely. So you just don't know. It could be just giving somebody a ride, something that seems so marginal when you think about making a difference. You just don't know.

Finally, what time frame are sponsors talking about when they try to evaluate a project? There's good reason to believe that evidence of IHAD's impact will keep rolling in for years and years after a kid's formal completion of the program. Hal Davies kept annual notes about each dreamer after they graduated, which enabled him to share news with mentors and tutors, and to keep his eye on overall group patterns over time. He'd begun with forty-seven children in the sixth grade, forty of whom were considered to be core participants (six disappeared and one died). Fourteen years after the program began, when the kids were in their mid-twenties, Hal could report that thirty-eight (95 percent) of that core group were "on a productive track (fifteen succeeded in college and twenty-three others have full-time productive employment)." But among his dreamers he often asks himself which child is more "successful" – the one who now plays for a professional sports team or the very limited young woman who is faithfully holding down a job at a convenience store and maintaining her own apartment and solid relationships with friends.

Long after a project officially ends, sponsors keep getting news about their dreamers. One told me,

> One of my dreamers got her master's degree this spring. She has just started work as a project coordinator in a new IHAD program. She's thrilled and I couldn't be more proud of her. Interestingly, kids continue to graduate from four-year colleges, and these are kids who started graduating from high school ten years ago! Another is working on her master's in finance while she holds a job at a big hospital in a financial/administrative capacity and she's thinking about going to medical school. Another one of the girls, who was completely blindsided by the death of her young daughter from asthma four hears ago, has gotten herself back on track and is in nursing school.
>
> It's so wonderful to see the program work even though everything seems to take much longer than we anticipated. There's so much to make up for. Some kids are still struggling to get their GEDs, but the fact that they are still trying seems to me to indicate that the program did have a powerful impact on them, even if they may not be in the best column statistically.

Mara Emerson, who would agree, wrote recently,

> My Dreamers—twenty-six of them—are in college this year, and six are in the military. A few are still to graduate high school and many are working. All are still dreaming!

No matter how this "brand" of engaged philanthropy is evaluated, what seems to happen is that as IHAD sponsors begin to understand all the things their dreamers are coping with, they just dig their heels in and insist on staying the course to make a difference. Perhaps, as Walter King suggests, it's not the most accomplished kids who are most influenced by IHAD—they may have made it anyway. And it's not the most troubled ones either, he says, because most of these were beyond reach of his program. Most likely, as he concludes, it's the many in the middle who benefit most from IHAD: the kids who might slide down or slip away, unnoticed, without the structure and attention of the program. After keeping very careful records about all his dreamers, Walter concluded, in the newspaper piece he wrote, that numbers don't matter:

> The accomplishments of our DREAMERS cannot be measured by where they started out in life, nor by where they are at present, but by the distance they have traveled in between. Most of our DREAMERS have come a very long way, and the most important outcome may well appear much later in their lives, as they have an opportunity to influence their children, and others around them.

Sponsors know that the makers of public policy rely on numbers, telescoped findings that can't possibly capture the complexity of an IHAD intervention. But some numbers, Lang believes, should be very persuasive. Though it now costs about $450,000 to sponsor a project of fifty to eighty dreamers for at least ten years, he argues that this amount is much less than it costs to keep one teenager in jail for the same amount of time, noting that 82 percent of all the people now in prison are school dropouts.

Even as they offer public officials encouraging numbers and hard evidence that their projects are helping disadvantaged kids become self-reliant adults who can contribute to society rather than become a burden on it in one way or another, sponsors express concern, even outrage, that not enough is being done on a large scale to solve the huge problems caused by poverty and inequality. Sure, one sponsor told me, his project "has produced seventy-five kids who will become productive and have a better quality of life. But that's not the answer to the big picture!"

In spite of their frustration, however, after years of devoted efforts with children they come to love, the determination of most sponsors to make a difference just grows more intense. As Pamela Marconi says, "Having the experience of IHAD sponsoring makes you more optimistic about the future, but you just wish you could do it in greater numbers."

CHAPTER 6

LESSONS LEARNED

I honestly think that I learned more from the kids than they learned from me. That's the real world there and we don't live in the real world. We thought we did but it just kind of takes over when you realize how bad it really is.

—Ann Hull

"The first twenty years of IHAD have been a collective learning experience," says Eugene Lang.

Early on we realized that to most dreamers the promise of a college opportunity six or more years down the road was readily neutralized by current environmental influences. It was up to us to make education and the college promise continuously meaningful and to recognize that college may not be for everybody. Turning off to college does not make any dreamer less worthy of our concern. We learned that effective mentoring and other support efforts require regular, individual, and sustained attention. We learned the importance of parent involvement, and the difficulties of achieving it.

We learned, and not always very well, to communicate with our dreamers. We also learned how precarious it is to presume agreement. We learned to value the differences between us and to work to understand how dreamers' perceptions sometimes differed from our own.

In this statement, Lang summarizes the collective experience of the program's many sponsors over the last twenty-five years. They learned—not always easily—that their original hopes of higher education for all their dreamers were sometimes unrealistic: we've heard them explain how they revised their models and goals. They learned about the problems and pressures low-income families face, and about the ways these problems are interrelated. And they learned about the far-reaching consequences of poverty and inequality in our society—both for the dreamers and for themselves.

But engaged philanthropists are risk-takers, they're committed, and they're inventive. They are also life-long learners who, as one IHAD sponsor put it, "don't think you can come to a solution until you understand what the problems are." And as they developed meaningful relationships—with dreamers and their families, with their PCs, and with others who work with the kids in their schools, community-based organizations, and housing developments—they began to draw on their problem-solving natures to craft solutions that would help the kids overcome the disadvantages they were struggling with. Relationship building and problem-solving were tightly woven together as sponsors began to understand and confront the challenges they and their dreamers faced.

This chapter focuses on several themes that run through sponsors' comments on what they learned about "real life" in poor inner-city neighborhoods—and how they have responded.

THE CRISIS OF PUBLIC EDUCATION IN THE INNER CITY

First of all, most sponsors were stunned by what many, including Richard Joseph, came to think of as a "dysfunctional, broken school system that needs major systemic change" and by "the low regard in which educators hold children like our dreamers." Several sponsors told me that when they visited each other's sites in different cities, they were amazed to find that conditions for poor children everywhere seemed to be the same or even worse than in their own under-resourced communities. Though a few had worked in public schools or community agencies before getting involved with IHAD, most sponsors—particularly first generation ones—had no idea, as one put it, how damaged educationally the kids were, how they could be so buried and forgotten by the system. We had so many illusions about working with the public schools and about the resources that would be needed.

Most sponsors—not all—had had positive experiences with schools when they were young. So they began with "illusions," and perhaps without such illusions they might not have begun. But once they were in—once they found themselves facing obstacles that threatened their strategic plans and promises—their characterological tendency was to "roll up their sleeves." As Will Christopher told me, "We're just not going to accept that."

Many sponsors, especially the first generation ones, found they had underestimated the extent of their dreamers' academic deficits. Within a year or two they began to amend their original projects, increasing the range of services and supports for their dreamers. Sometimes, as noted previously, they moved certain children out of the public schools or worked to get children transferred to stronger middle and high schools, even though, as Sam Hull said,

> This makes it a lot harder for us to keep track of the kids because you have to go from one school to another and another, and try to keep our kids in the same homerooms, wherever they are, so we can still meet with them regularly.

Simply keeping track of students was a problem most sponsors were unprepared for. After all, none of these people are educational researchers. They had not studied under-resourced schools, they didn't know about high rates of absenteeism and student mobility, and many were dismayed to discover, for example, how frequently teachers and administrators do not know the whereabouts of children missing from classes, especially once youngsters reach high school.

How do sponsors interpret this simple problem and other, more complex ones they encounter? Remember, most are people whose take-charge attitudes have been shaped in the business world and who have low tolerance for inefficiency and neglect. Many IHAD sponsors, even those who had been strong supporters of organized labor unions in other settings, began questioning their past allegiances. Will Christopher told me,

Before getting into advocacy issues, I had no idea how strong the teachers' union was. I find it despicable that it carries the strength that it does nationally, in impeding the progress of the public school system. The whole bureaucracy stinks! And I don't think it's any different in any of the big cities, from Boston to Los Angeles.

In a way, it's not surprising that a group of people from the management side of business come to fault the unions, as some sponsors do. In trying to understand what's gone wrong in their dreamers' low-performing schools, they draw on their experience with competition in the private sector. As one argued,

> One crisis we have in America is education. Our inner-city kids are not getting an education. Everybody knows this. And I don't think this will change. In twenty or thirty years, I believe, it's all going to be privatized. I don't think the public, the government, can educate kids. If I had to look ahead fifty years, I don't think you're going to see government in the education business. Because I don't think it's capable of doing it, because of the unions.

> In this city, basically we allow teachers to choose what school they want to teach in. So we inevitably end up with a system that can't possibly work. After one or two years, any good teacher leaves. So what happens? The school that needs the best teachers has the worst ones. And the school that doesn't need the very best teachers, the one with the best students, also has the best teachers. You know, in business, if someone owns ten McDonalds and one of them is doing badly, he puts his best manager there, not his worst manager. So that's inherently a problem. How can it work?

> Another thing about the system: new teachers make, say, $25,000 and old teachers make $75,000. When the state has no money, which is most of the time, it comes along and says, "Well, let's get as many of the $75,000 teachers as possible to retire because we can hire three new ones for every one that leaves." They go to the teachers and say, "How about this? We'll give you two extra years on your pension.

Why don't you retire?" So they "incentivize" the best, the most experienced teachers to retire.

It's frustrating! I don't know how you can make the system work. And the reality is that rich people don't send their kids to public schools. They don't really care. I just don't see how this is going to change in an environment that the union controls. I'm not an anti-union person. But this is one industry that should not be unionized. The teachers' union has to go. My prediction is you will see the privatizing of education as time goes by. I think it's inevitable. It's a rough situation in the inner cities especially, because in order to be a useful citizen more than ever now you need an education. You gotta know how to work a computer. Factory jobs don't exist. And the jobs that exist require an education.

This man's frustration is clear. Like many other sponsors, he's seen what his dreamers need to prepare for full and productive lives and he's come to understand how far from ready they will be if all they have to draw on is an inadequate public school in a poor district. Sam Hull complains fiercely, "It's as if education is only a middle-class value!"—as if low-income children weren't just as entitled to good schools as everyone else.

The Hulls, like several other IHAD sponsors, have built upon what they learned by becoming actively involved with charter schools.[39] While acknowledging that charter schools may not be the only answer to current difficulties, many see them as "a first line of a competitive structure that can help change the massive elephant that's sitting there: the public education system." Again, it's not surprising that entrepreneurial sponsors see competition as the most efficient way to reform schools.

On the other side of the debate, there are strong criticisms of charter schools. Some argue that charter schools draw public money away from already impoverished school systems, just as they are likely to pull away the most motivated children and families, the ones who are most likely to thrive in and strengthen public schools. This position strikes Richard Joseph as outrageous. Readers will recall from Chapter 2 that because of the bureaucratic roadblocks they had to navigate to provide a good-enough education for their dreamers, he and his wife, Laura, later established two charter schools in the community where they adopted their cohort of dreamers. Asked about the opinion that charters represent a threat to the prospects for improving the public school system, Richard is blunt.

> Excuse me, but I think that's bullshit. First of all, we take all our kids [in our charter school] by lottery. And we have a dozen kids applying for every seat. I mean, people break into hysterical glee when they get in, or mournful sobbing when they don't. And they look at going back to that public school as if they are going to prison. Are you arguing that they should be in prison because there are more committed families there?

> These families have no opportunity to improve the schools! They're just trying to get for their kids what all of us tried to get for our kids: a decent education!

In fact, the convictions of sponsors like Richard seem to be driven by their successes in the competitive world of business. As another sponsor who shares Richard's point of view explains,

> The essential, systemic reform of public education can only come from competition. If you want to save kids, take them out of the schools that don't teach them and put them into schools that do. There are millions and millions and millions of kids who are being destroyed by dysfunctional inner-city programs. I consider it to be a moral outrage that in a free and rich country like ours, we allow this to happen. It's our country and we're responsible for it!

> People in the inner-city public school system are like all other people: they're good, normal people. But if the people who run inner-city schools have a monopoly, they're going to run it like monopolies always have been run. Everywhere and forever. You get a shoddy product at a high price. When you introduce competition into that world, the people who are incompetent leave, or are forced to leave, because they go out of business.

The assumptions that inform this argument clearly reflect a belief in the superiority of an individualized, private enterprise system. There's no expressed faith here in the notion that it is the responsibility of government to create a public system that supports the education of all children. At the most, if pressed, sponsors who espouse this view would probably say that the private way can become a model for public endeavors.

But not all IHAD sponsors have given up on the public schools. They do not all accept arguments that favor solving public challenges by moving to privatized models like charter schools or voucher programs. Many, like Gene Lang himself, espouse an enduring commitment to the public system. Passionate about finding new ways to resolve the perverse problems in the schools where most kids actually are, they want to strengthen the existing system. And they see that when they are able to provide extra support, and work with teachers and administrators within existing public schools, the high school graduation rates for their dreamers far surpass system averages.

PROBLEMS ARE ALL ENTWINED

As we've heard, many IHAD sponsors grew up facing scarcity and adversity themselves, but most are astounded to discover "how much trouble there is in the world today," as Lou Irving says. Another sponsor, humbled by what he feels is the hopelessness of many children's situations, told me,

> People don't understand what these kids face. Nobody cares. The most successful people these kids see are drug dealers. The kids don't have any idea what's available to them if they do get an education. I think the thing that surprised me, and everybody else in our church, was grasping what these kids faced. What a hopeless situation most of them were in, with a terrible school system, no role models, and, in most cases, almost nobody who cares. And even if they do care, they don't really have any ambition for the kids. I had not understood the depth of that.

Poverty has a fracturing influence on young people—and it can be difficult to pick up all the pieces. In most cases, the specific structures and activities of the IHAD projects evolved as sponsors and staff began to understand how many obstacles their kids were struggling against and how entwined they all could be.

Like many others, Pamela Marconi began her project with tidy contracts that asked children and their families to do their part to insure the program's success. While she always emphasized the primary importance of education, it didn't take her long to discover that her kids' needs were not confined to schools and that many "extracurricular" problems were interfering with their academic success.

> Parents were responsible for providing a clean, well-lighted place for their children to do homework. Six months later, I started doing home visits and realized there's no such thing when five, six, or seven people are living in two rooms and the only light is an overhead light in the kitchen. That was my first awakening to the fact that we were dealing with more than an education program.

> I started out thinking this program would be a nice enhancement program. We'd go to museums, do some career stuff, and have pizza! Well, you know, as it turns out, we're going to the dentist, to the court, to the maternity ward. You find yourself doing all kinds of family stuff, and you may sometimes even become the surrogate parent. But you realize that, for instance, these kids never sit around a table where a parent or elder is saying that taxes are going up again, or complaining about how the government is spending tax money. They never have that opportunity. To them it's all a kind of nebulous system that has buckets of money and they're entitled. It's a real problem.

> You learn from getting to know other sponsors that you are not alone in experiencing this. That was the good news. But that was also the bad news. You come to understand that the same problems that plague urban kids here are happening across the country, everywhere, whether it's pregnancy, violence, or the lack of role models. Whatever it is, it's the same across the country.

The sponsors I interviewed talked about getting crash courses in all kinds of things that many didn't know about—drug and alcohol prevention programs, learning disabilities, residential treatment programs, teenage pregnancy, abuse and neglect, the juvenile justice system, family courts, domestic violence. Many described how their expectations that they would be running an educational project were turned upside down. Richard and Laura Joseph found themselves setting up "a mini social service organization. It took a great deal more than we had imagined to keep our kids on track and going in a positive direction." As his understanding of the interrelatedness of children's problems grew, another sponsor talked about his new respect for "the concept of the whole child."

> You could see that tutoring alone wasn't going to help. The PC got increasingly pulled into the family dynamics. We had to come up with a way to think about that and provide supports without getting ourselves sucked into situations that we just couldn't get out of. We did a mission exercise halfway through our first program, which has really helped us. Now basically our mission is to have every child graduate from high school ready, willing, and able to succeed. Under that we have three priorities in descending order: academic excellence, respect for self and others, and career- or horizon-broadening.

Revising original goals and objectives, as this man did, is one response to the multiplicity of challenges in kids' lives. Engaged philanthropists are fixers. Once they see how much is needed, they tend to revisit early assumptions that put them on a certain course and change the particulars of their models.

As they began to understand that the challenges facing poor kids were larger and more complicated than they had expected, many of the sponsors I spoke with also realized that they couldn't solve all these problems by themselves. Many ended up expanding their initiatives, bringing in providers with a variety of skills to design interventions that are effective for kids with multiple needs. One who did so told me,

> What my IHAD experience taught me was that you can have the greatest intentions in the world but your impact

will be zero unless you develop the right skill set and goals, and unless you learn the importance of teaching, mentoring, and guiding well.

For the first group of founding IHAD members, none of us had any training, any background in social work. None of us knew how to deal with teenage pregnancy, drug addiction, truancy, broken homes, a whole variety of things. That early study of the program[40] confirmed something I'd been saying anecdotally about my own class. As a consequence, we made a big shift in our program to become very goal-oriented, to quit being kids' friends and, instead, to be kids' teachers, to set a variety of educational goals, and again, as a mentor and a manager, to see that the kids acquire the skill sets to help them better themselves academically, educationally, and socially.

Just writing a check and saying, "I'm a sponsor," or promising the kids that if they graduate from high school you'll put them through college has about as much impact as spitting on a griddle. It has to be combined with an intensive, holistic approach towards helping those kids shape their lives in a fashion that will allow them to achieve academically at their highest potential. And this is obviously different for each kid. So this means packaging together a whole set of social, psychological, and educational instructions adapted for each kid. It's a huge undertaking.

One result of their personal involvement for many sponsors was a new appreciation of the specific skills and expertise of professional educators and human service providers who work successfully with low-income children.

A more complex understanding of the context of a child's life was another. As they got to know their dreamers better they found themselves thinking about things like "Who's with them when they wake up in the morning and go to sleep at night?" "How do they get to and from school every day?" "What kinds of streets are they walking down?" "What are they eating for breakfast and what emergency room do they go to?" "Who else is in their immediate family?" "Is there a state social worker who visits them regularly?" "What do they do on weekends and during school vacations?" Where do their grandparents live?"

The Hull family offered vivid examples of situations that helped them come to see the realities of their dreamers' lives in new ways. These vignettes also shed light on why IHAD experiences drive some sponsors to become seriously interested in alternative schools and/or more extensive involvement in community efforts.

> One of the kids in the class was Eddie . . . [who] wasn't doing very well. He was getting lousy grades and I don't remember just how we came around to getting his eyesight tested, but it turned out that he couldn't see! This is sad, of course. It turned out, though, that he'd had glasses and they broke, years before. We figured we would get him glasses. And the problem would be defined and solved!

> But no, that wasn't the problem. His mother didn't want him to get glasses, because if he went to school then he wouldn't be available to stay home with his younger siblings and therefore she would have to take care of them. But she'd rather go down to the corner saloon and drink with her buddies. This is the kind of thing that makes you begin to understand that these problems are far more complicated than you thought. You sit there and say, "Gee, there's a health problem," or "That's a housing problem," or "It's learning disabilities." That's a lot of crap. It's a whole series of issues, intertwined, that make everything so impossibly difficult.

> Here's another example. A gal wasn't going to graduate because she wouldn't take gym. She wasn't going to graduate from high school. You wonder why, thinking, "Gym is the easiest thing in the world." Well, one of our mentors was taking her out regularly. They were getting along well, and finally the girl admitted that her mother's boyfriend was beating her and her legs were horribly abused. In gym you're required to get undressed and showered. But this would reflect badly on her. So her mentor, who'd become like a big sister, got her a pair of skin-colored tights, explaining what was happening to the PE teacher and asking her to

accept the child in tights. Your first reaction was to think this kid was really being obstinate, that she just didn't want to go to gym. In fact, it had a lot to do with an abuse situation, with the girl's self-esteem, and with a whole series of other major problems.

You go through the experience of trying to get a class of kids through school, and you realize that the host of issues they deal with go way, way beyond the school. It's not just a question of the "good school" not being there—it's the gang problem, it's the drug problem, it's the healthcare problem, [it's] the "Mom and Pop" or the "Mom and no Pop" problem. You start to see how abuse and public housing are all part of living problems. You come to have a much fuller realization of just what these challenges are and to see that there's no simple silver bullet.

CONNECTING WITH FAMILIES

The two stories told by the Hulls capture another issue that featured in the anecdotes of many other IHAD sponsors: the difficulties presented by the parents of some of their dreamers. But, again, it's important to remember how different sponsors' own personal experiences as children may have been. We all know that the degree to which adults have "great expectations" for children has much to do with young people's later success. One particular sponsor spoke for many others in saying,

When I was growing up it was assumed I was going to college. This was not an option that was open to me. Everybody in my family went to college—for the last generation or two; I can't go back much farther than that. But in these particular families, no one went to college. When someone has, or when the parents do want their kids to succeed, we can see that what we are doing makes a kid's success much more likely. But when parents don't care at all, it's all up for grabs. The kid may make it or the kid may just not make it. We can see the difference.

Expectations are very important, not only in relation to school but also as they bear on other aspects of children's futures. And many of the people I interviewed attributed the lack of great expectations for these children to parental resistance—particularly as it played out in relation to their projects' outreach efforts. If parents really wanted their kids to succeed, they reasoned, they would grab at every opportunity to get them help.

Linda Martin has sponsored three IHAD programs in her community. Though she began in a school, she redesigned her second and third projects to address family resistance. She had come to understand the value of intervening while children are still young and believed that moving her "home base" from a school to a housing development would make it easier for dreamers to participate. At first, when most of the children were young, this seemed to be a wonderful way to engage children in all kinds of afterschool programs. But perplexing sponsor-family dynamics lingered, leaving Linda with much disappointment and a bit of resentment.

> This was a very difficult clientele to deal with, a real welfare . . . "what-are-you-going-to-do-for-me-now?" group. The mommas would ask the kids, "What did she bring you today? What did she do for you today?" Sometimes they wouldn't even walk across the street for a meeting. It's a really difficult neighborhood. When mothers won't get their children up to send them to school, or take themselves right across the street to a school meeting, or make sure their children are there for a lot of the activities, it's hard. You can walk 'em, talk 'em, call 'em, do all that—and we tried every gimmick we could. But it just seemed to get harder.

> Sometimes I think the children from welfare families are just as spoiled as we are on the other, up-end side of town where some kids get a BMW when they go to high school. Not everybody is spoiled, but you can see it happening. Some of these children we work with may not be getting BMWs, but they're getting designer clothes and shoes when the parents are on welfare or food stamps. There's a disconnect. Nothing is earned. That has been hard for me.

You know, we've grown up in families where you get up and your job is to go to school or go to work. This is just not negotiable. But in these communities, things seem to be negotiable every day. There's no basic commitment that says, "We're going to school," or " I'm going to keep this job." Sometimes you help parents get new jobs, and they're whiny or complain. You know? That kind of attitude. Not, "Who am I? I don't have much education and the way I get better is to go to school, to hold a steady job."

That's very hard to get through. Sometimes I think the biggest mistake we may have made is doing too much for some of these families. Being an advocate is one thing. But you can't do everything for them. They have to learn to make the calls to agencies for help themselves. It's hard to get them to do it, but it's like with your own children. Do you tie their shoe, or do you teach them how to tie their shoe? In the end, you've got to teach them how to tie their shoes and take care of themselves or you've done them a tremendous disservice. You're picking up the pieces for them whenever they stumble, filling in the gap and saying, "Oh, I'll take care of that." And that's not good.

Linda's impatience with the differences between her world and the world of her dreamers hasn't been sufficient to dissuade her from doing additional projects, but she's honest enough to acknowledge that she sometimes gets angry and discouraged.

Another sponsor told me that she dislikes the feelings of inadequacy that seem to be triggered within her by parent resistance. Understanding how important the mother's role is in dreamers' lives, she struggles with the fact that when mothers don't support the project there's a limit to what she can do.

The really frustrating thing to me is that no matter how much we want to do, or how hard we try, we are still just the benevolent auntie. Some things are totally out of our hands. We can make great suggestions. We can know what would be best. We can cry, cajole, threaten, treat, do all those things. But mama has the last word. I've seen it. They can have an

alcoholic father, a dysfunctional family, all of this, but if they
have a mother who's in their corner, they've got a chance.

There's nothing autocratic or insensitive about this woman. In fact, she
wants to understand parental resistance so she can build a strong relationship with families that will enhance the success of her dreamers.
But she struggles with the frustration of not being the "mama" who
has the last word, and with not always being able to reach the parents
when they stand between her and constructive relationships with the
dreamers.

Another sponsor thinks some of the resistance she and others
encounter has something to do with the way IHAD is often introduced at the beginning.

> There are these fancy people coming in to announce, with
> a lot of fanfare, that they're going to do something special
> for the kids that the parents themselves can't do. It sets up
> a bad dynamic from the very beginning.

But there are other reasons for parent apprehensiveness. Tessa Bloom
points out that part of the challenge for sponsors is to understand how
often families may have been disappointed in the past.

> We work very closely with our parents and we have about
> seventy-five percent of our parents coming to anything we
> ever do. That's very good. But I still think the biggest hurdle
> a sponsor has to overcome is this feeling that parents have,
> "When are they going to leave us? When are they going to
> walk away?" . . .
>
> Once the parents saw that we were here to stay, that the
> PC was there to stay, that someone had really made a com-
> mitment and was not letting [them] down, then they really
> became very, very involved in the program. The parents are
> so grateful, so appreciative, and extraordinarily supportive.
> They love it. And when they're in need and they have to
> have help, we do things for them too. We really feel we can
> change the whole community by teaching the parents that
> they can take control of their lives. It's not that they should
> be grateful that they've got a good school for their kids:

that's nonsense. And just because they're poor doesn't mean they don't have expectations.

Richard Joseph has come to believe that some parents feel threatened by knowing that their kids are having meaningful relationships with people who are in positions to offer them more than they can. Moreover, these relationships may ultimately pull the youngsters away from their families.

> You have to give parents an extraordinary amount of support, something I didn't realize when we started this. What you are doing is offering something to their kids that they did not have. On the surface this looks like a glamorous gain. But in their hearts this can be a loss to the parents. This child is not going to be like them. In fact, the kid is probably going to leave the neighborhood and go on to develop in a very different way. I think many parents are a little bit conflicted about that.

Thus we hear a variety of tones and themes in sponsors' observations about dreamer families, ranging from frustration to worry that family dynamics can ultimately limit what a project can do for a dreamer. Most sponsors, like Tessa and Richard, search for ways to understand and address the possible motivations behind resistance. How individuals cope with frustration varies, of course—and our tolerance for frustration can be different from one day to the next. But the most difficult aspect of families' resistance for sponsors is that it can determine how long it will take the dreamers themselves to engage in genuine, trusting relationships with them and their PCs and staff. "Getting the trust of the kids and the parents who participated was the most difficult thing of all," one sponsor told me. Another observed,

> If kids feel support and encouragement and loyalty from adults they respond. If they don't feel it's there, then they don't respond. But they're very skeptical in the beginning. It took three or four years to get a lot of these kids to believe we really meant it, that we were with them.

It takes time for parents and kids to trust these new people who have come into their lives. But it also takes time for sponsors to understand that what may appear to be a suspicious, even greedy response to an IHAD activity can be fear in the hearts of dreamers and their families about what may happen in these new relationships with people from such different worlds. The Hulls recall how long it took them to learn this lesson.

It took us at least two years before the kids and especially their families believed that we were still going to be there. They think that if anything good happens in the neighborhood, because somebody has given some money or something, it will go away. Promises have often been made and not kept. Well, we didn't go away. I think that was a first for this particular housing project. At the beginning, they really didn't have much faith in us. You know, they would hide things. Then, as the years went by and we would learn about problems, if there was a way that we could help, we would.

In the beginning we were very stringent. When we were taking a bus to the museum, for example, we would say, "This is only going to be for the dreamers." But some of them would have a brother or sister tagging along, and if there was room, we'd take them, you know? Why not? You had to. Because sometimes the dreamer wouldn't be able to come if the other kid didn't come, too. Some families have a lot of very definite dos and don'ts, and if the brother's there, they know the sister won't get away with anything. When you start understanding all this you become more relaxed. But at the beginning there's a lot you don't understand—like the fact that these kids have never had to be accountable for anything.

It's hard when you come from the upbringing that we have all had to be dealing with kids who have never done anything that they didn't want to do. But you start to see that often this is because most of the kids bring themselves up. Many of them are being raised by their grandmothers, because their mothers were having babies at fourteen and fifteen. They didn't know how to take care of babies, so they turned them over to their mothers to bring up.

It's a whole different world. It's not just that they weren't taught manners: they didn't even know that manners existed. It's a whole new perception of life. It's hard to understand that a parent wouldn't tell their kids to wash their hands, or keep themselves clean, take a bath, a shower, because it doesn't occur to them, because their parents never taught them. But this is what happens. And there are very few fathers. I mean, if you haven't walked in their shoes, there's so much to learn.

Indeed, walking in another's shoes is the central issue. The people I interviewed for this book had become IHAD sponsors with very conventional assumptions about serving and helping. It took some of them years before they started to understand that whether kids are clean when they come to school may have something to do with whether there is a working tub or shower in their home. Or that a child's dirty clothes may mean that there's no adult at home who has time to go to the laundromat. Or that parents may not cross the street to come to meetings because they're working three jobs, or have had terrible experiences in schools themselves when they were young, or don't have what they consider appropriate clothes or even warm coats. Everything is connected, and some sponsors seem to be able to look beyond their initial impressions and/or frustrations more easily than others.

COPING WITH "THE SYSTEM"

In this country, the poor are inadequately served by social service systems that have been structured in what is sometimes called the "silo" model. That is, each problem is addressed in isolation from every other one, evaluated and diagnosed categorically, without reference to multiple contextual factors. Difficulties are isolated. People are sent to "specialists" for help, referred to particular agencies—welfare, family support, health care, afterschool programs, juvenile court, community center, school, for example. These agencies are often legally and logistically unable to share relevant information with each other, so each specialist is expected to solve a problem without being helped to connect the dots between one difficulty and another.

Sponsors discover the inconsistencies of these policies in many ways. One described to me something he had learned about the irrationality of certain state and federal scholarship policies.

> For example, this state's compensation packages are crazy—so shortsighted. After high school, the state pays enough to let you go to a one- or two-year college with childcare, but not a four-year college. One of our dreamers needed $135 to take the state exam to get certified as a nurse's aide. This was a program the state would support, but it wouldn't lend her the money to take the test.

> It puts things into perspective, I'll tell you. . . . It's so appalling to me to look at the political landscape, from the president, to the secretary of education, to the governor and the mayor. Not one of them has a clue about inner-city education. It is just frightening. The whole world is different. When you're living with parents who aren't working, a mother who is a whore and a father on drugs, and there are five kids—well, this is a world they just can't understand.

Understanding may not change systems, although as a result of what he learned as a sponsor, one man told me that for a while he had thought about going into politics. The learning curve can be very steep. As Hal Davies says,

> I've been learning about a part of life I'd never have had a way to learn of. You get to see the world through very different eyes. And you understand how things are, not how people say they are. I know how our city school system works—and it's not the way people say it does. I know how the welfare system and social services system works, and I know that none of these things works the way people say they do.

> I've learned to be an advocate for these kids and their families, and this is really what the sponsor is: you get in there and you fight. I know I have the skills not to fight

the system: I have the personal contacts and the experience to know how to get around the system and to make things happen. But every time you started out, you saw what they saw, what they face; you understand how these programs, all designed to help people, don't do it nearly as much as they say. You end up with an enormous amount of knowledge in your head and you want to say, "God, someone listen to me!" There's so much you can't say, because it's not politically correct. But now when I read in the paper of some kid having trouble, where I may have condemned him before, I don't condemn him now. I look at him to try to figure out what broke? How did he get there?

It's interesting that Hal says he has the skills *not* to fight the system. He's banking on the bedrock notion that "personal contacts" will help him "get around the system" on behalf of his dreamers. Central to sponsor frustrations about parental resistance and other roadblocks to their kids' success are the structural inadequacies of our existing human service systems. But while engaged philanthropy can have an enormous impact on a donor's capacity for empathy and compassion, it does not seem to be an experience that turns many sponsors into political activists. They become more passionate advocates for children, but few join large-scale, activist movements to reform our inadequate human service systems. Those who have become engaged with the charter school and voucher movements are the exception to this. In the end, individual relationships with their dreamers are more important to sponsors than anything else.

LIVING WITH DIFFERENCE

Many sponsors are shocked to discover just how far most low-income children are from what they assumed to be the cultural and economic mainstream of the country. One spoke of how difficult it was—in unexpected ways—to "cross racial lines."

To see where the issue of race is in this country, at this time, has been a real eye-opener for me. To understand how much resistance there is among kids to learning and to doing well in school, and how negatively they can be seen by their peers if they happen to get a good grade—this has been very important to me.

Another told me that she sometimes feels a "vast cultural divide" separating her from her dreamers.

> When I started, I had no idea how isolated these kids are. I've had kids come over here who have never seen things like a blue corn chip! Like it's food from Mars.
>
> And there are many things like that. The cultural divide is vast. It's there in tiny, specific ways and huge, broad things. Sometimes the kids have no idea about the kinds of things that might be important to me. For example, if I do something special for someone I never receive a thank-you note. I know that sounds ridiculous, and I sometimes ask myself why I would expect a child who is fifteen years old to write a thank-you note. But at the same time, it's a cultural norm where I come from.
>
> Sometimes when I speak with them I feel, "Wow, this is great and I'm making progress." But at other times I walk away thinking, "They hate me." There are certain kids, especially the boys, who won't even look me in the eye. Part of it is, I'm sure, that they're too shy to talk to me. But another part of it is that they don't like white people. They don't want to talk to me. They have so much anger. And a lot of it is really valid. Sometimes I doubt that having me come down to visit with them is going to heal the anger that they have.

This sponsor's observations that dreamers may not have seen blue corn chips or don't know that they should write thank-you notes are trivial compared to her deeper worries about how the kids may perceive her and the fact that she will be unable to "heal their anger." What she is really talking about is a sense of powerlessness about how wide the gulf of class and culture between her and the dreamers is, and about how it makes her feel.

A number of sponsors acknowledge being surprised by the many ways, large and small, in which this distance manifests itself. For example, when they take dreamers to restaurants, bring a few

kids home for a Thanksgiving dinner, enjoy small group birthday celebrations, or take groups to visit workplaces in the local community,
they may discover that the kids don't always dress appropriately, are
unfamiliar with simple courtesies, or have trouble making themselves
understood clearly. These differences seem to be less troublesome
to sponsors when the children are young than they become later, as
dreamers move into adolescence. In fact, some seem to grow less comfortable with their dreamers' ways of being in the world at the same
stage that inter-generational relationships get testy in many families:
the stakes begin to feel higher, just as they do for parents of teenagers.
The closer kids get to "leaving the nest," the keener sponsors are to
know that their dreamers will really be able to fly.

In the case of the sponsor I quoted above, her own children are
still very young. She may be less familiar with the intimately ambivalent
turmoil of affection and frustration that is stirred up between parents
and adolescents. But it is not uncommon for sponsors of adolescent
dreamers to sound angry at times. Will Christopher, for example, is
frustrated by what he identifies as one persistent consequence of segregation in our society.

> What we initially found, which pissed us off, was the inner-
> city lack of trust. As if the kids and their families were say-
> ing, "Who are these people anyway?" In a way I expected
> that. But hey, I wanted them to know, "I'm for real, guys. I
> don't know what your other experiences were but, come on
> guys, I'm for real!"

> Cultural differences, socioeconomic differences presented
> barriers we didn't anticipate. It all just made us roll our
> sleeves up even higher and say, "Come on now, we're going
> to lick this!" But talk about a segregated society! In our
> city, when you cross the river and go into the neighborhood
> where most of these kids are still living, it's all one color.
> This is segregation! Just like in other cities.

> So, in the third and fourth and fifth grade, we'd expose them
> to the airport, to simple things on this side of the river, not
> just the monuments or the museums. On Thanksgiving we'd
> bring five or six kids to our house, asking different kids every

year to expose them to our environment. And all of a sudden we began to realize that with our neighbors and friends we are starting to give these kids a clearer picture of a different world. Now they're in high school and they obviously have a better feel for it. But at first we'd come home after a simple visit in their community and say to ourselves, "I can't believe this! These kids live in this big city! All they have to do is get on a subway or bus—forget driving—to see everyday things. But they never see what we see." They were only used to a one-color environment, and it wasn't very healthy.

Like others, Will was impatient. He was also a little naïve. He wanted to be accepted by his dreamers, but it took time for him to realize how often they'd been promised things and then forgotten. Drawn to engaged philanthropy with low-income children because of genuine sensitivity to the pain of social injustice, he and his wife, Carol, were determined to reach out and connect with people across difference. Will's irritation—and that of others—partly reflects a sadness about discovering that in spite of all their efforts, and in spite of the fact that they have started to love their dreamers, the kids remain vulnerable to pressures that keep them "isolated" from the mainstream worlds in which sponsors live. What's more, these dreamers are going to grow up and graduate from the program. There will be a limit to how much Will and Carol can do.

Although the many-headed hydra of racism, in all its ugly forms, complicates sponsors' efforts, many of those I talked to expressed optimism and gratitude for the ways in which their experiences have enriched their own lives by enabling them to cross the divide. Sam Hull told me,

> One of the wonderful things about the IHAD program is that it's had a profound effect on the number of people that are involved, who have found additional ways to express their concern about the disconnection between whites and "others," apart from whatever they were doing as a formal part of the IHAD program.

Another sponsor said she now realizes that "a lot of our race relations problems would absolutely vanish if we knew one another." And yet another found himself wincing at the glib way that people in his community talked about the subject.

> We don't have "poor" race relations here. We really don't have *any!* But with our project, I think what happened was that an awful lot of people took on the concerns and problems and solutions for a lot of other people's problems.

> And the ones that really benefitted the most are the mentors, not the mentees. They grow so much—in ways that would never have happened had they not had these opportunities. These mentors come up to me in the street and say, "Guess what? Remember old Sam, or Lakeisha? Do you know that he or she is now doing such and such? He graduated from this place, and she's doing great! We talk to her all the time—she was out for dinner with us the other night." Those kinds of things just don't happen around here.

All in all, while they're pleased to think that they are making strides to fight racism in their own communities, many sponsors continue to be saddened, often outraged, by the complicated consequences of racism on our society. They become increasingly aware of ways that it reinforces low expectations: families and peers can sometimes intensify a dreamer's distrust or despair. Though the instincts of action-oriented sponsors are to meet and solve problems head on, understanding the enormous reach of racism can be transforming.

In their projects, of course, they're attempting to create a positive peer group and provide good role models. But what also seems to happen is that, as the projects evolve and children grow, sponsors begin to feel greater urgency about holding dreamers just as accountable for their actions as they do their own children. They refuse to let young people off the hook by blaming racism for all their problems. As Richard says,

> One of the biggest things that I've learned, from the beginning, is that it is reasonable and caring and loving to have high expectations, to be demanding of young people, rather than to say, "Oh, they're poor and black, or poor and Latino. What can you expect?" I think the whole social movement that began in this country out of

good will, thirty to forty years ago, has had a sort of condescending racism about it. All of us that went into this
thing wanted to help and to do good. And sometimes we
see that the best way to do good is to have high standards.
That's what's really important for children.

This is a huge, humbling lesson for many sponsors. In most cases, it
hadn't occurred to them that pure compassion alone could undercut
potential.

When Will and Carol's dreamers were young and sometimes
uncooperative, psychologists advised them to "turn the other cheek."
They were encouraged not to blame the kids or get angry. Rather they
should think about the kinds of barriers these kids were up against and
interpret the difficulties that might come along as the consequences of
complex social influences. But when the dreamers got to high school,
Will and Carol became less patient with taking this kind of perspective and began instead to have tougher, franker conversations with the
young people and their parents.

When they started high school, we told our dreamers they
were going to be held accountable. We've held them to that.
We told the parents and the kids, "Look, you're always welcome in the program, but nobody's going to force you to
study. If you're not going to study, why don't you just get out
of the program until you're ready to be held accountable?"
We don't hold back any more. "You want to serve French
fries at McDonald's the rest of your life? Be my guest. You're
old enough now to determine your own destiny. If you want
to take advantage of all the things that we can offer you, we
welcome you with open arms, but we can't force you now."

We find this approach to be effective, even with kids that
we'd given up on. Our PC keeps reminding us to accept
one foot forward as a success factor, not to keep looking a
mile down the road. She tempers my expectations. We have
changed our feelings and attitudes about this culture.

Will keeps on "looking a mile down the road," as infused with
great expectations for his kids as ever. But when his dreamers hit adolescence, he is giving them exactly the kinds of care that many experts

say teenagers need. This means attention coupled with limit-setting, goal-setting, and constancy. The shift in his stance may reflect the developmental shift in dreamers. But it may also mean that once the dreamers have developed trust in the sponsors—who have learned to "turn the other cheek" and understand the kinds of obstacles kids are facing—then the sponsors can be more demanding and even, if necessary, appropriately punitive.

In part it's a matter of accepting limitations—one's own and those of others. Another sponsor told me about what he feels to have been a kind of change of heart as he became "a little more hardened to the fact that you just can't save them all, even when a kid doesn't want to do it and when you know it's not his fault, you know? You have to consider that." He continued,

> I'm a liberal. But the liberal argument is "Don't blame." Well, I think we've learned from the conservatives that there's something to be said for taking responsibility for your actions. We can't just keep making excuses for kids, saying, "Well, the reason they rob people is because their parents didn't care, or their mother was a drug addict, or their father's in prison." It's probably all true. But you can't excuse it, because it's not fair to the kid who *doesn't* rob people, the one who has the same background but somehow wakes up in the morning and isn't a drug dealer.
>
> I find now I'm more willing to adopt what I would have thought of before as a conservative viewpoint. You know what I mean? You've gotta take responsibility for your actions, and you can't expect society to just excuse what you do because you came from a poor family and a poor neighborhood. I'm not conservative. But I just believe that you can't save everybody, and that you can't use trouble as an excuse. At some point you've gotta either fish or cut bait. And you give a kid a chance—every chance you can, you give him.

Even with this new perspective and resolve, this man went on to muse that maybe if he'd been able to take the most difficult kids home with him, they "would all have made it." He has not given up wanting to help. In fact, he has recently started another IHAD project.

Sponsors do not necessarily find their politics changing. Walter King, for example, always conservative, became increasingly impatient with advocates for bilingual education. The longer he followed his dreamers, the more strongly he felt that English is the language of opportunity and assimilation is the fastest way to success for his kids. Getting tangled up in the "heritage issue, which is often referenced by bilingual education advocates," he says, is misguided, because

> communication is the source of much apprehension and worry. It's wrong to obsess about identity. I always wanted my program to be proactive, not reactive. If we have to spend all our time in court arguing about this, we won't be able to get momentum going for the kids.

Rather than leave them in a system that, as he saw it, was bogged down by bilingual education requirements and the lack of high expectations for its students, Walter moved some of his dreamers into private schools.

However they choose to respond, what seems to happen is that as sponsors come to understand the degree to which low-income, minority children live in strictly segregated environments, their feelings about the injustice of the status quo intensify—on all sides of the political spectrum. Sometimes viewpoints sharpen; sometimes attitudes shift. Before they began their IHAD projects, some sponsors told me, they worried that feelings about "ethnic differences" on both sides could inhibit strong connections between themselves and their dreamers. As Lou Irving said, "All of us are ghettoized in this city. I didn't want them to think of me as a rich honky. I wanted them to think of me as a guy who was there to help them." But over time sponsors most often discover that ethnic differences don't preclude long-term bonds between them and the children they are trying to help. Mike O'Donnell told of being thrilled by what happened when he was coming home from a college trip with his dreamers on a bus and a group of white kids got on.

> One of the girls in the back said, "Look at those honkies." And another one said, "Shh! There's Mike!" But Tiger jumped in and said, "Mike's no honky. He's a brother." And it really did feel like being an older brother.

George Norman remembers that before he began as a sponsor he was nervous that his own whiteness might constitute a barrier between him and the children of color who would become his dreamers.

> The reason I didn't adopt sooner was that I was a white person and I felt they would feel they were being better served by someone of their own color. But this really has nothing to do with it. When you get right down to it, it has nothing to do with color. In fact, Eduardo said to me, "You know, it took me a year to trust you because you were this white guy from the other side of town. And I didn't believe that you would really be here." Most of the kids had that same feeling. But once you develop the bond, we are all the same color.

In the end it's the passing of time that proves the truth of a sponsor's promise.

It's not easy for any of us to face personal feelings and attitudes about racial, ethnic, and cultural differences. It takes time and courage to understand what our assumptions and biases are, let alone how they may influence our behavior. But many of the people I talked to spoke of how necessary and transformative it is to do so. And it was easier for sponsors to talk about ethnicity than class differences. It was Chuck Peterson who pointed out that many sponsors had unconsciously relied on the apparatus of class for their sense of identity and social standing. Now, with their dreamers, it soon became clear that it wasn't the "toys" of class that made sponsors "cool or acceptable in dreamer eyes." As he says,

> Having to sit down and relate to a kid who doesn't share your assumptions, world view, or experiences reduces you, if you're a guy who's used to being powerful, to feeling like a fool. You try to impress them by paying, you know? By doing things you've always thought have impressed people. You take the kids out to a restaurant and they've never seen a cloth napkin. You get box seats to the symphony, thinking they'll be impressed with how cool you are. And you even find yourself seated in the box next to the governor.
>
> But these kids have never heard of the governor, and they don't care. They just think it's all kind of boring. You are

pretty quickly stripped of the insignia of power and success that matter to upper-class, white, over-educated Americans. These kids have never heard of the schools I went to. And so what if those places were the most important things in my whole life? Guess what: they aggressively don't care!

What they do care about is: Do you sit still? Do you listen to them? When you offer to do things for them, do you actually do them? Because, my God, if you can do those things, then you walk on water. With precious few exceptions, it seems, no one in their lives actually listens to them or says they'll do things and then actually does them. It takes a long time of watching their surprise grow as they realize that this random rich guy who dropped out of the sky into their world actually will do something for them. It challenges all their assumptions about the world. Not because you're rich and white—but because virtually no one they interact with on a daily basis engages in altruism. And over time, you realize that you're being a goofball and trying to show off for the kids, the way you've done for others before. The real challenge for the sponsor is to confront the fact that you're not being altruistic. You're just trying to impress these kids, like you've tried to impress everyone else in your whole life. And it's the attention that matters more than anything.

Once they throw themselves headlong into long-term relationships with the dreamers, sponsors find that what the kids care about most is constancy and connection. When they see how glad the kids are to see them regularly, they understand that barriers of color, religion, and class can be dismantled.

Sponsors' behaviors and perspectives change. Advocacy feeds itself. The higher the stakes get—the more they learn and the more they come to care—the more active many become. More alert than ever before to the consequences of segregation for young people, some have become actively involved in "think tanks" with various political orientations. And most would identify with Sam Hull when he says,

You know, most of us are from the suburbs. And when your friends sit around and come up with simplistic answers to these big problems, you now know enough to say, "Now hey, wait a second. That just isn't true. Come with me if you're really interested. I'll take you down town and let you see for yourself." Your perspective on major public policy issues is just changed.

Ours is such a segregated society—racially, socio-economically, and otherwise. You've got people sitting around deciding things for parts of the population that they have really very little real world contact with. There need to be more, not fewer people, who have respect for what is happening and can join conversations wherever they are going on, in kitchens and in policy offices, who can say, "Gee, that's not been my experience, for what it's worth." Because doing this, you begin to start really building some interconnects, unlike many whites, who have become totally disconnected. They want to ignore it all, rather than say, "My God, this is a human tragedy, and we have a moral and economic imperative to do something about it."

MOVING BEYOND IHAD

The kinds of things that engaged philanthropists learn as a result of their personal involvement—about the current state of public education, the reality of life for low-income children, the interrelatedness of needs in poor communities, the impact of segregation and racism—lead some to expand their efforts. This is true even for those who were previously actively committed to their communities in less direct ways. Like the Hull family, Richard and Laura Joseph started charter schools. They also created a new foundation dedicated to promoting the healthy development and education of low-income children.

The energy level of some of the sponsors I met was simply dazzling. Because of what he learned about the specific skills and expertise his PC and project mentors needed to have, one sponsor restructured the original IHAD model, turning it into a long-term mentoring and support program that serves an open-ended group of children. He credits his IHAD experience with his subsequent creation of a major foundation that gives away more than $30 million to people in poverty each year—but he's still working with kids directly as well.

> IHAD was important for me. It's part of a larger philan-thropic fabric that I have woven, but it was certainly my first step down that road. It taught me that you can have the greatest intentions in the world but your impact will be zero unless you develop the right skill set and goals and you learn the importance of teaching, mentoring, and guiding well.
>
> I'm now more involved in my foundation that's dedicated to helping people under the poverty line. But my experi-ence with IHAD had everything to do with starting this foundation. When I first came to the community in 1986, it didn't take long to look up and down that street and see, all of a sudden, how much need there was in my city. That's what got me involved in this foundation. Which is wonder-ful, fantastic, I love it. But IHAD is a lot more fun because it's more hands on, more one-on-one, and it's much more personal. Being able to have the foundation is great. But supporting other organizations doesn't give you the per-sonal feelings and experiences you get when you work with the kids every week.
>
> I love working with the kids. I go out there every week; I email them every day. I now have so many that it's hard for me to keep them all straight. We've got probably eighty kids in our afterschool program and another hundred kids in college, and it's just hard to keep them all straight. I have so many kids now I can't always even recognize them all by their faces. And I've also got four kids of my own—all under eleven. It's hard to balance it all, along with a com-pany of three hundred people. Somewhere I like to have some time for myself. It's a big juggling act.

A gifted multi-tasker, he's open to learning and change, even invigo-rated by the way engagement can restructure one's life.

George Norman, whom we've heard from before, is another example of someone whose life has been made more complicated— and richer—as he's gotten progressively more involved in engaged philanthropy. You'll recall that he'd started his own business as a junior in college and dropped out of school to build it up. Before his own two children were born, he became actively engaged with low-income children by becoming a mentor to two youngsters in a housing development. He grew so fond of the kids and so impressed with the mutually meaningful process of mentoring that he and some business colleagues began to develop similar initiatives. Then, abruptly, a potential IHAD sponsor abandoned a group of dreamers whom he'd promised to adopt. Because of their positive experiences as mentors, George and his wife decided to take over the project. When we spoke, he recalled a recent conversation with a friend who has been frustrated that it's taking so long to see clear and positive outcomes coming from a charter school in which he's invested. If the man really wants to make a difference, George says confidently,

> He should come work inside the system and get involved with the superintendent. He'll be amazed at what he can accomplish, with probably half the money he's invested in charters. IHAD has shaped my business and my philanthropic career outside of IHAD. So much of what I am now is because of this program.

> First of all, IHAD really focused me on education. It first led me to a local high school near where I work. I started volunteering there ten years ago. The governor heard about what we were doing at that school and came out to our plant, with his entire cabinet, to learn what we were trying to achieve. We were calling our project School to Career then, and six weeks later he invited me to sit with him on the National Governors' Association School-to-Career Round Table. The goal was to get a twenty-five million dollar grant for the state. He and I literally traveled the state, talking in small and large communities about the importance of project-based learning and of thinking about careers. We stressed that school is not just about college. It's also about what we are training kids to do, and how we can make what they're learning in the classroom something that will hold their interest. That was an important piece of what I learned and what we were doing.

Then, about four or five years ago, I was asked to chair the United Way campaign in our town. I was by far the youngest [campaign] chair they had ever had, and I ended up chairing the board. We restructured the whole program around two platforms. One was something we call Safety Net, a traditional platform intended to provide . . . for those people who have fallen, who need help helping themselves. But the other piece was something we called Bright Futures, which had four elements: teaching, nurturing, protecting, and mentoring. Those were the elements that I knew from IHAD really worked.

We reformatted how we looked at United Way and how we described it to our donors. And last year we were among the top three or four chapters in the country in terms of increased fund-raising support from the community. This happened because we were able to talk very tangibly about what it is United Way does that really helps kids make a better life for themselves. Each Bright Futures feature came right out of my experiences with IHAD. As board chair, I could often be asked to be the agency speaker, because I could always tell real stories, talk about what happened last night, say, with the dreamers.

Those are some of the things that I've been involved with. In fact, I was asked by the school board president earlier this year if I'd apply for the superintendent's position. Certainly that never would have happened if IHAD hadn't happened to me. I really want to do that. But I never graduated from college myself. What I want to do is go back to school.

I need to sell my company: that's the first step. I'm on a three-year exit strategy. I really would like to do something like that in the future. But would I have ever thought, in my wildest dreams, that I would ever consider even wanting to be a superintendent of schools? No! What the recruiter said, when I met with him, is that of all the people he inter-viewed—and he does this on a national basis—he typically doesn't see the passion he saw with me. That's because I've lived through it. It's such a great experience. Without it I doubt that I would be as involved in the community as I am. In fact, there's a group of sponsors here now who have said to me, "We don't think we would have known how to do this if we hadn't watched you guys over the last several years." Another friend of mine who's on my board of directors has also decided to sponsor a group. And when I chaired United Way another friend gave our first million-dollar gift for Bright Futures. We had invited Lang to speak at our United Way and after that he came up to me and said, "You know, the reason my wife and I have done this in part is because of what we've seen you do. Thank you." The guy contributed a million dollars! And he's very involved in the system now.

George's life is very different from what it would have been without IHAD—and so is the United Way organization in his community. He has assumed major civic responsibilities. And although he himself never finished college, he was asked to apply for the job of district school superintendent because of his proven passion and performance on behalf of his city's kids. Now he plans to sell his business and focus even more exclusively on educational issues. He's certain that his experience as an actively engaged philanthropist gives him the kind of clout that will enable him to work effectively for change.

Lou Irving and Tad Johnson have each started scholarship funds for low-income children. Two other sponsors now spend time consulting to younger entrepreneurs who are starting new schools and looking for guidance as they try to design successful programs. Others have started new businesses that focus on helping young people. Tad Johnson's communications, public speaking, and life skills program, which we described in Chapter 2, is one example. Another is that of Hal Davies. When his dreamers were getting ready to graduate from high school, Hal founded a new business management firm in order to realize his "life-long ambition" to combine his "wealth of knowledge in business and finance" with his "ability to get things done for people." The organization provides a wide range of planning services—financial, investment, business, legal, and personal—for gifted young people, athletes in particular, who may find themselves coping

with the consequences of material success before they are quite ready
to manage it. It's an endeavor, Hal says, that reflects much of what he
learned from his valued firsthand relationships with youth.

As noted throughout, several sponsors go on to begin second,
sometimes even third IHAD programs. Ken Robinson, Tad's philanthropic mentor, was the first IHAD sponsor in his city. He was so
impressed with what he saw happening to his dreamers, so enthusiastic about what he was learning, that he used his sharp business
skills to replicate his own project ten times locally. When, in the early
1980s, he became a devout Christian, his related decision—to donate
one tenth of everything he made to charity—meant that he began to
spend a great deal of time finding new efforts to support.

> I've been in marketing all my life, and I know. In sales, it's
> not what you can earn through your own efforts. It's what
> you can earn through the combined efforts of many people.
> I wanted to multiply what I had done. My goal was to bring
> in nine other IHAD sponsors in the area, which ultimately
> I did. I brought in nine others and got the tenth class myself,
> with a new working sponsor/partner.

Not only did Ken bring nine other sponsors to IHAD, but he
created one of the largest local IHAD programs in the country. Will
Christopher has been the director of that chapter for about five years.

For most of his life, Will had worked in a very successful business that he started himself. In Chapter 3 he called it an event-planning
business, but when we last spoke he described it as a "destination management company." With offices around the world now, the business
helps independent hotels book major meetings and conferences. "Not
paranoid about making humongous profits," Will now says he wants
to be "remembered on my tombstone for helping to educate inner-city
kids." This intention now informs a great many of his activities.

> I really didn't roll up my sleeves until the IHAD program.
> That just opened the floodgates for a whole bunch of other
> things. At this point, as much as thirty or forty percent
> of my everyday life is spent in educational arenas, helping
> inner-city kids. After getting in the trenches and seeing
> how bad the inner-city schools were, the first thing we did

was to put together a group of very influential people in this city. I was the ringleader, the orchestra leader, and I was ready to sue the mayor—who was doing nothing about our schools—to create all kinds of hell-raising until somebody cooler than me said, "Hey, Congress just passed a law that allowed us to open charter schools. Let's be constructive." I brought two guys to town who had opened a charter in the east, and then I got some high net worth people to write some serious checks.

The long and short of it all was that we opened two high school charter schools right here in town, both of which have gone on to be fairly successful. I sit on the board of one of them right now. While it has a few problems, the fact is that under a charter school umbrella, with our efforts, we are helping to educate roughly six hundred kids who are getting better educated than they would be in this city's public school system.

That was first. Then, two, though I supported it individually for a long time, I recently went onto the board for the School Reform Initiative, a national advocacy group that talks to the nation and to Congress about the importance of educational reform. All the issues are on the table: vouchers, charter schools, rebuilding school boards, whatever the educational reform movement is doing. So now I'm heavily involved in advocacy.

And three, I've recently joined the board of America Teaches, an organization that I absolutely love and that I frankly think does more than IHAD in the way of influencing inner-city kids. For a number of years, I've sat on the board of the Children Grow Foundation. Now I've revamped that board. We've really picked up a lot of money and consequently make grants and offer scholarships totaling about $150,000 a year. This is money that primarily goes to underprivileged kids involved in our programs, helping to support their college education. Do you see the common thread? Every one of these things means being involved in education and is devoted primarily to inner-city or under-privileged kids. But that was not my life before IHAD.

Engaged philanthropy teaches people a great deal about the world beyond the relatively comfortable realm in which they've lived. When the floodgates open, as Will put it, the way they spend their time and money changes. What engaged philanthropists learn from being personally involved in hands-on efforts can intensify their impatience with both public and private systems of support in this country.

Once you have new children in your lives and hearts, you come naturally to resent the fact that institutions that are supposed to help these children—schools, welfare offices, and hospitals, for example— can be overly bureaucratic and seem unresponsive to human needs. You may well begin to appreciate the limitations of any one particular approach, and you may find yourself involved in multi-pronged attacks on the consequences of poverty and social neglect. You may chafe at the fact that so many people in positions of power seem neither to understand nor to care about the kinds of everyday difficulties that low-income children face.

Seeing that "the cup is half-empty in the macro arena of educating inner-city kids," however, does not stop people like Will from dedicating their lives to strengthening education for poor children. When you become close to children, when you understand the obstacles they are up against, and when you see what a difference you can make, you have greater expectations—in spite of the odds. You believe that all kids can succeed. And you fight out of a conviction—not a dream— that systems and institutions can change to meet the needs of the people they are designed to serve.

CHAPTER 7

THE RICHES AND WONDER
OF ENGAGEMENT

*I am a true believer in the power of this model—not
just to change kids' lives, but to change the lives of the
sponsors, staff, volunteers.*

—Chuck Peterson

The engaged philanthropists I interviewed for this book talked about how they learned new things about the realities of life in low-income communities, and how they developed new ideas, theories, and programs to try to change the lives of children and families for the better. But in addition to describing what they learned and what it was like to have new "day jobs"—new tasks, external associations and commitments—they also identified new feelings about themselves and their place in the world. In fact, the kinds of shifts sponsors find most precious about their IHAD experiences—personal growth, a sense of efficacy and hope, and a keen appreciation of the sustaining value of relationships—are the same benefits they want most for their dreamers.

It's a bit arbitrary to try to distinguish cleanly between learning that happens in the head and learning that happens in the heart. When we love a landscape, a song, a person, we love with our whole being. Nevertheless, this chapter tries to unpack the meaning of the heartfelt emotions that these sponsors experienced because of their involvement in IHAD. When they talk about the personal impact of their extended experiences with their dreamers, they show us something essential about the intimate rewards of direct engagement and investment in philanthropic efforts.

THE SURPRISING PRESENT

We start with surprise, returning again to Gene Lang's own descriptions of amazement and improbability. Sometimes, he says, he feels that his whole life has been a living dream, "improbable." He remembers what he did, fumbling his way into making a spontaneous promise and then waking up that night "with a chilling thought," or, as we also heard him say, feeling that he had elected to be on the receiving end of a javelin throw. Decades later he adds,

> Only four years after I made the first promise did I realize the impact it could have. I never envisioned that it would be anything more than a relationship with my dreamers. I saw what happened. I was learning a lot.
>
> I had a chance to be a father over again in ways that made me feel good about myself. And I realized that if I could do it, so could others. Now my dreamers still come to see me on Saturday mornings. I've seen three just in the past month.
>
> You never know where things are going. You just never know how one person, without intention, can have meaning for another. . . . Years ago, if you had told me I'd ever do something like this, I'd have said, "You're out of your mind. It's the last thing in the world you'll catch me doing!" And now I often find myself thinking, if I hadn't done this, I don't know what my life would mean.

Without his promise, without his dreamers, Lang doesn't know what his life would mean. And other sponsors, even those who took the leap later and with more knowledge about what it would entail, echo what he says about the meaning of engagement. Sponsoring is "life-changing in terms of impact," says one. Another describes sponsoring as "a lot of work, all engrossing, wonderful. Probably the ten best years of my life." A third says of herself and her husband that the IHAD years were the "ultimate mixed blessing of [our] lives: how could we abandon it?" A fourth, a man who has given large amounts of money to many charities and built major civic structures in his town, has this to say:

The bottom line, as everybody will tell you, is that for those of us who were sponsors, this was an enriching lifetime experience. We got more out of it than the kids did. For anybody who's rich, it's pretty easy to write a check. That's no big deal. But if you're able to really give your time, energy, guts, your abilities to help others, well, that's the true meaning of giving. The reward.

Had these sponsors ever gotten this kind of "return" on a single investment? What was so "enriching" about it? What exactly do they mean when, one after another, they insist that they got more from the sponsoring experience than their dreamers?

George Norman was much younger than Lang when he became a sponsor. He's told us that the business he started in college always had very strong links to the community. But when he thinks about his IHAD experience he sees it as "a first step" that "addicted" him to life-long community leadership. For him, participating in the program reinforced what he knows will be a sustaining relationship between him and the world.

> I didn't really expect the impact IHAD would have in terms of how addicted I would get to wanting to be and remain involved in community. It just sucked me in, and willingly. There's so much opportunity to do things. That first step opened up all these avenues. Instead of being like some of my friends who spend all their time building their businesses, I chose to do that half-time, and spend the other half [of my] time in the community. And that decision just opened up this avenue that I've never wanted to step out of again—this avenue of engagement.

> It's not that I didn't realize that these problems or these hardships existed. But the understanding is just on such a different level. You see what it's like: being in somebody's home year after year after year, watching as people move from the projects to their own little first house, bailing out a kid from jail, going to court, visiting a kid in a juvenile detention center—you see what it all feels like.

> It all gives so much more dimension to who I am as a person. I can speak from experience now. You know, you can read it in a book but until you've smelled it, felt it, seen it, it's different. In many ways I think I'm much more believable now because I didn't learn this second hand. My experiences enable me to be a much more effective leader. I'm not sure I can predict the future right now, or what exactly I want, but I know I want to continue giving back to the community.

For George, philanthropic engagement has opened up "avenues," giving him one opportunity after another to gain firsthand experience that adds legitimacy to his role in the community. He hadn't expected it, but the process of personalized, extended giving actually strengthens the connections between the giver and the present moment in which he lives.

Living intensely in the present is one hallmark of the persistent youthfulness referenced in Chapter 2 as "neoteny." It seems characteristic of IHAD sponsors—and perhaps of many engaged philanthropists. Across the lifespan, it appears, they spend little time looking back. One sponsor in his early forties says he "can't remember what life was like without this program and these kids in my life." Nor is another, nearly seventy, at all interested in thinking about what an unengaged life might be like.

> First of all, I'm sixty-nine years old and I look at this project and say to myself, "If my church doesn't sponsor another class, I'm going to find something else to do. I am going to have to stay involved somehow, some way. There are just too many problems out there not to try to do something about them."

> I don't look back. I'm here, I'm now. I recognize there are all kinds of problems out there, and I have a personal feeling that the way to solve most of them is to deal with the children. You just have to get involved with them, in their lives, because nobody else is. You do this because you can change lives, and the kids benefit. In the end, you benefit so much. In the relationships that you develop with the kids and the things you learn that you just never knew before.

There it is again. "In the end you benefit so much." To some, the benefits, the enrichment, seem to mean a terrific invigoration that comes from their direct personal involvement in their projects and in the world today.

Lang, an archetypal example of enduring youthfulness who is now in his eighties, has thrown himself into creating another bold, hopeful venture, called Project Pericles. This initiative aims to persuade colleges and universities to make institutional commitments to community service in a way that moves beyond perfunctory efforts and truly integrates service experiences with classroom pedagogy and student learning. Lang continues to be passionate about providing young people with what he has had: meaningful opportunities to make the world a better place. Though frequently urged to write about his life by friends and family, Lang says he is far too busy, too immersed in the present, in his work, in his relationships, and in learning new things "to take the time to go back over the past." What's more, he worries that people, particularly his dreamers, might misunderstand any kind of account of his life. If they were to read it as a reductive, self-serving attempt to celebrate what he has done, that would be a catastrophe, he says.

> The experiences, the relationships themselves, are too intrinsically precious and personal to me. The way I see it, if I can do this, it's the right thing to do. Having money is not enough. You must know how to use it. I get such great pleasure from using it as I have—not for my ego but because it's the right thing to do. I only wish other people would know how right Thoreau was when he said, "When you give anything, you give a piece of your soul."

> Once you begin, this is something that captivates you— for all the right reasons. Its spirit has wings—like a virus, a good one. Viruses mutate to accommodate to each situation. This idea brings everything together for people. It becomes a kind of envelope into which anything can fit, and everyone becomes better for it. Personally, I just try to deal with life in a meaningful way, where there's room for the right kind of actions.

It is clear that the "right kind of actions," for Lang, means, above all, building relationships. This is one meaning of the word "enriching." Lang has found that when relationships grow from giving they carry a captivating kind of contagion that can infect others "for all the right reasons."

In their own ways, IHAD sponsors say that because of what they have learned and discovered from personalized philanthropy, they will not step away from the present moment—the one life they've been given. Engaged philanthropy has created a vitalizing, robust connection between them and the world. In some ways they're saying they are more fully realized as people than they would have otherwise been.

To the sponsors I interviewed, "enrichment" means other things, too. For one thing, they have been very moved to see how their commitments to philanthropic engagement have influenced those to whom they are closest—members of their own families. Secondly, as Lang has said, they treasure the enduring relationships themselves—the loving bonds that have developed for them through giving and getting of sponsorship. Thirdly, a number of sponsors suggest that, in some way, engaged philanthropy has fed their spirits. And, finally, many find deep comfort in knowing that at the end of their lives they will be able to see themselves as people who have made a difference in the world.

SEEING CHANGE CLOSE TO HOME

There's a difference between the kinds of "ripples" described in the previous chapter—when an intervention influences people and institutions—and seeing that something we do has an impact on members of our own biological families. The latter often affects us deeply.

The Hulls, as we know, undertook IHAD sponsorship from the beginning as a family. They have told us how much the experience has shaped the work of their family foundation. While the three Hull daughters watched their dreamers mature and finish high school, each was pursuing professional advocacy training in different professions—education, public policy, and business. Now they are all actively invested in nourishing and empowering residents in the low-income community where the foundation has strong commitments. At the 2003 IHAD sponsor conference, when Sara Hull was asked to speak to new sponsors, she likened her family's then eighteen-year relationship with IHAD and its impact to holding a comet with incredible heat and energy and light, streaking across the sky with a tail sixteen times as long as the comet itself. It just never, never ends.

My sisters and I have talked about it. When our kids are a bit older, we'd like to take on an IHAD dream class going forward. Because there's just nothing better. I feel selfish saying this, and I don't mean to minimize the effect we've had on our dreamers. But IHAD has had a profound, absolutely transformative experience on all of us. What a lot you have to look forward to!

When you ask Ann Hull how it feels to have such a validating family, she smiles quietly and says very simply, "Lucky."

Many sponsors told me they wanted to pass their convictions about justice and equity on to their children. One woman whose children are still young believes that example is the best teacher.

For me, I don't think you can really teach your children by telling them things. I don't think they really listen. The only way you have an impact is through your own actions. Watching you, your children will one day grow up and realize, "Wow, my mother did lots of really good things. That's what I should do with my life!" I feel that's the only way to teach them.

Others confirm her hypothesis. One woman recalled the many times when her daughters chose to go with her to dreamer award ceremonies rather than join their high school friends for football or basketball games. Laura and Richard Joseph described daughters who have created various projects that draw on entrepreneurial and philanthropic aptitudes that they seem to have learned, at least partly, from their parents. Frank Matthews, whose children all served with him as mentors in the early years of his first project, doesn't doubt for a moment that "your kids are watching." One of his sons is now a missionary in Peru.

And then there's George Norman's story about his four-year-old son, Charlie.

Our kids have grown up with these kids, and it's been a really special thing for them. Most kids coming from where we come from don't get exposed to "that world." As a result, they don't see it as "our world." But my kids do. They're learning so many lessons. When we have pumpkin parties or birthday parties or any kind of celebrations with the dreamers, my own kids are always there. They have been through the good times and some of the tough times with our dreamers.

They think about one dreamer, in particular, as a member of our family. Here's the best example of what I mean. When our dreamers were younger, whoever had a birthday each month we took out to dinner and to a bookstore so they could buy a book for their birthday. After one of these trips, my wife was headed home. It was the middle of winter, near Christmas. Right outside the project where our dreamers live there was a homeless man and a small boy who was probably about four—the same age as my son at the time. They were standing on the corner and the little kid didn't have a coat on. My wife turned to my son and said, "Charlie, that little boy is homeless and doesn't have a coat. Would you mind giving him your coat?"

So Charley thought for a moment and then he said, "Okay, Mommy," and they gave him the coat. About two weeks later they were at a mall nearby. It was around Christmas so there was a Santa Claus there. My son said, "Mommy, I want to go talk to Santa." We're Jewish and my son goes to a Jewish day school, but my wife said, "Well, I guess so."

So Charlie went and sat on Santa's lap and proceeded to tell him, "Santa, I'm Jewish, so I don't believe in you. But a couple of weeks ago my Mommy and I were driving down town, and there was this little boy and he didn't have a coat and I gave him my coat because he needed it. I don't think he's going to have a very nice Christmas, and I was wondering if you would stop by his house and make sure he gets presents." At four years old he has that awareness. That's one of the gifts we've gotten through sponsoring. I think for my son to recognize these things at this age and then independently to do something about it is spectacular.

George is right. It is unusual for a four-year-old to understand and act on empathy. This incident speaks volumes about the power of example to build the capacity for compassion, particularly when the modeling is going on within a child's immediate family.

Stories about how sponsorship may have influenced the philanthropists' children are complemented by other vignettes about ways that their engagement also seems to have affected their parents and others close to them. George's father, for example, has become more generous in the community than ever before. His parents had no history of being involved with youth in the city, but, George told me,

> Over the last five years, my dad has really changed. He didn't give money away at all, but now he writes a lot of checks to a lot of different things. He's changed.

In previous chapters, Chuck Peterson told us how I Have a Dream became a way to cross political divides within his family. In both his family-owned business and in private life, Chuck is an ambassador for community awareness.

> There are stories in the news all the time about places like Chechnya and East Timor. The people I work with are astonished that I even know where [these places] are. There's a secretary here with a map on her wall, and I win trivia contests with her all the time about things that are on the local radio. She keeps saying, "How the hell do you know?" And I say, "See it right here? That's East Timor. Start listening for it, and I promise you'll hear a story about that on the local radio." And then three days later she'll come into work saying, "Oh my God! Did you hear what happened in East Timor?"
>
> That's the point I'm always trying to make. It's on the radio, but because you don't know where it is, it doesn't mean anything to you. And this is the same thing that happens in our own world, right here at home. Our dreamers are from a

neighborhood in this community, less than five miles from where I grew up. But because my family never knew where it was or who they were, it didn't mean anything to them. We can execute kids, we can put them in cages for their lives, we can under-fund their schools, we can abandon their neighborhoods—and it might just as well be happening in East Timor for all they know. This is not an indictment of my family. It's a comment about humans and their ability, or inability, to process things they don't know anything about.

For me and my mother and now—finally, after years of work—my brother, we are paying our social mortgage. It's a personal investment that is not just money but exposure. It's taking a risk to try to do our best to do something, to give back something in response to centuries of racism and deprivation and impoverishment. For my surviving grandmother, my stepfather, and my stepsister, IHAD is a hand up, not a handout. It's opening a door that the kids have to walk through, a non-governmental, local, private initiative, voluntarily helping the public schools to do what they ought to do: provide opportunity—not equality of results, perhaps, but at least opportunity. And boy, have we had discussions about this, over and over and over!

At our annual family gathering during the past few years I've made up little cards with pictures of all the dreamers in their graduation gowns, saying what institutions they're at. As they open these cards, I know that different members of my family see different things: injustices remediated or opportunities opened. All I care about is that there have been more faces, more gowns. And that I've actually had some small hand in doing something concrete that was good. This program has allowed me to sleep at night. Without it, I couldn't work at this family business company, and I couldn't be a member of my family without being at constant war with myself and my family over our success.

To me, the most profound effect I hoped this program would have on my family is that when they hear the evening news and there's a story about a teen mom, or a welfare queen, or a kid shooting somebody, or a drug dealer on the corner, there's now a real face and a name attached to the incident. They connect our worlds and say, "Wow! I know kids who live on that street! I've been in that neighborhood and I know the pressures and challenges that those kids face. I know a kid who grew up in that neighborhood and has made it and works in our business today. I know another kid who knew us and worked with us and is now in jail." For my family, there is now some texture to the human reality of poverty. It's no longer just something you leap over.

Chuck is determined to make the people around him regularly aware of the reality of hardship and inequity. He cares deeply for people in his workplace and his family, and he has changed the consciousness of many of them. For his own self-respect he needs to know that his family business is engaged in more than profit-making, that it is using engaged philanthropy to bridge differences and strengthen bonds within his community and his family. As many of us know, in most families it can be very difficult to connect across political differences—even to talk about them. But Chuck continues to remind people that we're all standing on common ground, together. As people become aware that hardship is real, they understand its implications for us all. And they can find themselves drawing on their capacity to make a difference.

IRRESISTIBLE RELATIONSHIPS

Lang isn't the only sponsor who speaks of philanthropic engagement as a "captivating" experience. When IHAD sponsors talk about the rewards that they have gotten from their personal involvement with their dreamers, there's a tone in their voices that implies a kind of inevitability, an *irresistibleness* about both the children and the process. It's almost as if it goes without saying: once you start down the path of personal engagement you'll never turn back—it's too rewarding. As one told me,

> You cannot meet these children—who, at this young age, really are open to almost anything—and know you can help them without getting involved. You just can't help it.

Tessa Bloom speaks about the experience this way:

> We get far more out of this program than our dreamers.
> Without question, this is the most rewarding philanthropic
> group I've ever been involved with.
>
> My husband and I do a lot of philanthropic stuff, but this is
> the one that makes the difference. Just to see these kids, to
> see the look in their eyes and the appreciation, to know you
> can really change the life of a person in such a simple way: it
> makes you feel it's almost a scandal that this is all it takes to
> change life for these children and their parents. I love these
> children! I love to look at them. And I find myself thinking,
> "These are such beautiful, kind, wonderful kids. Where
> would they have been if we hadn't had this program?" From
> the ways the kids respond, it just proves that if you just give
> someone an opportunity, you know, they can succeed!

While many sponsors say they think of themselves as the primary beneficiaries of IHAD, only a few are as open as Tessa in talking about how much she loves these kids. She loves looking at them. She loves knowing that something she's done—which, from her point of view, is very simple—can help them to succeed. She frames it as the giving of opportunity—which is how Lou Irving sees it, too.

> For me it just simply boils down to this: if you give them
> a chance, they can do it! Just give them the opportunity!
> I don't care who they are or where they come from! Given
> the opportunity, they can succeed, and some of them splen-
> didly. I love these kids! I don't care if they go to college, all
> of them. I want them to be better people. And the qual-
> ity of their life, I know, is measurably better than it would
> have been otherwise. They understand certain things. They
> understand about helping other people. And they under-
> stand about being helped.

Lou and Tessa aren't patting themselves on the backs for having put these children on a path of possibility. They're searching for ways to articulate what they themselves have gotten from seeing dreamers succeed where so many kids fail. Lou's dreamers showered him with birthday cards for his eightieth birthday. He confesses that he loves them, describing them as the "blessings" in his life, and is sure they have no idea how much they mean to him.

From a distance, these anecdotes may seem to be suggesting something about pure charity at its core. As we're often told, "Virtue is its own reward." "It is more precious to give than receive." But the personal gratification of engaged philanthropy can be so profound that the data encourage us to ponder these old adages, to explore the meaning of "reward" and "enrichment." We know that altruism always bestows some benefits on the altruist. This is very lucky for all of us because, as Bill Shore reminds us, "Altruism has its limits but self-interest rarely does."[41] As Lou says, "The more kids we can help, the better off we're *all* going to be." And it is certainly true that intervening effectively with low-income children is a win-win proposition for all of us. But, many sponsors also focus on the intimate joy of relationship—between them and their dreamers, and among the sponsors themselves.

Speaking of his fellow sponsors, Hal Davies says,

> One of the great joys of our life, and I think everybody in our program would agree, is the kind of people that the IHAD program attracts. You meet people from all different walks of life, all different backgrounds, all different breeds, people you never really would meet otherwise. And those friendships stand the test of time. It really is extraordinary. It's a wonderful group of human beings that you are just very proud to call a friend.

Hal is proud to be a sponsor and grateful to have colleagues who want to make the same kinds of commitment he does. As he and others say, it's valuable to have opportunities to become friends with a diverse group of people, including some whose politics differ from your own. Earlier we heard Tad Johnson say that from the very beginning of his involvement with IHAD, he has treasured his friendships with other sponsors—"the kind of people I want to run with."

> This is the kind of person that I was meant to be. They are making something happen. It's done my character a world of good. Knowing that there are people with the same desires to do something significant is like finding kindred spirits. It

makes you feel that you're not running alone. I know people of real substance and I really feel blessed that I can play in this game. I'm just glad to be on this bus!

In the same way that good friends can sometimes feel like mentors to one another, sponsors draw on what is best in one another. For Tad, being in the company of people he admires reinforces the importance and legitimacy of what he himself does. Another sponsor who is not inclined to pat herself on the back explains how much it's meant to her to be associated with such a dedicated group of people.

> Please understand that I'm not saying this to praise myself. But it takes a very special kind of person to do this, I think, because it's a very long-term commitment. You have to say to yourself, "I am going to do this, and I am going to be there for the long term. I'm really not going to get rich or famous or anything else out of doing this. I'm just doing this for these kids." It is a long time. But I have never met a group of nicer people anywhere, any time, through anything I've been involved with, in my life, than IHAD sponsors. They just are all such great people. It's been wonderful.

Here again we note that what happens to dreamers, over the course of their involvement with IHAD, also happens to sponsors. Positive, caring relationships solidify an individual's strengths and bring richness to one's life.

THE POWER OF CONNECTION

Some years back, in an op-ed piece for his local paper, Mike O'Donnell wrote,

> The rewards? Getting a boy out of jail, seeing the charges dropped, and helping him get back into school. Watching a child who saw his uncle shot finish as one of the top 40 high school students in the district.

> Rafael stops my car and shouts, "I got an A!" Raquel is one of the state's young poets. And Pedro and Justin say, "Watch me!" when we go swimming at the Y. Isn't that

what it's really all about—young kids having someone to say "Watch me!" to? We are getting an awful lot more out of IHAD—in terms of affection, reward, the realization of human potential—than we ever put into it. Meg and I haven't lost our sense of wonder about these young minds, and no one is ever going to tell us that these Dreamers, given the same love and encouragement that we had when we were kids, are not going to make it.

Mike wants to bring some balance and fairness into the lives of poor kids. Why should they not have someone watching them learn to swim—just as so many others have had? And why should philanthropists not have the joy of seeing that with their "love and encouragement" poor kids can beat the odds? That's the point for Mike. He's a lawyer, and it's clear that he wants to see justice done. And for Meg O'Donnell, relationships are life's ultimate blessing.

> You don't know what a gift this is to us. You have to understand that this is something we were honored and privileged to be involved with.

> Every child invited us into their home, wherever it was, whatever the circumstances, whatever the numbers of parents and relatives. They invited us into their hearts and their lives. I have a phone message upstairs right now that I left on my answering machine—I often leave messages on for a long time, because I think we need to be reminded of people and voices and hearts and souls. Right now there's a message from Jose saying, "Hello, Meg! Hello, Mike! I love you! Here's what's happening."

> Hearing that voice brings right back every memory we have of Jose and his terrible problems. For one thing, he had a terrible eating problem. We'd take him out to a restaurant or a picnic and there would be cakes in his pockets, oranges in his pockets, every opening filled with food. Dear Jose! What really made an impression on him was becoming a member of the Boy Scouts, where he had victories. He got medals. He succeeded in areas where he'd never succeeded before. We are so proud of him. But we've sort of changed

with the kids. People are always saying "Aren't you wonder-ful for doing this?" And I always say I've gotten more out of it in terms of gratification and reward than I ever put into it. I'm sure that if you ask any of the other sponsors, they'll all say the same thing. . . .

To have them accept us in their lives reminds me of the story about the starfish, you know? That guy who's taking starfish off the sand and throwing them back into the water, one by one? Another guy comes up and says to him, "There are probably eighty trillion starfish on this planet. What are you doing?" And he says, "I'm saving starfish. I'm saving the lives of the ones I'm throwing back, even if I can't save them all."

What do we hear? That sponsors don't want to let go of dreamer voices on the answering machine. They hold on. They don't want to forget how far the kids have come. They feel hope and pride in their young successes. And deep down they treasure knowing that they are welcome and valued in a world where many children are in great need of the same kind of support from adults that they had as kids.

More than a decade after Hal Davies first met his sixth-grade dreamers, four of the men—they are now in their late twenties—come to his house every six weeks.

[We] watch football, have a beer, and talk about life. To be able to talk about any subject in the world with these guys without have to worry about being politically cor-rect—just to talk about life, to find out what's going on in their community, to keep understanding their frustrations and joys—it makes me smarter, wiser, more sensitive to the world I live in. This is one of the greatest rewards of the program. What good luck it is. True family.

What's happened here? Dreamers have become like cherished family to Hal. Their continuing presence in his life keeps him alert to what's happening in his city and "smarter, wiser, more sensitive" to the world he lives in. Many of us value the ways that children—whether they are born to us or not—keep us in touch with the world as it changes. Such connections enable us to keep translating who we have been to the next generation—and to understand the challenges that we all face together. What could be more precious, more enriching, than lifelong learning and strong connections with people we care for, and who care for us?

At this point we must approach the delicate concept of "love," though it makes some sponsors uneasy to use that word. While it may be more comfortable to talk about "empathy," "compassion," and "attachment," most sponsors agree that, whatever we may decide to call it, a deep mutual regard between them and their dreamers is the strongest determinant of dreamer success. As Laura Joseph says,

> For want of a less smarmy word, I think it's about love, I think it's about connection. That's the miraculous part to me. Children who have been abused by society still have enough trust to let some other stranger in, and they do that because they feel a genuine connection with someone else.

This kind of connection is not a one-way phenomenon, especially when it lasts for years. We've heard Tessa and Lou comfortably say they "love these kids." And no matter how sponsors frame their testimonials, their voices ring with deep affection for their dreamers.

During the first year of sponsorship, Mara Emerson started baking Christmas cookies. There were seventy-one new children in her life.

> I love to bake. I wasn't big on cookies, but I love to bake. The first year I said to myself, "I think I'll make Christmas cookies." And by the time I was done I'd baked one hundred dozen assorted Christmas cookies and put them all on little plates. One was a sugar cookie, decorated with the kid's name. I handed them out on the last day before Christmas vacation started. They were a big hit. And in September of the next year, the kids started saying, "Are you going to do that again?"
>
> You know, you can freeze most cookies. But the first year I didn't know that. The first year I was a little nuts. And that was not something I could ask the national office how to do. By the third year, when I had eighty-six kids in the sixth grade, I was up to one hundred and twenty dozen: it

took me three weeks. And I just loved it! I went to the kids and I said, "I know you've all had store-bought cookies and sometimes somebody at home makes cookies, but nobody makes cookies like I do. What do you think I put in the cookies?" And they'd tell me they have sugar, eggs, flour, and chocolate. "Yes. But what else?" I'd ask. I'd say, "My cookies have ambition and success and honesty and caring and a sense of humor in large doses! So you be sure to eat them up!" And they do!

And I'm still doing it. I make about one hundred dozen and they know what's in there: lots and lots of love. They're always afraid that I'm going to get tired of it and not do it again. Now I make a big plate for the transportation department, a plate for the guidance department, a plate for administration. And they all know that they're loved. It's personal. They know that it takes time and caring: I didn't just go out and buy them. And it makes a huge difference. I want to tell people how much their participation and caring means to me, and this is just a little something I can do, a labor of love.

Mara's precious recipe helps us understand what engagement means to other sponsors, too. It includes a host of hopes—ambitions, success, good humor. Mara is as nurtured by her attachments and connections as are those to whom she is so devoted. Like the other sponsors, she is giving and getting back, caught up in the irresistible web that binds dreamers and sponsors together in attachments that generate meaning for many years.

"YOU CAN'T DO IT ALONE"

If love means many things to people, so does faith. And though some IHAD sponsors talk about the meaning of sponsoring in relation to deeply held religious beliefs, for many the word "faith" is not necessarily associated with organized religion. In trying to understand this delicate aspect of enrichment, we must try to parse out what sponsors mean by "faith" and "spirit."

In the previous chapter, we heard sponsors express frustrations at feeling powerless in certain situations. Some were angry about school bureaucracies, some about the power of the teacher's union. Others complained about the heartbreaking inefficiencies of human service systems, about the isolating consequences of racism, and about how little most people seem to care. Feeling powerless is not easy for any of us and, partly because they are so action-oriented, IHAD sponsors chafe fiercely when they feel helpless. Although they may quickly begin to understand why things are the way they are, coming up against the limits of what they can do for their dreamers can make them rail against what they call "the culture." Some, like Will Christopher, place part of the blame for the problems of poor children—teen pregnancy, crime, and drugs, for example—on what they see as a tendency for low-income people to be passive rather than proactive.

> The inner-city family has broken down. It accepts single parenthood as a norm, having guys wear clothes that are intimidating as hell to white people walking on the same side of the street, the worship of destructive role models. And the whole culture is one that pisses me off now because it's perpetuated. These are the kinds of things that are so painful.

> Enormous amounts of people's money and time have been spent on these seventy-five kids. But this certainly can't be the answer to the "big picture" problems. I don't have the answer to all the problems for all our inner-city kids, but the strength of the family unit is really important. And when we look at the bigger picture, this project is such a small microcosm of effort.

Will gets terribly impatient with what he sees as people's limited capacities to fight against the bad influences that are handicapping their youth. He wants to make a bigger difference than he can because of circumstances that seem beyond his control.

Sam Hull's perturbation is intense too, but it's focused on how few people are willing to get involved.

> This experience—giving, getting back, and growing with dreamers and your community—becomes a complete part of your life. I know not everybody wants to do it. But unfor-

tunately most people who could afford to do something don't want to. That's the sad part. There are a lot of shallow people, a lot of people who are very wealthy who don't even give very much to charity. I don't know what they're saving it for.

Others I spoke to agreed. Now that he understands all the things that dreamers are up against, one man said, he becomes angry at what he perceives to be many wealthy people's self-serving ways. They are more devoted to

> trying to figure out how they can avoid paying estate taxes and pass the money on to their children than worrying about saving the world. I can't understand it. . . . I always felt sorry for the underdog. And I just enjoy giving money away. Maybe it's genetic.

This last comment, not spoken at all in jest, reflects the frustration many sponsors feel about the limits of their own power and about the lack of interest on the part of most of their financial peers in helping the poor. The intensity of their distress echoes the intensity of their engagement with the dreamers.

When patience and the search for understanding don't seem to be enough, some sponsors find themselves looking for more encompassing ways to counter their sense of their own limitations. One is simply having faith. Many sponsors would interpret that term in a very secular, humanistic way; for others the faith that sustains their efforts is rooted in their religious beliefs.

Ben Howard, one of several sponsors I met for whom religion is central in life, described the very singular pilgrimage he found himself taking when he became an engaged philanthropist. Initially, he had a very specific, pragmatic reason to become an IHAD sponsor. As a member of an old political family, he was thinking about running for elected office. His intention was to campaign as a successful businessman who was not only an entrepreneur but also someone who was actively involved in serving the poor. Like other sponsors, he launched his dreamer campaign somewhat hastily, but his business was thriving and he felt confident that he could solve any problem that came his way.

I had a beautiful house, a beautiful wife, and I thought I could do anything. I wanted to go to Congress to solve problems, to use my influence. I thought that problems could be solved systematically, with legislation and programs and policy. But what happened? The more I learned about the problems, the more I learned that people in government are fairly impotent. The reality of these kids' problems moves you away from thinking [in a political] way. You discover that most problems are not resolved by legislation but by relationships.

Life is so bizarre. I always wondered, "What are we doing here?" I mean the wife, the family, the Volvo? At some point, it's all going to go away. The reality is that life is miserable for people on the top and on the bottom. They both share a certain kind of knowledge that no one loves them. . . . It's very comforting to think you can have a plan for these children's lives. But the reality is so humbling! As somebody told me recently, "If you want to hear God laugh, tell him your plan."

The faith perspective has become mine since this project began. I hadn't understood the concept of grace at all. But I became a born-again Christian ten or eleven years ago. I came to understand that God doesn't want me to visit the person in prison because he wants me to do everything for the prisoner. He wants me to do the work so that He can be with me. The problem with *noblesse oblige* is that it's up to me to do everything. Then if it doesn't work, I'm a failure. But I can't do everything.

Somebody was just pointing out that there's a big difference between whether you try to take life's problems and hold them all in your own hands or extend your hands, hold them palm upwards and open. When you open your hands, you're not giving the problems back to God. You're just saying that you can't hold them all yourself. If you try to do that, your hands get very, very tired. "These are your people," you want to say to God. "But I am your person, too, and it doesn't look good right now. You love these people,

God. Please help me to let go. Show me how I can help these people to help themselves, with your support." The purpose of life is to glorify God, as someone told me about eight years ago. This simplified all sorts of things for me.

We all know that poverty is ugly. And I think we all will acknowledge that poverty won't go away. Christ said, "The poor will always be with us." But they don't have to be naked, hungry, cold. There's a feeling of devastation that comes from feeling powerless. The sense of powerlessness that comes from trying to help and finding yourself completely inadequate is enormous. IHAD sponsoring makes you go to places your life would never have gone. It teaches you that growth is painful. And that the absence of pain is the absence of growth. In the end, you really learn that giving is the reward.

Ben's intimate account of his spiritual transformation is generous in its detail. It helps us understand how belief systems do assuage the pain of powerlessness. And it also illustrates the kinds of burdens imposed by a social code like *noblesse oblige*, which, in Ben's case, encouraged him to think he could fix any problem that came his way. It was not only his own impotence that pained Ben but also the recognition that even government, in which he had previously had great confidence, cannot simply step in and instantly "solve" the problem of poverty. Ben's born-again belief system has given him access to a higher power that allows him to transcend the intense distress of limitation. And he has turned his pain into the lesson that, in the end, "giving is the reward."

No other sponsor told me of such an intense or dramatic spiritual transformation during the course of sponsorship, but several others spoke of the importance of religion in their lives and philanthropic efforts. In Chapter 5, we heard Frank Matthews explain the logic behind the explicit evangelizing that he and his fellow mentors do in their third neighborhood project, but what's relevant here is that his religious faith also helps mitigate his distress about most people's selfishness and enables him to find joy in his own good works.

You know, I often think Lord looks down on us and just kind of giggles a lot. Because we learn one thing and we talk it, but we don't do much of it. If our goal as Christians is to become like Jesus, we're not carrying out that kind of life. We've got a long way to go. When we see people in need, we walk right by them! Jesus never would have done that. Never! So what are we to do? Are we just supposed to say, "Well, that's not my responsibility?" Well, it is your responsibility. . . .

I see the things happening around me, and they disturb me, but none of them surprise me any more. When people come up to me and say, "What you're doing is so wonderful," I say, "Get your checkbook and the keys to your car and get down to the south side of town. You're wasting your life and you're being selfish and you have no idea what the rewards are!"

Growing old can be a tough maintenance problem, but maturity is different. I feel privileged. I'm just a lot more interested in others than I am in myself. I really have a joy in my life now that I never had when I was young. This is who I want to be. It makes me very happy.

Ken Robinson shares Frank's beliefs. He has also discovered that the experience of giving and caring for others in the world has enriched his later years.

You know, you go along through life and God opens up different avenues for you to go down. Now I'm involved with other grassroots things. Not big charities, but basic stuff like feeding centers, prison ministries, a children's home, a city ministry for people in horrible circumstances. Simple programs where I can make a difference, things that are successful.

You see, making money is success. . . . But there are so many multi-millionaires who are totally empty, totally bored with their lives, who don't live a life of significance. They have the million-dollar house or two, the apartment in Florida, all the cars they need. And they find out they are still empty, still unfulfilled . . . You know, as you come to the end, your life is centered around things that really make a difference. You want to move from a life of success to a life of significance.

And you want to help others and change other people's lives
so that they can live a life of significance too: this is one of
the things we have a high degree of interest in doing.

The common themes return. Making a difference is the goal. As is
moving beyond the self-centered, unfulfilled, empty life. Like Frank,
Ken sees it as part of his mission to motivate others to discover the joy
of giving.

Not surprisingly, sponsors have many different relationships
to what we are calling faith. Many refer more to a sense of destiny or
spirit than to the tenets of any specific religion. Mara Emerson's statement that she always felt her relationship with her dreamers was "just
meant to be" is one example. Another woman told me,

> Problems come up, when we are trying to figure out how to
> do something. And then suddenly something will happen
> and we'll see the solution. Sometimes we all look at each
> other and say, "You know, that was nothing that we did.
> We're not that good. There's a hand in this that goes way
> beyond us."

George Norman's project has never had any affiliation with an
organized religion, but sometimes, as he watches the transformations
of his dreamers, he says he feels something akin to awe. George thinks
it's important to distinguish between "spiritual" and "religious."

> Sitting down, reciting the same prayers year after year,
> doesn't do a lot for me. "Spiritual," though, means putting
> the words of the prayers, the values they represent into
> action. This is the work I do in the community.

> I think it all boils down to making the world a better place
> by being there, by being a part of it. That can be some-
> thing as simple as picking up litter on the ground or raising
> money for United Way or mentoring a kid. Each person, in
> their way, in their own place in life, can make the world a
> better place by doing very simple things. And it all depends
> on who you are. You know, for some people it's very easy to
> write a check for a million dollars. In fact, that may be easier
> [for them] to do than it is for someone else to volunteer in a

classroom, or actually spend time with a kid, or help elderly people in an old folks' home. But there are many different ways. It's not how much money you give, it's how much of yourself that you give, to make this world a better place for all of us. That's what counts.

There's much that joins George both to more religiously observant sponsors like Ken and Frank and to those whose faith is essentially secular. They all share a kind of pity for the person who feels satisfied by simply writing a check. They are passionate about wanting to make the world a better place, and over and over again they emphasize what engagement—their personal involvement in their projects—has given back to them.

Without exception, in one way or another, IHAD sponsors "thank their lucky stars." Richard Joseph says he's always felt he's led "a charmed life." But these philanthropists do not take their good fortune for granted. Even those who say that their philanthropy is the result of a kind of obligation to "give back" use phrases like "by an accident of birth," or "There, but for the grace of God, go I." Even sponsors who have no interest in organized religion feel a kind of humility about the extraordinary luck that has put them in positions where they can act "to make the world a better place."

When Laura Joseph speaks about the kind of joy she has experienced during her many years with dreamers, she says, with some embarrassment, that it sometimes feels as though the work is "directed," "done through you." She's uneasy about this feeling—as she was uncomfortable using that "smarmy" word, "love," to describe the kinds of relational joys she has gotten from engaged philanthropy. But she echoes comments I heard from many other sponsors when she says,

> You can't do this work alone. Whatever your motivation is, it's a communal effort, from the time you have the idea. There's Mother Theresa, and Gene Lang, but they couldn't do it alone either. They need us as foot soldiers.

> It's kind of a soupy thing to say, but I think it's a long chain. We all have ancestors in whatever we do. Let's say you're seven years old and someone gives you Clara Barton to read. I remember this quite clearly. I thought to myself,

"Oh! That's what I want to be!" Of course it gets erased.
But now I'm watching it in my grandchildren.

Our children take their children into retirement homes. They
draw with the elderly, or bring them cookies on Valentine's
Day, or pictures. One of our daughters supports a community
action for the arts program that's designed around the idea of
supporting social change for the disabled. I didn't teach my
kids this. They're just doing it. It's not accidental. Embarrass-
ing as this is, I think it's directed; I think it's done through
you. If you're really lucky, you get directed. You wake up one
day and you think, "I couldn't have done this! Where did I
get that idea? Why am I doing this?"

It's all about being connected to the universe. That's the
basis of it: being in connection. Take our dreamer Kenny,
back from college and graduate school as a social worker.
Here [he] is now, in his old neighborhood. He's going to
have to learn to straddle both worlds. But he can. Because
he came back to us wanting to give his experience back to
the next set of kids. It gets passed on. The work goes on
from one generation to the next. If you can reproduce that
a couple of times in your lifetime, it feels pretty good. But
it's not because of you. I just read something from an Indian
philosopher that I think explains it all: "Whatever is not
given is lost."

So for Laura—and for many engaged philanthropists—the sensa-
tion that good work has a way of carrying its own momentum may or
may not have something to do with organized religion. But there is a
kind of wonder about how things work out and about how profoundly
enriching it is to give of oneself as well as from one's pocketbook.

LOOKING TO THE FUTURE

Philanthropic engagement is invigorating. It has impact not only on
a target cause or community, but also on one's family. And it brings
something like irresistible love and spirit into one's life. In short, it's a
good way to live.

IHAD sponsors are vivid examples of people who have achieved in their lives what Erik Erikson and other stage theorists call generativity and integrity: they see their own lives in perspective and have become committed to guiding the next generation. These are people who make big promises—not just to dreamers, but also to themselves. They are zealous entrepreneurs, determined to beat the odds that threaten so many of their dreamers, and they often go on to tackle other big challenges. They have a tremendous zest for living.

> I enjoy my life! I love it! I enjoy getting up every day and coming into this office. And I have no desire to retire. I'm blessed by circumstances that got me into this crazy business in the first place—and it's fun! It's intellectually stimulating! And all my life I've been blessed with a lot of good things.
>
> So much of life is luck! I can't say everything we tried in business was successful. If I threw things against the wall, and tried them, and they weren't successful, I had the right intelligence to cut my losses pretty quickly. It's a nice life, but I'm not money hungry. I don't go around pushing and driving for big yachts, bigger houses. That's just not my style. I happen to believe in living every single day to the fullest. That's been my philosophy for as long as I can remember. It's the way I've been living almost my whole life.
>
> You know, I didn't have the greatest upbringing. So maybe I decided, well, I'm going to maximize my life, learn from other people's mistakes and my own. And it's been phenomenal. I'm lucky! You know, this is no grand design I have. But [Carol and I] can wake up every morning and look in the mirror and know that some of these kids would not be where they are today if it were not for our program. And if I were to die tomorrow, I wouldn't have any regrets. I would say, boy, I've lived life just the way I want to!

This statement from Will Christopher captures much that is true about his fellow sponsors—and perhaps for engaged philanthropists in general. A combination of random good fortune and hard work has convinced them that it's not only possible but also essential to move beyond material obstacles. This is a conviction that they want to pass on to others, including people who are less fortunate.

Despite their frustrations and complaints, all the sponsors I interviewed seemed heartened by a real sense of accomplishment. They might not choose that word because, from their point of view, there's always so much more to do. "Efficacy"—the power to produce an effect—might be a more acceptable term. And of course positive efficacy is one of the things sponsors want for their dreamers. In return for their investment, financial and personal, they feel they've received a tremendous return. Mara's joy is now and in the future.

> This experience has kept my brain from turning to oatmeal mush from lack of use. But it has also made me feel good that I'm going to leave this earth in a better way than it was before I came, or than it would have been had I not been here. And most of all, the days I go to school are the days I wake up with a smile on my face.

Her reflection about leaving the earth better than it was before she came along is sandwiched between two statements about how much she has learned and the pleasure she gets from going to school. This is typical of IHAD sponsors. They are willing to speak confidently about how their experiences have affected them, and acknowledge that it feels good to have made a difference, but they do not want to take too much credit for what they've accomplished.

For one young sponsor, still in his thirties, it might seem a little early to be thinking about the end of his life, but already he feels that making a difference , no matter how small, will matter to him then.

> I really feel that, though it's not a huge group of kids, even with this small group of kids, I'm making a difference. What's that quote about? "You make a life by what you give?"

> Basically I feel that, even though I've got family and friends and work, this is something I can do. I can't do anything about systemic change. I can't do anything about world poverty or about war. But I can raise a little bit of money and help this group of kids and do it in a way that improves the likelihood that it can have a positive impact on them. To improve the chances that these kids will have a productive,

happy life is very gratifying. I really feel, at my core, that this is a good thing for me to do—the right thing to do—and that when I close my eyes to die, I will feel I have had a good life. IHAD is a big part of the reason for that.

A much older sponsor, who's now in his sixties, feels exactly the same way.

> Sponsoring is a great experience. As I see it, I'm one of the few people who will be able to look back and think about lives I have made better. I have to believe that.

> I'm not going to make it to ninety, but I have to believe that I'll be able to look back and really say I made a difference, as opposed to just giving money to a charity. When you do that, you don't really know where your money is. If I give money to the Salvation Army, I can't say that I made a difference. This is really different. I'm optimistic that I'll stay in touch with some of these kids in later life. And in my mind, there's no question that some of these kids who would ordinarily have fallen by the wayside will turn out to be productive kids because of this program. That's a good feeling.

It's important to notice that not only are kids empowered because of this man's engagement, but also that he is looking forward to staying in touch with them "in later life." Over time, he doesn't expect to let go of the young people he's met through his project. That too is enriching. It feels good to look forward to the end of your life as a time when you will have continuing relationships with people who mean a great deal to you.

This is a study about more than good works. It affirms some very old truths with new twists. Hard work pays off—in more ways than one would have dreamed. It's far more precious to give than receive—in ways one can't imagine in advance. Risk on behalf of others can bring immeasurable rewards.

Eugene Lang tells an eloquent story about one of his first dreamers, Ramon. I include it here as an example of the surprising legacies that sponsors find themselves inheriting from active philanthropic engagement.

When I first met Ramon, in 1981, he seemed like a born loser—no father, a part-time mother, subsisting in two rat-infested rooms of an old tenement. I didn't know it then, but the school system had classified him as "special ed"—a boy who, for whatever reason or disability, was considered just about hopeless. He hated that . . . systemic designation that made him less than the others.

"Tell me, Ramon," I asked, "what's your dream?" He couldn't think of any. However, when he told me he enjoyed drawing, I suggested that he might consider becoming an architect—and I explained how architects design beautiful buildings. Ramon liked the idea and, without further ado adopted architecture as his dream. From then on, I never saw Ramon without greeting "my favorite architect."

One Saturday morning about a year later, Ramon visited me and I asked him about school. As usual, everything was fine—great—until I asked, "How are you doing in math?" He looked at me—surprised—with a vague sense of guilt. "Math? I'm not taking math." I said, "What do you mean, you're not taking math? If you want to be an architect, you've got to take math!" He said, "But Mr. Lang, I applied for math but they told me at school that the math classes were full and they said I should take social studies instead. They said it didn't matter—that I'd get the same amount of credit for my diploma. I did what they told me."

There was no point in getting mad at Ramon or the school. That's the way the system can function. As for Ramon—he accepted its dictum and there was nobody home to suggest otherwise. Well, I was upset, and bright and early on Monday morning, I called the school—talked to the principal—and as politely as circumstances suggested, proposed that they damn well better get math on Ramon's program. They did—no problem! After all, the school had no reason to know about Ramon's dream to become an architect. Somebody just had to tell them.

Another year went by and one afternoon I got an urgent call from Ramon. "Mr. Lang, I gotta see you right away." He came to my office and told me the problem. "My mother's boyfriend threw me out of the house. Where can I live?" That threw me, but I remembered that one of my dreamers lived in a large flat with his working mother, who I had come to know. I called her . . . and hastened to tell her about her son's classmate, Ramon, and his need for a home. She responded with heart-warming enthusiasm, "Oh, I know Ramon. Send him right over." That was that. A wonderful ending. What made it particularly wonderful—Ramon, an Hispanic Catholic [was] taken in by a Black Muslim mother. Mrs. Walker needed no sermon on love and brotherhood.

Two more years went by. Ramon got his diploma. He couldn't qualify academically for a good engineering school. However, I arranged for him to take a technical program at . . . Valley Community College. I also arranged with a neighboring engineering college . . . to accept Ramon if, after two years, his academic deficiencies were resolved. So, full of hope, Ramon went off to Valley and I subsequently got this letter. I'll read part of it.

"Dear Mr. Lang,

" . . . I thank you for giving me this opportunity for making my dream a reality. I'm now at the very start of my dream. I'm sure that with your inspiration, you would be my guiding light. I hope that some day I would be able to design your future dream house. Even if you would pass away, God forbid, I will still design your house, with your name engraved on the side. 'The man who opened many hearts and dreams for children of America.'

"Love Always, Your Son Ramon." [42]

This story captures much that is both wonderful and challenging about IHAD. A sponsor from far away enters a world that has, for years, been foreign to him. It's a world where household vermin and educational neglect alike reflect the indifference that society shows toward low-income children. The sponsor is confident. He comes into the child's life with great expectations—both for the child and for the systems that are supposed to serve that child. And his crash course on the reality of life for many low-income children begins. Astonished and frustrated by obstacles that soon appear, he does not become paralyzed by blame or outrage. He draws on his problem-solving expertise to forge ahead, insisting as forcefully as ever on the legitimacy of his great expectations: that every child can become a productive and responsible adult. The sponsors looks steadily ahead, planning a future, maintaining his faith in the boy, and holding tight as a wet knot. He never lets go.

Over the next few years, Ramon and Gene Lang each learned something about limitations and possibilities. And for them both, the result is at the same time real and ineffable—solid as a documented track record and as ephemeral as hope. Whether or not the dreamer becomes an accomplished architect, the child's message back to the sponsor is clear. In his heart, he and his sponsor will share a home together, forever. Put differently, the boy will be at home, within himself, with a new-found sense of confidence, possibility, and connection to someone who "opened many hearts and dreams" for children. And what does Lang himself make of all this?

> The story is still unfinished. Whether I will live to live in the dream house—who knows?

> But . . . the story is a parable for our time. It relates to the infinite worth and dignity with which every young life is endowed. It relates to the lives of millions of children across the country who have priority claims on our consciences, commitments and resources. It relates to a challenge whose immensity must not intimidate us or immobilize us from doing what we can. It relates to our ability, perhaps as mentors, to make a fulfilling difference. And, above all, it relates individually to our will: have we the will to make that difference?

CHAPTER 8

THE WORLD BEGINS TO SHIFT

*Through what we earn, we make a living. Through what
we give we make a life.*

—Winston Churchill

Admittedly, this book reflects a personal bias—the belief that helping poor kids to beat the odds is a win-win situation for everyone. From a purely utilitarian point of view, giving gets return: it builds the prospect of a hopeful future to look toward—for ourselves, our children, and our grandchildren. But engaged philanthropy takes us a step further. It's my hope that this book will help many different kinds of readers—people of modest income and those with money to spare; human service professionals, teachers, researchers, and policymakers—think in new ways about what giving means. And that it will invite readers to consider where they are in relation to the people whose stories are told here.

We have learned a lot about what makes engaged philanthropists tick. They are pragmatic, bottom-line business people, but they are also visionary entrepreneurs. They like to be autonomous and in control, but they also treasure the unpredictable challenges and joys of being in mutually enriching, enduring relationships. They like to take risks, but they feel deeply grateful for the stability in their lives, for the good fortune that enables them to steer a steady course even when the waters get rough. The sponsors I interviewed for this book are compassionate and modest. Their hearts beat with a strong pulse for lifelong learning and the solid conviction that things can get better.

This book has focused on exploring the personal meaning of engagement to those who give from their hearts as well as their wallets. But we must not forget the kids. Like the sponsors, young dreamers are also risk-takers. It takes tremendous courage for them to enter into relationships with "outsiders"—people who will make serious demands of them over time—and to maintain those relationships no matter how frightened, distracted, sad, or angry they may become during the turbulent process of growing up. The stakes of connection and commitment are high for everyone.

PLAIN FACTS

In 2003, Joe Harris—who had been the project coordinator for an early IHAD project in his large Midwestern city—met with a group of new sponsors to tell them about the kinds of things they could expect from their involvement with the program over the coming years. Joe was now one of the three principals of a charter school located in one of the city's poorest neighborhoods, the school mentioned in Chapter 5 that was created in 1998—in an effort led by the Hulls and other local family foundations. "You're a strange bunch of adults," Harris told the new sponsors.

> How many people in your group of friends or families are making longitudinal commitments of finance, organization, heart, and soul to enter into tough conversations with adolescents of different races, socioeconomic status, cultures? How many have the preposterous notion you have—of creating a pathway for a kid to have a full-grown life when they're born into hells? Born into places that piece by piece disassemble and fracture what's most special about them?

> You're crazy to take this on—and I don't know how America will stay together as a functioning democracy without you. IHAD is an experiment in democracy. It's a chance to find common ground between people that have no business talking to each other, to build an ark, to create hope. And there are a million reasons why the kinds of connections you are setting out to build should fail.

The kids put more on the line [in] loving you than you do. In fact, they're the real heroes, because these are kids who are trusting middle-class white people when most of their experience with people like us has been very bad. There's the social worker who threatens to break up the only family they know, the teacher who should have retired years ago and yells all the time, and the cop who is certainly not Officer Friendly. But when these connections work, it's because of love. At the end of the day, the most important treasure you put down is not the financial backing. It is love. I know it sounds like hearts and flowers, but it's tough work. These kids go out of their way to love us back, and this is what fuels the whole thing.

In fact, not all IHAD sponsors are white (though at this time most are), and *upper*-middle-class might be a more accurate way to describe many of them. But by pointing to the fact that IHAD is a program that involves mostly white people who care intensely for mostly poor children of color for many, many years, Joe invites us to review some of the facts about our society that we too often and too easily avoid.

Let's think clearly about the facts of life for poor children of color in our country today. In the cities where the IHAD sponsors I interviewed adopted their dreamers roughly one-third of the children under eighteen live in poverty. What does this mean? According to the 2004 U.S. government census, a family of four with two children under the age of eighteen is designated as "poor" if they live on less than $19,289 a year. A mother with three children under the age of eighteen is the head of a "poor" family if she earns anything less than $18,725. Meanwhile, in Washington, D.C., for example—the nation's capital—in 2001 the median income of all families with children was $34,000. Forty percent of that city's children were living in families where no parent had full-time, year-round employment.[43]

In schools, various government formulas determine whether children, as members of families that are officially "poor," are eligible for free or reduced-price lunches at school. It is common for educational researchers to use the free or reduced-price lunch index (FRL)—which tracks how many are availing themselves of this program—to capture the extent of poverty and socioeconomic hardship in a school or district. Actually FRL figures tend to underestimate poverty because when kids get to high school, many don't like to be seen as needing a free or reduced-price lunch.[44] But however you choose to define poverty, statistics show that across the country school achievement is lowest where poverty is most concentrated. Again, taking the example of the nation's capital, 71 percent of D.C.'s eighth graders, in 2003, scored below standard expectations for their age group on basic math tests.[45]

In several places in this book, to make the point that IHAD programs were beating local norms, we've referred to average graduation rates. To understand what that means, we need to consider some basic realities about secondary school education in this country today. Nationwide, the percentages of children who enter ninth grade in the public schools and graduate with a regular diploma in twelfth grade are troublingly low. These rates are even lower for black and Hispanic students. In our largest cities, where the dropout problem is concentrated, about half the public high schools actually graduate fewer than 50 percent of the youngsters who begin high school in the ninth grade. Furthermore, students who do graduate are much more likely to be white than children of color. Among all children of color, boys do worse than girls.

The achievement gap between white children and children of color is increasingly acknowledged in public discourse today. Sometimes people refer to test-score differences; sometimes they illustrate the gap by referring to differences in the graduation rates of white kids and children of color. Once again taking the numbers from the nation's capital city—where the majority of kids in the public schools are black—in 2001, 11 percent of the city's teenagers were on record as dropouts.[46]

Across the United States, in schools where 90 percent or more of the students are children of color, only 42 percent finish twelfth grade. According to researchers Gary Orfield, Dan Losen, and Johanna Wald,

> Every year across the country, a dangerously large percentage of students—disproportionately poor and minority—disappear from the educational pipeline before graduating from high school. Nationally, only about 68 percent of all students who enter 9th grade will graduate "on time" with

regular diplomas in 12th grade. While the graduation rate for white students is 75 percent, only approximately half of Black, Hispanic and Native American students earn regular diplomas alongside their classmates. Graduation rates are even lower for minority males.[47]

"Nationwide," Christopher Swanson recently wrote in *Education Week*, "minorities have little more than a 50–50 chance of earning a diploma."[48]

In addition, there is reason to suspect that, as well intentioned as current education reform policies may have been, threats of punitive action against schools or school leaders who cannot document "adequate yearly progress" have, perversely, become an incentive for some principals and superintendents to encourage dropping out. This practice has actually been quietly in place for some time, particularly in large, over-crowded, under-performing, under-resourced high schools.[49] But some researchers believe that new accountability pressures are contributing to a tendency for school leaders "to push low-performing students out the back door" so they need not be counted when annual statistics are reported.[50]

We need to look at these realities head on. The good news is that this information is trickling out. The bad news is that most people don't believe it. Those who can bear to think about it understand that failing to graduate from high school today means having virtually no opportunity to earn a living wage. When Bill Gates, chairman of Microsoft and cofounder of the Bill & Melinda Gates Foundation, went to Washington in February of 2005 to talk to the nation's governors about the obsolescence of today's high schools, his comments echoed the complaints of some of the visionary entrepreneurs I interviewed for this study. Putting it strongly, he insists that the failures of the American public school system "ruin the lives of millions of Americans every year."[51]

> We have one of the highest high school dropout rates in the industrialized world. . . . [T]he United States has now dropped from first to fifth in the percentage of young adults with a college degree. The percentage of a population with a college degree is important, but so are sheer numbers. In 2001, India graduated almost a million more students from

college than the United States did. China graduates twice as many students with bachelor's degrees as the U.S., and they have six times as many graduates majoring in engineering. . . . [O]nly half of all students who enter high school ever enroll in a postsecondary institution. That means that half of all students starting high school today are unlikely to get a job that allows them to support a family.[52]

When Gates talks about the economic and moral imperatives confronting those of us who are trying to look squarely at public education today, he proposes a "new three R's" as the fundamental elements of good schools:

> Rigor: making sure that all students are given a challenging curriculum that prepares them for college or work;
>
> Relevance: making sure kids have courses and projects that clearly relate to their lives and their goals;
>
> Relationships: making sure kids have a number of adults who know them, look out for them, and push them to achieve.

These are the same principles that have guided IHAD projects—and similar efforts, public as well as private—for the past two and a half decades.

Gates exhorted the governors to face the music—to demand that voters in their states agree to "spend real political capital" on public education. Like Gates, we must all be very clear: the neglect of public education and the failure to respond effectively to the grim and interrelated realities of poverty constitute a crisis in the country that has a direct bearing on the future for all of us. Another way to put this is to suggest that each one of us is in possession of social and political capital that must be spent.

THE MODEL EVOLVES: VARIATIONS ON A THEME

Whatever age they may be when they are first adopted, by the time dreamers get to high school most of their sponsors have come to understand that Lang's original vision—to pay for everyone's college education—may not be the single best way to nurture responsibility and help each child succeed. This does not mean giving up on any child's potential. On the contrary, creating strategies and objectives tailored to each individual dreamer reflects a new, more comprehensive definition of success.

Three other specific features of Lang's original model have proved problematic for some sponsors in ways that have caused them to make adjustments to it. First of all, many worry about the randomness of the selection process, which they sometimes fault for the frustrations they have with particular children and families. If they'd had more control over the composition of the dreamer group, some speculate, they would have had "more success." Secondly, some find out rather quickly that they are not personally equipped with the kinds of skills that are most helpful to dreamers. After all, they were not trained as social workers, special education teachers, or guidance counselors. So, though they had not always anticipated it, they can find themselves scrambling to assemble and join extensive student support teams. Thirdly, the original estimates for the costs of adopting dreamer classes tended to be unrealistically low. While these factors have sometimes led to frustrations, they have also contributed to some constructive variations on Lang's original design.

DREAMER SELECTION

The original selection process—traditionally sealed by a surprise announcement at a special school event that a certain group of children will be supported for many years, with college as the long-term goal—strikes some sponsors, after a while, as being problematically exclusive. Some therefore choose to proceed differently, as we know. They may site their projects in housing developments, keeping basic agreements and services the same but adjusting the structure or the format for a dreamer group defined by geography rather than age. (Lang himself has never been particularly keen on this approach because an important feature of his own dream has always been the reform of public schools.)

Most sponsors who decided to stick closer to the original model now choose their schools very intentionally. In fact, they sometimes look for schools in neighborhoods with slightly less poverty, where chances for a strong return might be better. One first generation sponsor sometimes finds herself wishing she had done that—"begun at a school where there were fewer parents at the bottom of the social strata, more who valued education more, and more children for whom college was a dream." When she thinks about the individual successes of her dreamers she is very pleased, but she's also sad that she couldn't make her own dream come true: to see all of them go to college.

Rob Mitchell, whose story we heard in Chapter 3, connected the original random selection format with his frustration about how hard it was to get many of his dreamers and their families to commit themselves wholeheartedly to the program.

> As IHAD sponsors, we look down from on high and say, "I am going to choose you to be a dreamer. This will entitle you to many things if you want to take advantage of them. And it means getting a college or vocational scholarship." But now I know about another program that says to kids, "We want you to be part of our program, but you have to work two hours a day extra, before or after school. If you do this, we'll help you build a better life." It doesn't promise a scholarship.
>
> Why is their program successful? Well, think about it. If I were going to shake your hand, you would probably put out your hand halfway. But with IHAD kids it often feels like we're chasing them or prodding them. Gene would argue vehemently that the IHAD class has to be all-inclusive, that it has to be random. But maybe having some measure of control over which kids actually want these benefits would be helpful. Then you'd get kids who really want to be there. I've heard sponsors talk about spending thirty, forty, fifty percent of their efforts on that small group of kids who, in the end, don't make it. Maybe the other kids would have benefitted more if you'd had more time to spend with them. At some point maybe this is a numbers game, but it's tough. I always felt that if you could have kids who said they really wanted to be a dreamer, for whatever reason, you would have greater success.

As you'll recall, Rob is a self-described "contrarian" who has always followed the beat of his own drummer. So in some ways, it's not surprising that once his first class of dreamers graduated, he was ready to try another approach. That first class had done very well—95 percent graduated from high school and 75 percent went directly on to college. Now Rob, who wants the very best return on his investment, has begun a different kind of program in his community. Earn and Learn is very selective in its approach. Working very closely with the local school district, the project has begun to serve a targeted group of motivated students and parents. As described in the local paper,

> The program will work with middle school students and encourage them to succeed in school with a unique work/incentive program. [Rob] will "hire" each student as an "employee" and the employee will commit to specific requirements as to schoolwork, behavior, attendance, timelines and bi-weekly meetings with the "employer" [Rob]. Failure to meet these standards could lead to suspension without pay or termination. The awards will be at [Rob's] discretion and students are required to put at least ten percent of their "income" into an Education Savings Account at a local bank. If they save more, [Rob] will match up to thirty percent.

During the first year, the school referred only four children to the program. These were eighth graders, each of whom had significant histories of behavioral difficulties—frequent referrals for disciplinary infractions and counseling. And in the second half of the year, after these kids started in Earn and Learn, the number of times they got into trouble dropped dramatically. However, once these four children got to high school, two had trouble honoring the original contract and Rob had to "fire" them. They can apply for reinstatement within a certain period of time, but they can only return to the program if they fulfill certain requirements. The two other kids have done very well. One is a child who has struggled with all kinds of family difficulties and suffers from Tourette's syndrome; the other is a girl who often finds herself challenged to fight but (so far) has been able to find new ways to avoid conflicts.

Rob's greatest frustration now is with the school district, which is so encumbered with all kinds of desperate fiscal crises that the school board—which must approve the referrals to Earn and Learn—has not been able to find the time to vote on the next group of children to be referred. Remember, before Rob became an IHAD sponsor, he had never been seriously involved in the education of any children besides his own. He was not an educational philanthropist. But now he's in it for the long haul, determined to keep searching for effective ways to help poor kids find good futures. If the school board doesn't deliver soon, he will take Earn and Learn to another district nearby. "I don't give up," he says.

TEAMWORK

Soon after they began their projects, many sponsors discovered they didn't have the skills to effectively support their dreamers on their own. So, despite the fact that most are individualistic entrepreneurs who are accustomed to being in charge, they have found themselves working collaboratively, together and with professional staff, for the good of their dreamers.

Remember the project we briefly described in Chapter 5 that was headed by a sponsor who adopted a class in 1990 with two other people—one of whom pledged to cover college costs, and one of whom contributed her services as an experienced psychologist?. Together they created an impressive variety of services and supports, including a team of providers who opened a drop-in center for dreamers and, at times, their friends. The psychologist, a highly skilled professional, spoke to me about how the initiative has fostered her own continuing education and growth.

> I'm very glad to have done it. I find it very satisfying in a lot of ways. I like working with graduate students from the universities. It sort of keeps you in touch with professional life. I like the feeling of ongoingness. And I like knowing all about our kids but not having to see them myself in treatment directly. It's also a very effective position because I can focus on helping the staff to focus on particular problems.
>
> Not being directly in the middle of everything, I find I have [a] freedom to think that is quite useful to the general running of the project, and that one often doesn't have when

one is doing direct service. The project needs someone to be in this position and I've learned a tremendous amount. . . .

The main thing that IHAD offers is the chance to make a difference in a person's life through relationship. We're always thinking about kids' lives from many angles. We try to figure out how we can provide just what they need, as if we were Mom. I've always thought that if a person hasn't had good relationships somewhere, it's probably hopeless. But maybe it isn't.

What's especially astonishing is seeing that when you have ten people thinking together, you can really solve problems!

For this woman, the continuity of the work and the value of teamwork in problem-solving are major themes, though the latter is often not the first instinct for either single-minded entrepreneurs or for traditionally trained mental health professionals, who tend to focus more on individual than on group solutions. But by putting together a team of people with different kinds of expertise, these and other sponsors have found that they can construct philanthropic initiatives that have a capacity to evolve and reflect what they are learning about how best to serve poor kids.

On a somewhat larger scale, the same thing happened when the Hulls made their community commitment to one of their city's poorest neighborhoods. A significant piece of this initiative is Northside, the charter school where Joe Harris works. The funders who joined the Hulls in creating the school knew that it was possible to hold their dreamers together and address their inter-related needs effectively while the children were still in elementary schools. But placing them in better than under-performing high schools, where they would have good chances to actually succeed at getting into college, was very difficult. And they were also concerned about the numbers of young people who make it to college but then drop out. So, at the same time that the state was passing its charter school legislation, this group of funders, including the Hulls, decided to establish a high school that would not recruit college-prep students, but produce them. The founders of this effort are determined to demonstrate that it's possible to run a successful, high-quality college preparatory school in a very poor neighborhood without spending any more than regular public schools spend on their students.

Northside realizes three principles that are at the core of the IHAD model: relationships, high expectations, and an orientation toward the future. Because its founders understand how essential human connections are to children's healthy development, the school is committed to remaining small so faculty members can get to know students very well. Daily and weekly schedules are structured so that staff has frequent opportunities to gather and talk in detailed ways about meeting the changing needs of particular students. And, most critically, Northside's staff includes five counselors—each a licensed counselor or social worker, and each assigned to one group of youngsters for five years, that is, through their first year of college. One of these, also assigned to alumni support services, continues to be available to young people as they navigate through college. These counselors, selected because they understand the importance of relationships in adolescent development, provide traditional kinds of academic counseling, clinical counseling (for individuals, groups, and extended family members), case management, and developmental support. The money to pay for this support team reflects a deliberate decision to use the $500,000 routinely spent by most inner-city public high schools on metal detectors and security staff in a different way, to create a connected, safe school community.[52]

Expectations for students are very high at Northside. Because students enter with a variety of deficits and strengths, the rigorous curriculum is "scaffolded." As Joe Harris explains,

> You have to meet kids where they are. You have to find teachers that understand that curriculum can't be "dumbed down." You must have high, incremental expectations, along with resources to help the kids. You can't set the bar over the roof and then not give kids a ladder to help them climb.

According to Joe, 91 percent of the school's graduates are in college and "we can tell you where every one of our kids are, whether they're working, what their grade-point averages are, and what their progress toward college graduation is. We all stay in touch."

Like IHAD, Northside continuously points young people toward the future. A good example is its Phoenix Rising developmental summer program. After their first year, many freshmen participate in leadership and team-building programs in different parts of the country. After sophomore year, eligible students attend academic enrichment programs offered by universities in New England, New York, the Midwest, and the West. And a good number of juniors spend their third summer in paid internships at local institutions (both corporate and nonprofit ones). In a school built around relationships, where educators and children work together to build a community of peace, young people are planning ahead. As Joe says, "You can't keep your eye on the future if you're always watching your back."

Joe Harris was a Catholic priest before he became affiliated with IHAD. As happened to many sponsors, his life changed dramatically because of his involvement with the program. And, like many of sponsors we've heard from, he sometimes finds himself looking at former colleagues who are plugging away at the same jobs they've had for forty years, and feeling sorry for them.

> I've been out now seventeen years and I'm as happy as I ever was as a priest in my parish. When I look at a lot of my classmates stuck in their rectories, I sometimes feel sorry for them. Their vision is skewed, and they don't know it. Things have changed in the world for many reasons. But IHAD has given me a chance to be part of a community that is devoting its vital energies to a very noble cause. And it helped me understand that I could still do ministry but not have to wear a collar. It became a way for me to continue aspects of my ministry in a non-denominational way, to answer the gospel's call for social justice and care for those who are peripheralized.

Both Joe Harris and Sam Hull are now engaged in initiatives that are much bigger and more complex than the discrete IHAD projects that first captured them. They are sharing their skills and commitments with others who are similarly determined to turn things around for poor children. And, as Joe points out, because IHAD sponsors are often powerful people in their communities, the impact that sponsoring has on them can in turn be significant for many others. Sam, for example, whose daughter Sara is an active board member at Northside, is heading up the school district's big campaign to raise money for new schools. As Joe says,

What we're doing is smart, it's replicable, and it has some chance of affecting a whole system. And with [Sam Hull] working in the district, we're now talking about 450,000 kids who may be touched because of what he learned as an IHAD sponsor!

COSTS AND BENEFITS

Finally, what about the cost of these commitments? Of course IHAD sponsoring is more expensive now than it was twenty-five years ago. Apart from inflation and the increased costs of living, many sponsors now start their projects with children in the early grades—or with groups of dreamers of different ages who live in housing developments. These demographic shifts make original budget predictions very outdated. But even among the first generation sponsors I spoke with, there was surprise about the real costs of their efforts—partly because some couldn't bear to put up with the realities of what Bill Gates would call an obsolete public school system. As Richard Joseph says,

> We spent about four times as much money as was advertised. But we did a lot of things that were not part of the program, that we thought made sense as we went along.
>
> We sent a lot of children to private schools—because their neighborhood junior high school was far from "exemplary." We sent a couple of kids away to school because of difficult home situations—and we weren't always able to get much scholarship assistance for that.
>
> In one way, I think it was a weakness of the IHAD program that, if you adopted a class of kids and they had no commitment to the program, you might find yourself running an afterschool program at your nearby community-based organization which could benefit thirty children—but then only three showed up. Since we were going to the effort and expense of offering these things, we decided we should offer them to more children. So we created a special thing called Friends of the Dreamers, for friends and acquaintances of the dreamers who wanted to participate in the program. We

actually developed a process where we interviewed these kids and their parents and got them to sign an agreement. We made no commitment to send them to college. But then we had a bunch of self-selected, committed youngsters. And some of our biggest successes—a young woman now in medical school who graduated from [a prestigious private university], for example—came through that way. Actually, nearly all those kids went on to college and were successful.

While the cost factor surprised them, Richard and his wife, Laura, went on to amend other features of their project in a variety of ways that increased their prospects for success. The original model, after all, is scant on formal requirements. As we've said, this gives sponsors a great deal of autonomy—an important aspect of IHAD's appeal to them. So when sponsors send dreamers to alternative schools or open up project activities and services to dreamer relatives and friends, as some did, they end up spending more—and enhancing the prospect for greater returns. Those who adopt children in younger grades do so knowing that the scope of supports children will need over what can be fifteen years will be much more extensive and expensive than what was required in Lang's original model. It's not surprising that sponsors now often enter into the commitment with others who will share the financial responsibility for the project.

But the single sponsor survives too. Among those whom Tessa Bloom's example has inspired in her community is Ed Montero, now thirty-nine, who adopted his first group of dreamers six years ago, when they were in first grade at Tessa's school. The following year he adopted a second class of first graders at the same school. Now, with his first two classes of dreamers in the sixth and seventh grades, Ed will adopt three more first grade classes in the neighborhood where Tessa plans to begin her second group with another couple. Ed's new dreamers will be first graders in three different schools, with about sixty children in each grade.

Ed graduated with a scholarship from a five-year university program that combines the bachelor of arts degree with a master's degree in business administration. He went straight to Wall Street, spent a few years paying off loans, and made enough money to start his own financial services business. After a few years of nurturing his new company, he was confident enough about its financial well-being to say to himself, "I'm just going to jump in with both feet!" Now pleased that he jumped in when he was so young—because he can apply what he's learning to new projects—he's concentrating on hiring good program coordinators, and he's looking for people who are prepared to stay with the children for fifteen years.

There's a fundamental difference between Ed's approach and Lang's original model because, though Ed meets with groups of his dreamers every six weeks, he is not their primary adult connector. As he sees it, his job is to "drive" the projects as a whole. He gets employees in his business involved. He oversees staffing. He has hired an executive director at his place of work who spends half her time at the schools. With three young children of his own and an actively growing business, Ed feels his primary responsibility is to keep telling the dreamers his story.

> I'm the guy who comes in and talks to the kids about their future and about the importance of college education. I give them my own story about how I was born in Latin America and grew up in a low-to-moderate-income home with parents who urged me at every turn to go to college. I watched them struggle financially. They ingrained in us that education was critical to accomplishing what we wanted. And this is what I thought was important: to help other kids use education to lift themselves up from a difficult situation. I tell them about how I went to university on a scholarship with lots of financial aid and graduated and went to Wall Street and made a lot of money. About how that could be them.

Ed's account is not so different from some others we've heard in the book, though the speed at which he's moving is breathtaking. Obviously he's too young to have ever been involved in major philanthropy before he began IHAD. But full-fledged philanthropic engagement fits perfectly with his beliefs. A risk-taking, energetic, value-driven entrepreneur, he is extremely positive about what he's doing.

> I am absolutely confident that we are going to impact future generations. The important ingredient to success is making sure that the kids understand the future is out there.

There are a lot of afterschool programs and other things that try to help these kids. But what makes IHAD unique is the long-term commitment that it makes to the children. The college scholarship is huge. If you just offered that and didn't provide all the services along the way, you'd fail, I think. But it [also] wouldn't work if you only provided the services without tying the kids into the long-term commitment—so they know that you've invested in them, that they have a future, and that they have to do their part to get there.

I really love the model: I'm a big believer in the whole package. It's cost-efficient and very effective. I understand why it's hard to replicate, why the public schools can't just make it all happen by themselves. But because I feel it's absolutely doable, it's a responsibility to do it. Because we can. Because we're lucky. I feel very good about doing it, and I believe that if others felt there was a clear way to make a difference—in a way that is meaningful and efficient and successful—people would open up their pocketbooks. One of the reasons people hold back is because they're not confident that writing the check is going to do any good. But this works!

Though Ed's approach differs somewhat from Lang's in terms of the parameters of his personal involvement, he has made sure that the core elements of Lang's model are intact—long-term relationships, coordinated enrichment and support services, and an orientation toward the future based on academic success. He is determined to address the evolving challenges of cost by keeping his focus on "driving the project." Test scores from his first two dreamer classes confirm his sense that his investment is paying off. Many people in their thirties and forties have more money today than was available to the same age group twenty-five years ago. Ed's confidence that things can get better for poor kids beckons these people to join him, at whatever level their resources permit, in ensuring that a good future is indeed possible for all children.

Lang himself is gratified by the success of the initiatives inspired by the work that he began in 1981. [53] I Have a Dream, he says, "has gotten things done." Though he may have been frustrated by the obstacles that his own city's school system kept throwing in front of his dreamers, he knows that by refusing to accept the status quo he has made a contribution.

> IHAD has helped to change the course of education in the U.S. For every project we started, dozens of others have begun—just because we brought into focus a basic pro-posal that everyone recognized was important to the coun-try—something that, as human beings, everyone could feel attached to. We highlighted a problem and showed we could do something about it—establishing relationships. It was spirit, purpose, idealism that impelled us to do things. It was a jolting reminder of something everyone was aware of—but somebody had done something to light the fires. You have to not only recognize the need and be concerned but *do* something! And if you ring the bell of conscience, emotion, and feeling, then you've got it!

> I know I have a mission. I'm lucky to be able to inspire and motivate people. I don't want to let that go to waste. I couldn't do it if I were a shrinking violet: you have to be able to project your self-esteem. I can make you feel my joys and my sorrows, and you may not want to feel the sorrow but, when you leave me, you can almost taste the joy!

IHAD sponsors share Lang's vigorous confidence in their mis-sion, along with his energetic and contagious joy about the value of engagement. They are what Bill Shore calls "agents of conscience"— people who have become personally engaged in projects that change lives because they have seen the reality of need at firsthand.[54] What is more, one of the rewards of involvement comes from their direct expe-rience with efficacy: the knowledge that they can make a difference. All of us who are fortunate enough to have been able to work hard and achieve personal objectives know that we can "get things done." This sense of optimism and confidence is, of course, something we want to transmit to *all* our children.

AN INVITATION

Engagement is costly in many ways. But what are the costs of staying disengaged? The urgency of poverty bears down on us all. Remember Chantal, from the prologue to this book, who happened to be born in the wrong zip code? Sara Hull, a child of privilege, acknowledges her kinship with Chantal: the only difference between her and the poor kids at the school where she now works, she says, is "dumb luck: it could have just as easily been me. It could have been my kids who were born here in the Northside community."

Joe Harris, whose description of Chantal opened our prologue, has the same ability that Lang has—to make listeners feel his sorrows, taste his joys.

> You think you know about poverty but you don't. With IHAD, it gets up close and personal. You see things in a deep way. You see the human cost of poverty, how generational it is, how short the time frame is for those who are living in it, and how so many kids are born with so many disadvantages. At the same time that you see intractable misery, you also begin to find ways you can make connections.
>
> You see that people want connections, that kids can adjust to do-gooders in their life, and that do-gooders can be taught by kids. There are lots of differences between you and the kids—generational, social, economic, racial. But if you're a pretty decent human being, the differences don't matter.
>
> When IHAD really works, people get this sort of spiritual, nuclear energy in them. It splits your atom! You get mad. You find yourself saying, "I am not going to bear this injustice. I will not bear children's hearts being broken. I refuse to bear what happens to poor families in my country. I will rage, with intelligence and organization, but I will rage."
>
> And the world begins to shift. When someone becomes an IHAD sponsor, there ought to be a warning label. "WARNING: This experience is going to screw up your life." Your politics will be messed up. Your philanthropy will be scrambled. Your tennis partners won't know what

the hell you're talking about half the time. It'll change you. Because you are people who have chosen to see what very few people see. And it will make you different. With eyes that see and hearts and spirits that feel: that's how you'll stay connected for many years to all this.

For philanthropists who choose to engage with poor children, the shock of what they learn about the consequences of poverty is balanced by their own experiences with hope and promise. When Joe talked recently to prospective sponsors, he picked up on the image of the comet that Sara used to describe the impact of her family's eighteen-year relationship with IHAD. Getting involved was, she said, like "holding a comet with incredible heat and energy and light, streaking across the sky with a tail sixteen times as long as the comet itself. It just never, never ends." Far from being costly, then, Joe insists that personal investment, human-to-human connections generate tremendous energy. This happens, he says, because the eyes and hearts of sponsors open to the world, and because kids who have no reason to trust strangers "love us back. It's the comet's long tail. Luminosity endures." And changes everything.

Life, like that comet, is flying by. As I've discovered over and over again, time is the most precious resource of all. So reader, where are you in all this? Probably, like IHAD sponsors, you are neither saint nor hero. But the work you are doing in your life—the work we all do—calls on strengths within us that, over time, become integral to who we are. As we mature, these strengths are refined. We see paths more clearly. Were we each able to achieve what Joe Harris urges— open our eyes and hearts to the world—we might all do as much as we could to make the world a better home for low-income children. Their struggles challenge our futures.

Perhaps on the pages of this book you've met someone who reminds you of yourself. Maybe you'll want to gather up a group of children and help them become responsible, productive citizens. Maybe you'll become the hands-on sponsor for a project that serves a cause you're passionate about, mentor a child, volunteer in a school or clinic or hospital, or take on vigorous advocacy for public funding of programs that you know are effectively serving those in need. Now you know something about what to expect. The returns can be immeasurable. Wrestling responsibly with the problems of our world, moving beyond the edges of what's familiar to tackle the challenges of those whom we can help, brings many rewards. Not the least of which is hope. As Dorothy Day once said, "No one has a right to sit down and feel hopeless. There's too much work to do." Dreams matter. And so does waking up and getting to work. To be of use is one of life's greatest joys.

BIOGRAPHICAL NOTES ON UNNAMED SPONSORS

Here are some biographical notes on IHAD sponsors I have quoted but not named, or have not provided histories for, in the text of this book. As with the other sponsors, to protect their privacy I've given them pseudonyms, and their stories show at once how diverse a group they are and how much they have in common.

Paul Abramowitz has lived in his mid-Atlantic city since he was eight. His father, a Russian immigrant who came to the United States when he was sixteen, worked hard to develop a successful plumbing business, and Paul remembers spending summers digging ditches and carrying bathtubs. After attending public schools, he went to a local private university, working in construction the whole time he was a student and graduating with a major in government. During the last twenty-five years Paul has become one of his city's most important business and philanthropic leaders. The construction business through which he built his fortune is now helping to resuscitate its decaying neighborhoods. Paul and a friend adopted a class of fifty-nine fifth graders at a very disadvantaged school in 1987. Though they spent three times as much as they had expected to, his determination to help children in need is unlimited. He has chaired local drives for national and international foundations and poured enormous resources into his community, hoping to be a "catalyst to help turn the city around." But he is troubled by the shortsighted habits of its high-tech leaders, who, he believes, are not pulling their weight in the community. A self-described risk-taker, Paul believes that living is about giving, that nobody gives enough, and that the highest form of charity is anonymous. Proud of his Jewish heritage, he recalls the biblical command to leave a corner of the field unharvested so those who are hungry can quietly find food there, unembarrassed by their need.

Carol Bristol works full-time running a small entertainment marketing company on the West Coast. She grew up in New England and attended a private high school and university, where she majored in history and literature. When she graduated she headed west to start her business, married a childhood friend whom she hadn't seen for years—a television writer—and had two children. Carol's mother was a teacher, her father a lawyer, and her family one that was always very involved in "hands-on philanthropy." She is not inhibited about asking people for money: in fact, she feels she is doing them a service by telling them about important initiatives. When she began her IHAD project—in 1996, with fifty fourth graders, half of them black and half Hispanic—she turned to a group of friends and colleagues who all chipped in to fund the project. Young and energetic, she was asked to be the director of the local IHAD foundation, which has kept her heavily involved in fund-raising for local projects. She is also creating partnerships between projects and local universities, to strengthen staff's capacity to provide mental health and counseling services to dreamers and their families. One of the things that Carol says she enjoys about IHAD is that it attracts people from all across the political spectrum. And she treasures the fact that her family has friends in all parts of the large city in which they live. She believes that children learn what's most important by seeing how their parents live their lives.

Mary Carlson grew up in a Northern Plains state. Her father worked for the U.S. border patrol, and when she was thirteen the family moved to the Southwest. She attended a large state university, majored in home economics and education, and married her high school sweetheart. Mary's husband was in the military for many years, but in the late 1960s, when the Vietnam War was raging, he left the service and took up a variety of executive jobs working for hospitals and a construction company. Mary taught middle school students while her children were growing up. Eventually her husband became the owner and chief executive of a glass manufacturing company and, as a successful businessman, was invited to sit on the board of a local foundation. After a profitable year, the foundation's board decided to investigate initiatives serving low-income children. In 1992 they entered into a partnership with the local IHAD foundation, which was already running several projects in the area. Mary agreed to become the new donor's front-line sponsor for eighty-four dreamers, ranging from second to sixth grade. The foundation that funds this effort has established a partnership with a local college, building a much needed child development center which also houses offices for the ongoing IHAD programs in the city. Mary is now the primary sponsor for a second class, insisting that they start this time with first graders; she says she's glad to have a chance to do some things differently—better—this time around. Mary treasures her relationships with other IHAD sponsors, the "wonderful people" she has met both in and beyond her community. Always an active volunteer, Mary is a religious person, and although the agreement is that they never preach dogma, she has hired PCs for whom religious faith is also important. It's Mary who says that sometimes, when she and her staff discover unexpected solutions to tough challenges with the dreamers, they find themselves thinking, "This was nothing we did. We're not that good. There's a hand in this that goes way beyond us."

Carl and Deb Clark live in a very comfortable suburb outside an Eastern city where they raised their two children. The Navy had sent Carl to Ivy League schools to prepare him to be an officer, but World War II ended just before he completed college. He went to work for his father, who had never finished high school but owned a small hotel supplies manufacturing business. A few years later, his father died and Carl began work as a securities analyst on the bottom rung of the ladder at a large brokerage firm. There was no particular ethos of service in Carl's family of origin, but after their marriage he and Deb became active contributors to community charities—the local teen center and the YMCA, for example. In 1987, they adopted a class of fifty-two dreamers who were just finishing sixth grade at a school in a nearby "problem community" in their county, where the school district was spending $7,000 per student (as compared to $19,000 per student in wealthier districts nearby). The Clarks were regularly and intensely involved with their dreamers—many of whom have now graduated from college—and have started two other programs reflecting their enthusiasm for the IHAD approach. One is an arts program and the other, which they founded in 1999, is a growing scholarship initiative that gives $10,000 over four years to promising high school students from families living below the poverty level. The Clarks maintain direct personal contact with these students during their college years.

Carl is an active supporter of charter schools and has thought about getting involved in politics. Both he and Deb talk about the gratification of watching young people succeed and of hearing many say that they plan to give back to their communities once they are settled in their careers.

Phil Connelly rode the commuter train daily from the wealthy suburb where he lived with his wife and four children into the heart of an Eastern city's financial district. Proudly identifying himself as a conservative, a Republican, and a Catholic, Connelly has worked as an investment banker for decades, except for a few years when he served as economic advisor in Washington, D.C. On the train, he and a colleague began to talk about the remarkably run-down, crowded, and disadvantaged communities they travelled through every day. After reading about IHAD, they met with Lang and each agreed to start a project. But when Connelly saw what kinds of bureaucratic hurdles his dreamers were encountering in the public system, he placed many of them in parochial schools. Like his father, also a successful banker, he had always contributed to local philanthropies, including Catholic youth organizations and the private schools he had attended. But until he became an IHAD sponsor, Connelly had never invested in public schools or the education of low-income children. But he is passionate about freedom and, for years now, about what he sees as the "moral outrage" of denying a high-quality education to any child who wants it. Connelly is actively involved in developing private school voucher programs and oversees an initiative that finds tuition for promising low-income children to attend parochial schools where graduation rates are higher than in the public schools.

Linda Garnet and her husband grew up in the Southwest, where they returned to live after attending private schools and colleges in the Northeast. An attorney by training, Mr. Garnet later became a high-level executive with a major insurance company. The Garnets have two sons who were young when Linda served for ten years as president of her big city's school board, during a time when court-ordered desegregation was being implemented across the district. Her children went to public schools until high school. Linda's mother died when she was very young. She was raised by her father, who worked in the farm and ranch loan business, and a stepmother who was always active in the community; her grandmother had been an early leader of the town's charitable efforts. At the time Linda adopted her first class she also persuaded a local church to make a similar commitment. Within a few years there were four IHAD projects in town, including one of the first in the nation that would be sited in a housing development. The Garnets, who have now sponsored three IHAD projects, are active supporters of a variety of charities that include math and science enrichment programs, performing arts programs for children, an astronomy research center, the local symphony, international piano competitions, and the private schools from which they graduated.

Tim Jackson majored in economics at a Southern state university and began trading stock in a large Eastern city within a few weeks of graduating. He loved the energy level of the exchange, became a broker, and, as he says, "cut my teeth in two great bear markets." He started his own successful financial fund when he was twenty-six. Describing himself as a conservative investor who never likes to take risks, Tim became an IHAD sponsor in his early thirties, adopting a large group of eighty-five dreamers in a very disadvantaged neighborhood in 1987. In response to what he saw in his dreamers' community, he and two other young traders created a foundation that finances neighborhood programs and anti-poverty initiatives, an exemplary, activist venture philanthropy that gives more than $30 million annually to low-income children in their city. Two years after becoming an IHAD sponsor, Tim adopted a second group of eighty-five dreamers. He soon began requiring an application process that he believes has enabled him to find and work with those children who are most likely to succeed. Then he began to fill the place of every child who graduated from his projects with a new dreamer. By now he has been a mentor to well over four hundred and twenty-five children. Tim comes from a charitable family that was always involved with the church. From his perspective, "The most exciting aspect of the Christian faith is that it teaches you to love and to give at every opportunity." An avid environmentalist, he has four children of his own, runs a company with over three hundred employees, manages the foundation, and makes weekly visits to the low-income children who have become his friends.

Kitty Karlin adopted seventy-one sixth graders in 1987. She lives in a Midwestern city where, although she had established a local IHAD foundation and invited others to sponsor projects, hers was the only IHAD program. Kitty was always very close to her father, who came to this country when he was fourteen and worked hard to establish a workman's clothing manufacturing business. She completed her higher education at respected state and private universities in the Midwest before marrying, whereupon her husband went to work for her father. After her father died, Kitty and her brother established a family foundation that supports various community endeavors, including the local symphony and fine arts museum. It also underwrote her IHAD project. Her son, in addition to working in financial management, has developed a consulting firm that advises foundations and large philanthropies about ways to increase the social impact of their investments. One of the principles of the firm's strategic planning approach is the importance of having funders work directly and over time with grantees—in much the same way that sponsors work with dreamers.

Fred and Leslie Miller adopted a class of IHAD dreamers in 1987, just as the kids were finishing fifth grade. Leslie was born in the Midwest; Fred grew up in a coldwater flat in the large Eastern city that had always been his home and is now theirs. His sickly immigrant father, a tailor, was elated by his son's school successes. Graduating from high school at fifteen, Fred studied business administration at a local college and began working as an office boy for a talent scout agency. Within five years he had learned enough to start his own firm in the same field, and eventually he went on become the CEO of a major motion picture and communications business. One day, when he was sixty-one, he came home and told his wife that he had talked with Gene Lang and decided they would become IHAD sponsors. And, he announced, she would be in charge of the project while he continued to work as usual. It was a startling moment for Leslie, but once she stopped resenting the unilateral nature of Fred's decision, she threw herself into the project with terrific energy and affection. Dreamers came to her home; she met with them regularly at the community settlement house where the project was based, took them to museums, wrote them postcards from all over the world, and served for years on IHAD's national board. It's

Leslie who now calls her years with the project the "ultimate mixed blessing" of her life.

Matthew Oliver and a group of people in his church took on an IHAD class, in partnership with another church in a downtown, low-income neighborhood across the river from the comfortable, mid-Atlantic, suburban community where he lives. Matthew was born in the Midwest where he went to school and university, majoring in political science and hoping to go into government. But the times derailed that plan: military service came first, and after he returned he took a variety of jobs for large communications companies, working his way up to and eventually assuming top-level managerial responsibilities. Even before he married and had four children—"And how lucky I am to have raised four children, all of whom seem to have their heads screwed on and are doing well," he says—Matthew, now divorced, was always an active volunteer in his community. But it was his corporate experience as a manager in charge of a company division beset by racial tensions that influenced him to focus on issues of poverty, race, and social justice. Within the company he led the effort to develop classes about the nature of prejudice: "We have to start understanding each other," was his basic premise, "because we're going to have to work together." And so it was also with his church, whose mission was to do something for the community whenever it took on a project to benefit its own congregation. Though the downtown church provided the home base for the project, over a hundred people from Matthew's suburban church participated regularly and intimately, as tutors and mentors, with the dreamers. They took middle-of-the-night calls from dreamers in trouble, and, when the program ended, continued to "see the need." "They see the siblings of our dreamers," Matthew told me, "and wonder who's looking after *them*." Though Matthew's was a church-affiliated project, those who were involved always said they were not trying to "win converts, just trying to help kids get to college. Setting an example rather than preaching is what it boils down to." The group started with sixty-six youngsters, of whom forty-four graduated from high school and thirty-three went on to college. They also raised funds to send children to private schools whenever possible. At the age of sixty-nine, Matthew says he can't imagine not carrying on with another IHAD project and has indeed begun a second one.

David Peters grew up in a large Midwestern city. He went west to attend college and during his senior year was recruited by a major financial company, where he worked for a year doing investment banking. But that job wasn't a good fit for him and he left it for four years in the nonprofit world—first at a local city foundation and then in fund-raising and development for a large, established child-serving nonprofit organization—before going to business school. He and his partners now run a venture capital firm that invests in small software companies. David went into business school with fund-raising skills that helped him and a group of his classmates raise over a million dollars from wealthy individuals, foundations, and corporations in order set up their first IHAD project, which began with third and fourth graders in 1992. Their second project began with first graders in 2000. They also hired a wonderful program coordinator to structure and stabilize their effort, which currently uses about eighty business school students as mentors and tutors. These students receive training about "the whole child" concept, which became increasingly important to these sponsors as they realized how interrelated their dreamers' needs were. Their mission is to "have every child graduate from high school ready, willing, and able to succeed," a goal broad enough to include academic excellence, respect for self and others, and a focus on career. A first-generation American whose parents came to this country from the Middle East in the 1950s, David says that education was "a huge emphasis" in his family. It enabled his father, a retired cardiovascular surgeon, to come to this country, and his mother to become a teacher. David's brother, a doctor, and his sister, a lawyer, are also actively involved in community service and human rights. He and his wife, who has always had a strong community service orientation, have three young children. While he and another business school colleague have been the official IHAD sponsors, the PC and student mentors provide the most important personal relationships with the dreamers. Raising money for the project is a double blessing, as David puts it, because, in addition to helping the dreamers, "business school students are caught at a time when they're receptive to new ideas and are going out in the world to be business leaders who will want to give back to the communities where they work and live."

Greg Ralston lives in a large Eastern city. After working in construction, he joined his father in an old family business that combines real estate sales with a leasing brokerage. He and his two sisters grew up just outside the city and he went to public schools and a private college specializing in engineering. Greg hated school, never liked to study, and was a classic example of a smart boy whom teachers always said wasn't "living up to his potential." While he has raised three children (and, at sixty, has four grandchildren), he also raises horses. He also provides his sisters with extra financial support to make them comfortable. Greg got involved as a sponsor because the IHAD Foundation building was once located in one of his buildings. When he first met Eugene Lang, he told him how much he admired what Lang had done. Then, in the early 1990s, when Greg was fifty-two, someone who was about to become a sponsor of about ninety third and fourth graders in a nearby housing development backed out and Lang approached Greg to see if he'd like to take on a project. While several friends helped provide the initial backing, Greg became the primary sponsor. Greg says he had no idea what he was getting in for: "When you start out you think you're going to help all the kids and they'll [all] turn out well." But he's become "a little hardened to the fact that you can't save them all. We can't just keep making excuses for kids, though I'm a liberal. You've gotta take responsibility for your actions." He takes his dreamers out to dinner regularly, gets them summer jobs, is very pleased with the structure of services that he and his partners have been able to provide, and finds himself very attached to individual dreamers—even some who are beyond help. Greg has powerful feelings of obligation and says he doesn't understand why more wealthy people don't share them. "If you live the kind of life that we live, you should be obligated to give back because God has been good to us." Having always felt that "there are a lot of smart people with a lot of ability that just don't get that lucky break," and that poor people are "getting the shaft," he would advise anyone, without reservations, to get engaged with philanthropy because at the end of his life he knows he'll be able to look back and see that he has made a difference in the lives of kids who will still be his friends.

Mark Richards grew up in a small, supportive Southern town of 95,000 where his mother had been a teacher: she knew everyone in town. The only child in his family, he attended local public schools and had never met anyone who'd gone to a private school until he got to college thanks to a scholarship. The college he attended was allied with the Presbyterian church, to which his family had strong ties. Mark's father, who had been a comptroller, died when his son was still in college. Mark, a history and English literature major, signed up for ROTC and after graduating went into the military, to be trained in counter-intelligence. Living and working overseas broadened his understanding of others and increased his compassion for those less well off. After coming home to attend law school, Mark went to work for a fast-growing pharmaceutical company, helping to set up new policies and procedures and eventually overseeing local headquarters in Latin America, Turkey, and France. The Richards's four children were all born abroad. Eventually Mark became vice president for planning and development, settled in a Midwestern city, and found time to become more active in his church, which, in 1991, was looking for a new way to realize its community mission. By the end of that year his congregation collaborated with another to begin their first IHAD project with sixth graders, creating a 501 (c) (3) and enlisting a number of partners to help them provide support and enrichment services for their dreamers. After a few years, Mark was asked to serve as president of the city's IHAD foundation and by 2001 he was heading up another church-initiated IHAD project. At this point, drawing on federal community learning center grants, corporate and private donations, he is working with an array of neighborhood partners to build a permanent community center which, in addition to being a base for IHAD projects, will be home to a variety of community services for residents. Mark has contributed generously to the local symphony and has run United Way campaigns. Thanks in part to his efforts, the board of education, a local college, several churches, the local museums, volunteer mentors, and the YWCA are all partnering to support dreamers, their families, and the community as a whole. He is driven to continue these efforts for practical reasons because, as he sees it, "education is the force that will solve our socioeconomic problems."

Wally Roberts has never been an IHAD sponsor but has served as a kind of front-line manager for a project funded by graduates of Yale's class of 1956. (The lead sponsor for this project is a local African-

American businessman with strong feelings of loyalty to the community, a man who wasn't available for interviews.) Wally has spent his life in education—working as a teacher and administrator in junior highs and high schools, in curriculum development and college admissions. The IHAD project began at an ethnically diverse school near the university, where the principal was very interested in seeing that the fifty-six children going into fifth grade become dreamers. Before committing themselves to raise $800,000 for the project, this group of graduates had already started a summer fellowship program. It was a class of close friends, Wally says, and many of them went into education, law, and the ministry. He is the only member of the class on the IHAD board, which meets monthly; all the others are representatives from the community. For Wally, who has been in and around schools all his life, the success of this IHAD project has confirmed what he has always known—"that if kids feel support and encouragement and loyalty from adults, they respond." As of the time we spoke, of the fifty-six children chosen, forty-six had graduated from high school on time and were planning on college, technical school, or a military career. And over the years, when the class of 1956 has convened for periodic reunions, alumni have visited with dreamers and been inspired by the authenticity of the young people's hopefulness. One of Wally's classmates has taken up a second career in teaching.

Esther Solomon is a psychologist who partnered with Greg Ralston, as a co-sponsor, to develop a rich structure of support services for dreamers. The children were adopted in a housing development when they were in third and fourth grade. Esther is married to a psychologist and has two grown children and five grandchildren. Now sixty-five, she has spent most of her life in the large Eastern city where she still lives, With the exception of a few years when she was very young, her father worked in advertising and made volunteering a central part of his life as soon as he retired. As a child and young adult, Esther went mostly to private schools and to a private university. She always loved learning, and in addition to her doctorate in psychology she has master's degrees in English, psychology, and special education (which she pursued so she could learn more about how the brain works.) After her mother's death, she was able to invest some funds in community service. Inspired by Leslie Miller's enthusiasm for IHAD, she offered to help Greg develop a mental health component for his project. Esther is eager to follow up with her dreamers; she's kept test data and will try to look at the long-term outcomes for the kids, to get a sense of how effective the project was. Even knowing that there are some children with whom they have not succeeded, she says that coordinating and overseeing a team that tackles problem-solving has given her new faith in people's capacity to understand and respond effectively to the complex needs of low-income children. Esther says she has "learned a tremendous amount, and I'm very grateful for the project that has kept me in touch with life."

NOTES

CHAPTER I, THE JAVELIN

1. Bill Shore. *The Cathedral Within: Transforming Your Life by Giving Something Back.* (New York: Random House Trade Paperbacks, 2001), 199.
2. See Bonnie Benard. *Fostering Resiliency in Kids: Protective Factors in the Family, School and Community.* (Portland, OR: Northwest Regional Educational Laboratory, 1991); Robert S. Brown. "Challenges and Potential of Mentoring At-Risk Students: A Literature Review." *ERS Spectrum* (Spring 1996); Ronald Ferguson. *The Case for Community-Based Programs that Inform and Motivate Black Male Youth.* (Washington, D.C.: The Urban Institute, 1990); Marc Freedman. *The Kindness of Strangers: Reflections on the Mentoring Movement.* (Philadelphia, PA: Public/Private Ventures, 1991); Patricia A. Haensly and James L. Parsons. "Creative, Intellectual, and Psychosocial Development Through Mentorship: Relationships and Stages." *Youth & Society* 25 (December 1993): 202-221; Catherine Higgins, et al. *I Have a Dream in Washington, D.C.: Initial Report.* (Philadelphia: Public/Private Ventures, 1991); Nel Noddings. *Caring: A Feminine Approach to Ethics and Moral Education.* (Berkeley, CA: University of California Press, 1984); Jean Rhodes. *Stand By Me: The Risks and Rewards of Mentoring Today's Youth.* (Cambridge: Harvard University Press, 2002); Robert Reich. *The Work of Nations: Preparing Ourselves for the 21st Century.* (New York: Alfred Knopf, 1991); Joseph Shapiro et al. "Invincible Kids." *U.S. News & World Report* (November 11, 1996): 63–69; Cynthia L. Sipe. *Mentoring: A Synthesis of P/PV's Research: 1988–1995* (Philadelphia: Public/Private Ventures, 1995).

CHAPTER 2, OVERVIEWS AND CLOSE-UPS

3. Bill Shore, *The Cathedral Within*, 94.

   Consider also Michael Nakkula's good description of at-risk, lower middle-class children growing up in housing developments who have trouble seeing their futures:

"Many young people in lower middle class public housing develop-ments around the country grow up expecting to do what their parents have done. As our economy changes, however, requiring an ever-more educated workforce, children growing up in working-class families face the likelihood that the jobs their parents, uncles and aunts held will not exist when they are ready to begin working. As such, their aspirations and sense of possibility can be limited by the scarcity of role models who participate in the world these youth will enter. Implications of this can be seen early on in failing school performance and later in the struggles of joblessness, poor self-image, and attendant self-destructive behaviors. At other times, these children's struggles are hidden, as they slip unobtru-sively through the cracks of our educational and social service systems, never quite creating dramatic enough problems to grab our attention. But our attention is precisely what all of these children need: caring, safe attention that takes seriously their desires for affection, respect and guid-ance." (Michael Nakkula. "A Mentoring Project: Project IF: Inventing the Future." Unpublished proposal, 1996).

4. Joseph P. Tierney, Jean Baldwin Grossman, and Nancy L. Resch. *Making A Difference: An Impact Study of Big Brothers/Big Sisters.* (Philadelphia: Public Private/Ventures, 1995), 6.

5. Marc Freedman. *The Kindness of Strangers: Adult Mentors, Urban Youth and the New Voluntarism.* (San Francisco: Jossey-Bass, 1993).

6. Rhodes, *Stand By Me.*

7. Freedman, *The Kindness of Strangers*, 56–8.

8. Freedman, *The Kindness of Strangers*, 21.

9. Shore, *The Cathedral Within*, 122.

Also consider remarks by Harvard University's President, Lawrence Summers,

"The gap in income for going to college has risen from 31 percent in 1979 to 66 percent in 1997. Accompanying this change has been sub-stantial increase in inequality. In 1970, the top one percent of the popu-lation earned less than half the share received by the bottom 40 percent. The most recent data suggest that today the top one percent earn more than the bottom 40 percent. Or, to put the point differently, in the same period when the median family income was going up 18 percent, the top one percent of all families saw a 200 percent increase in their income.

Sharp increases in inequality and their relation to education are a seri-ous concern. They are even more troubling when one examines changes in intergenerational mobility. . . . The evidence suggests that intergenerational mobility in America is no longer increasing and may well be decreasing. One recent study found that a child born in the bottom 10 percent of families by income has only one chance in three of getting out of the bottom 20 percent. [Thomas Hertz]. Others suggest that Andrew Carnegie's famous line—"shirtsleeves to shirtsleeves in three generations"—needs to be revised to five or six generations. [Alan Krueger, NY Times, November 14, 2002]. More inequality and more persistence of inequality mean just this: The gap between the children of different economic backgrounds has sharply increased in this country over the last generation." (Remarks as prepared for delivery in "Higher Education and the American Dream." American Council of Education. 86th Annual Meeting, February 29, 2004, quoted by Office of the President Publications: www.president.harvard.edu/speeches/2004/ace.html).

10. Francie Ostrower. *Why the Wealthy Give: The Culture of Elite Philanthropy.* (Princeton, NJ: Princeton University Press, 1995), 139–141.
11. Russ Alan Prince and Karen Maru File. *The Seven Faces of Philanthropy: A New Approach to Cultivating Major Donors.* (San Francisco: Jossey-Bass, 1994).
12. Joseph Kahne. "Personalized Philanthropy: Can It Support Youth and Build Civic Commitments?" *Youth & Society.* (March 1999):367–387.
13. *Catalogue of Philanthropy: A Guide to Giving.* (Massachusetts, 2003).
14. Shore, *The Cathedral Within*, 188.
15. Shore, *The Cathedral Within*, 96–7.
16. Bill Shore. *The Light of Conscience: How a Simple Act Can Change Your Life.* (New York: Random House, 2004), 148–49.
17. Paul Schervish. "Adoption and Altruism: Those With Whom I Want to Share a Dream." *Nonprofit and Voluntary Sector Quarterly* 21(1992): 338.
18. Schervish, "Adoption and Altruism: Those With Whom I Want to Share a Dream," 338–39.
19. Schervish, "Adoption and Altruism: Those With Whom I Want to Share a Dream," 329.
20. Schervish, "Adoption and Altruism: Those With Whom I Want to Share a Dream," 338–39.
21. Schervish, "Adoption and Altruism: Those With Whom I Want to Share a Dream," 347.
22. Marc Freedman. *Prime Time: How Baby Boomers Will Revolutionize Retirement and Transform America.* (New York: Public Affairs Books, 1999), 247.

23. Freedman, *Prime Time*, 207.
24. Erik H. Erikson. "Identity and the Life Cycle: Selected Papers." *Psychological Issues*: 1 (1959), 97-99.
25. See, for example, Mary Belenky, et al. *Women's Ways of Knowing.* (New York: Basic Books, 1986); James Fowler. *Stages of Faith: The Psychology of Human Development and the Quest for Meaning.* (San Francisco: Harper & Row, 1981); Betty Friedan. *The Fountain of Age.* (New York: Simon & Schuster, 1993); Mark Gerzon. *Coming Into Our Own: Understanding the Adult Metamorphosis.* (New York: Delacorte Press, 1992); Robert Kegan. *The Evolving Self: Problem and Process in Human Development.* (Cambridge: Harvard University Press, 1982); Robert Kegan. *In Over Our Heads: The Mental Demands of Modern Life.* (Cambridge: Harvard University Press, 1994); Lawrence Kohlberg. *The Psychology of Moral Development: The Nature and Validity of Moral Stages.* (San Francisco: Harper & Row, 1984); Benjamin Lee and Gil Noam. *Developmental Approaches to the Self.* (New York: Plenum Press, 1983); Daniel J. Levinson et al. *The Seasons of A Man's Life.* (New York: Ballantine Books, 1978); Mary Lou Randour. *Women's Psyche, Women's Spirit: The Reality of Relationships.* (New York: Columbia University Press, 1987); Samuel Osherson. *Holding On or Letting Go: Men and Career Change at Midlife.* (New York: Free Press, 1980); Nancy K. Schlossberg, E. B. Waters, and J. Goodman. *Counseling Adults in Transition.* (New York: Springer, 1995); Gail Sheehy. *Passages: Predictable Crises of Adult Life.* (New York: Bantam, 1976); George E. Vaillant. *Adaptation to Life.* (Boston: Little, Brown & Co, 1977); Robert W. White. *Lives in Progress: A Study of the Natural Growth of Personality.* (New York: Holt, Rinehart and Winston, 1966).
26. F. M. Hudson. *The Adult Years: Mastering the Art of Self-Renewal.* (San Francisco: Jossey-Bass, 1991).
27. Warren G. Bennis and Robert J. Thomas. *Geeks and Geezers: How Era, Values, and Defining Moments Shape Leaders.* (Cambridge: Harvard Business School Press, 2002), 84.

    This adaptive capacity is also characteristic of people who derive profound satisfaction from work in multi-problem human service agencies and who, unlike many of their colleagues, don't burn out. (Margot Welch. "Thrivers: A Study of Job Satisfaction and Success in Multi-Problem Human Service Organizations," [Ed.D. dissertation, Harvard Graduate School of Education, 1990]).
28. Bennis and Thomas, 102.

29. Bennis and Thomas, 84.
30. George E. Vaillant. *Aging Well: Surprising Guideposts to a Happier Life from the Landmark Harvard Study of Adult Development.* (Boston: Little, Brown & Co., 2002), 48–49.
31. It is partly because of the new ground-breaking research about the psychology of girls and women, done during the last two decades, that students of human behavior now see development as an inclusive phenomenon that can not be well understood without taking lifelong relationships into account. See, for example, Mary Belenky, et al. *Women's Ways of Knowing.* (New York: Basic Books, 1986); Carol Gilligan. *In A Different Voice: Psychological Theory and Women's Development.* (Cambridge: Harvard University Press, 1993); Judith V. Jordan, ed. *The Complexity of Connection: Writings from the Stone Center's Jean Baker Miller Training Institute.* (New York: Guilford, 2004); Judith V. Jordan et al. *Women's Growth in Connection: Writings from the Stone Center.* (New York: Guilford, 1991); Peg G. McAdam. "A Question of Boundaries: The Dynamics of Power in the Clinical Supervision of Psychotherapy." (Harvard University, unpublished thesis, 2001); Jean Baker Miller. *Toward A New Psychology of Women.* (Boston: Beacon, 1986); Nel Noddings. *Caring: A Feminine Approach to Ethics and Moral Education.* (Berkeley, CA: University of California Press, 1984).
32. Anne Colby and William Damon. *Some Do Care: Contemporary Lives of Moral Commitment.* (New York: Free Press, 1992).
33. Erich Fromm. *The Art of Loving: An Enquiry Into the Nature of Love.* (New York: Harper & Brothers, 1956), 23–25.
34. Fromm, *The Art of Loving,* 127–29.
35. I have spoken, for various lengths of time, with representatives of eighteen first generation IHAD projects (a total of twenty-three people), and with sixteen representatives of second generation projects. Not all are given names in the text of this book. For brief descriptions of all the unnamed sponsors—under pseudonyms and with identifying details masked—see the "Biographical Notes on Unnamed Sponsors" at the end of the book.

CHAPTER 5, WHAT'S IT LIKE TO BE A SPONSOR?

36. The superintendent of Chicago Public Schools, Arne Duncan, who worked closely with an IHAD initiative before he became chief of the Chicago school system, is now applying some core IHAD principles to the district.

37. Nick Kotz. "Changing Lives." *The Washingtonian* (February 1998).
38. Ed Barlow, Bud Wagner and Bob Wheeler. "A Volunteer's Voice: Class of '56 "I have a dream" Project: A Success Story." *The Blue Print* (Newsletter of Association of Yale Alumni, New Haven, Spring 2003).

CHAPTER 6, LESSONS LEARNED

39. Charter schools, licensed by state legislatures since the 1990s, were developed as independently run schools that would offer choice for families and more opportunities for innovation in public education. Nonsectarian, they receive core funding from public systems, based on the per capita amount of money that a district pays for each student. People who develop charter schools tend to belong to one of three groups: grassroots organizations of parents, teachers and community members; entrepreneurs; or existing schools converting to charter status.

   Most charter schools accept students through a lottery. They are not bound by the regulations that apply to traditional public students. Their autonomy is highly prized – although this has led to some complications with the assessment of these programs. Charter schools are controversial. The National Assessment of Educational Progress issued a report in 2003 saying that the record of charter schools is very inconsistent, that the schools have done nothing to improve the performance of low-income minority children in the core inner city districts, that student performance at the schools is very uneven, and that they tend to take the most strongly motivated children and families out of the public system, leaving it even more disabled than it is. Teachers' unions have opposed charter schools. Supporters of charter schools allege that the NAEP report was politicized and that charter schools are indeed expanding opportunities for learning and access to quality education for all students, encouraging professional innovation, increasing parent engagement, and constructing systems of accountability.

   Regardless of one's position about charters, there is some agreement that insofar as charter schools have the capacity to present real alternatives to traditional public schools they may serve as important examples that, in the long run, may help strengthen the public system. (See, for example, www.uscharterschools.org, and "Book Faults Achievement in Charter Schools," *Education Week*, April 6, 2005).
40. Joseph Kahne, 1999.

CHAPTER 7, THE RICHES AND WONDER OF ENGAGEMENT

41. Bill Shore, *The Light of Conscience*, 239.
42. Eugene Lang. Unpublished speech at Harvard Graduate School of Education (1997).

CHAPTER 8, THE WORLD BEGINS TO SHIFT

43. Annie E. Casey Foundation. *KIDS COUNT, 2004 Data Book.* Available on line at the foundation's website, www.aecf.org.
44. Gary Orfield, Dan Losen, and Johanna Wald. *Losing Our Future: How Minority Youth Are Being Left Behind by the Graduation Rate Crisis.* (Cambridge: The Civil Rights Project, Harvard University, 2004).
45. Annie E. Casey.
46. Annie E. Casey.
47. Orfield, et al. *Losing Our Future.*

The implications of national statistics seem more immediate when we consider data drawn from smaller units—states and cities, for example. Consider information drawn from five geographically diverse states (compiled here from Orfield et al.).

State	% of All Students Graduating	% of Hispanics in Student Population	% of Blacks in Student Population	Hispanic Graduation Rate	Black Graduation Rate	Race Gap: Hispanic/ White	Race Gap: Black/White
Colorado	69%	22%	5.7%	47.6%	49%	−27.6%	−26.2%
Florida	53%	19.3%	25.1%	52.2%	41%	−5.7%	−16.9%
Illinois	75%	15.5%	21%	57.8%	47.8%	−25.1%	−35.1%
Mass.	71%	12%	9.6%	36.1%	49.4%	−37.6%	−24.3%
Texas	65%	40.6 %	14.2%	55.9%	55.3%	−17.6%	−18.2%

48. Christopher B. Swanson. "The New Math of Graduation Rates." *Education Week* (28 July 2004).

Of course, the term "minority" is a relative, shifting, and time-limited one: in many communities there have been more blacks than whites for many decades, in some counties and states there are now (and may always have been) more Hispanics than "Anglos," and immigration continues to make the population of our country ever more diverse.

49. Michelle Fine. *Framing Dropouts: Notes on the Politics. of an Urban Public High School.* (New York: State University of New York Press, 1991).

50. Orfield, et al. *Losing the Future.*

51. Editorial. *New York Times.* (1 March 2005).

52. Bill Gates. "Prepared Remarks for National Education Summit on High Schools." (Read at a conference in Washington, D.C., 26 February 2005).

53. As the school's grant renewal application says, they have been able to raise between $400,000 and $1,000,000 every year and consistently balance their budget. "The school has new science labs, a working auditorium (opened after 15 years of disuse), a new lunchroom and cafeteria, and $1 million of new wiring, thanks to a federal 'e-rate' grant." Committed to remaining small—never admitting more than 400 students—it regularly has a waiting list of over 400 applicants for 100 places in its freshman class. Chosen by random lottery from the applicants, all the children live within a ten-mile radius of the school. More than 90 percent of the children are eligible for free or reduced-price lunches, 14 percent are students identified as having special needs, and as many as 15 percent may be homeless. Again from the grant renewal application: "Most of our students arrive with poor reading and math skills, weak study habits, and little notion of what the future might hold for them." In 2004, 93 percent of their students graduated, and for the classes of 2002, 2003, and 2004, 100 percent of those who graduated were accepted to at least one college or university.

Many students arrive at the school with a variety of academic difficulties. The school hires teachers who reflect the demography of its students (65 percent of the teachers are minorities) and are skilled at communicating with "at-risk" teenagers. It has invested significant resources in providing professional development opportunities for its teachers, who are given time to work on pedagogical issues together. The school relies on constructivist learning theories that allow students to keep building on what they are learning even as they master new ideas and concepts.

Its inquiry-based curriculum is aligned with both state and national standards and invites students to explore new subjects and higher order thinking while they build strong foundations for more specialized coursework in the upper grades.

54. Good ideas do have a way of spreading, like viruses. Whether we call this a "tipping point," as Malcolm Gladwell has suggested in *The Tipping Point: How Little Things Can Make a Big Difference* (London: Little, Brown, 2000), or "thought contagion" that some social scientists are

investigating, it is true that sometimes innovation takes off. Lang gets pleasure from knowing that the basic impulse which drove him to start IHAD—that relationships and support are the most important factors in a child's success—informs a great many current public and private initiatives designed to meet the needs of low-income children.

In a new book by Oral Lee Brown, *The Promise: How One Woman Made Good On Her Extraordinary Pact To Send a Classroom of First-Graders to College* (New York: Doubleday, 2005), readers can familiarize themselves with another passionate, determined individual who acted on a good impulse to get and stay involved with poor children until they got through college. Brown shares many attributes of the engaged philanthropists in this book. She has tremendous energy, a deep understanding about the central importance of personal attention for children, and a need to change the "little corner" of the world where she lives—particularly because, like Lang himself, she believes that if she sees something that needs to be done and knows she can do it, she must forge ahead.

55. Shore, *The Light of Conscience.*